Roger Borniche, alias Roger Bor, is France's most famous policeman since the Second World War. With over 500 arrests to his credit, Borniche retired from the police force in 1956 and now runs a highly successful detective agency in Paris.

Flic Story, a sensational and true police-detective story can best be described in the author's own words: 'Until now, it's only the crooks who had their say. The police have listened silently to these hard-luck stories. My aim is to try and explain who these men are, these little known and less loved men, the cops, the fuzz, and now the pigs, *les flics*, without whom society – let's face it – could not live in safety.

I know about criminals. In my career with the Sûreté Nationale, I arrested 567 of them. The story I have to tell is about one of these, the most merciless killer in post-war France. This is the true story of a manhunt that went on for three years and which I have reconstructed in detail.'

'Has much of the fascination of a jigsaw puzzle and reveals as much about the ways of crime as it does about the quirky lives of top cops'
Publishers' Weekly

Roger Borniche

Flic Story

Translated by William Ross

PANTHER
GRANADA PUBLISHING
London Toronto Sydney New York

Published by Granada Publishing Limited
in Panther Books 1978

ISBN 0 586 04394 2

First published in Great Britain by Hart-Davis,
MacGibbon Ltd 1976
Copyright © Librarie Arthème Fayard 1973
Translation copyright © Doubleday & Company, Inc 1975

Granada Publishing Limited
Frogmore, St Albans, Herts AL2 2NF
and
3 Upper James Street, London W1R 4BP
1221 Avenue of the Americas, New York, NY 10020, USA
117 York Street, Sydney, NSW 2000, Australia
100 Skyway Avenue, Toronto, Ontario, Canada M9W 3A6
Trio City, Coventry Street, Johannesburg 2001, South Africa
CML Centre, Queen & Wyndham, Auckland 1, New Zealand

Made and printed in Great Britain by
Richard Clay (The Chaucer Press) Ltd
Bungay, Suffolk
Set in Monotype Times

CONTENTS

PREFACE

Until now, it's only the crooks who have had their say.

One after another, they have trotted out their memoirs, lectured on the difficulties of their profession, bewailed the hardships of prison life.

The police have listened silently to these hard-luck stories.

If I break that silence at a time when police prestige is at its lowest, it is not to justify the men who fight crime and murder. Nor am I anxious to tell the story of my life.

My aim is to try to explain who these men are, these little known and less loved men, the cops, the fuzz, and now the pigs, *les flics*, without whom society—let's face it—could not live in safety.

I know about criminals. In my career with the Sûreté Nationale, I arrested 567 of them. The story I have to tell is about one of these, the most merciless killer in post-war France. This is the true story of a manhunt that went on for three years and which I have reconstructed in detail. For obvious reasons, I have given false names to some gangsters who have done their time and to some police officers who are now retired.

As the case unfolds, you will see the cogs and gears of the 'Grande Maison'—the Sûreté Nationale—in motion. And you will see into the lives and hearts of those men whom society shuns: the police.

R.B.

A NOTE ABOUT MONEY

All the sums in this book are in French francs. Trying to find an equivalent for them in today's pounds or dollars is like trying to psycho-analyse a dead man from his laundry lists: the results have only the remotest relationship to the truth. In 1937, the franc was officially worth roughly twenty cents. In 1950 it was worth—again officially—less than a third of a cent. The combination of inflation, at different rates in the two countries, and shifting official values makes any firm estimate extremely risky. For the 1937 franc, in fact, it is hopeless, like trying to calculate how long it would take to ride a mule to the moon. The post-war period, though still economically remote, is at least dimly visible. Figure, then, that every 1948–50 franc Émile Buisson stole was worth a shade over one 1976 U.S. cent or a 1976 British half-penny.

W.R.

IN TRAINING

1

'Borniche, come into my office.'

Just that. Then he hung up.

I sat there for a moment with the receiver in my hand, staring at it. Then I set it back on the cradle, still surprised by the jarring curtness in his voice. Fatso was usually so unctuously polite.

The newspaper I was reading slipped to the floor. I got up and plucked my jacket off the back of my chair, checked to see if it was rumpled—Fatso insisted that his men be neatly if not elegantly dressed—straightened my tie and went out. A few strides took me across a corridor reeking of floor polish to the door of No. 522. I knocked twice, softly, and waited, my eyes following the movements of the cleaner as he busied himself in the hall a few yards away.

'Come in.'

Chief Detective Inspector Vieuchêne was seated behind his beechwood desk, looking bulky in his dark blue suit. A cowlick stood up like a crow's feather from a plumage of sleek, black hair brushed straight back from the round, smooth, pink face. His brown eyes, generally so affable, looked worried. He didn't ask me to sit down, just sat frozen in his chair, studying the official telegram he held in his thick, well-manicured fingers. Finally he looked up at me.

'Buisson and Girier have escaped,' he said, handing me the wire. I reached for it, still standing. The message said:

> *Prefecture of Police, Headquarters, Criminal Investigation Division, to all units Paris Police, Sûreté Nationale, Gendarmerie—stop—Request urgent search for Émile Buisson, alias Monsieur Émile, born 19 August 1902 in Paray-le-Monial (Saône-et-Loire Department), no known address. Height: five feet three inches; build: slender; hair and eyes: black—stop—This man was confined to the Villejuif psychiatric hospital for observation while serving a sentence*

*of hard labour and he escaped from there 3 Sept. at ten a.m.—
stop—The escape was made with help from outside—stop—
Buisson was accompanied in his escape by another convict,
whose description is as follows: Girier, René, alias René the
Exile, born 9 November 1919 in Ouillins (Rhône Department),
no fixed address. Physical appearance: height: five feet
eleven inches; build: average; eyes: blue; hair: blond, wavy—
stop—These men are dangerous and may be armed—stop—
If they are located, apprehend at once and immediately notify
Prefecture of Police, Criminal Investigation Division, 36 quai
des Orfèvres, Paris. Telephone Turbigo 92.00. Signed: Badin,
Assistant Commissioner—End.*

I laid the telegram on the desk. Vieuchêne leaned back in his
chair, his gut rearing up in front of him. He hooked his thumbs in
his waistcoat pockets and, deliberately biting off each word, he
intoned:

'I want—you hear me, Borniche?—I want you to find these
men before the Prefecture does, before the Gendarmerie does—
in fact, before anybody else does. I want to prove to them that
the Sûreté Nationale is on the map and that neither the quai des
Orfèvres nor the heroes in the Gendarmerie have any monopoly
on crime-busting. A word of advice, though, Borniche: watch out
for Buisson. He's a killer.'

Fatso dived back into his papers, repeating as he dismissed me:
'I said before anybody else. Don't forget it, Borniche.'

I went back to Room 523, my office, a ten-by-thirteen-foot
rectangle with buff walls. The Administration hadn't ruined itself
furnishing the place: two unpainted wood tables with matching
chairs, a wastebasket and a telephone, which I shared with my
partner, Inspector Hidoine. He was in his underwear when I
walked in. He changed clothes every morning when he got to the
office, stripping off his whipcord breeches, his riding boots and
his tweed jacket and putting on his work clothes, a brick-
coloured suit that was too big for him. He had explained this to
me when we began working together: he disguised himself as a
country squire in order to wow the girls in the Metro. He was a
tall fellow, dark and bony, with delicate features and lively,
laughing eyes. Nothing at all like the standard image of a cop.
Whenever he was worked up over anything, he would shove his

upper plate out of his mouth, popping it in and out with nimble flicks of the tongue. I tried repeatedly to convince him it was a disgusting habit, but Hidoine never managed to overcome it. Repulsive.

'What did Fatso want?' he asked as he pulled on his trousers.

'Buisson.'

Hidoine turned and looked inquiringly at me. 'Who's Buisson?'

'Haven't a notion. This is the first I've heard of him. But I can tell you that Fatso seems to be obsessed with finding him. He made a huge song and dance about how we have to get him before the Prefecture does. He still can't stand them. Presumably if we can bring in his precious Buisson it will somehow set the seal on his promotion. Especially with nominations due for seven new superintendencies.'

Hidoine nodded and sighed, 'I get the picture. No more peace and quiet for us. Bye-bye pinball machines.' Hidoine was a pinball virtuoso, the unchallenged champion of matches everyone conceded in advance.

I took two green slips out of my desk drawer. In the corner of each I wrote PJ/1, standing for Police Judiciaire (Criminal Investigation Division), First Section. My section. On one of the slips I wrote Buisson's first name, last name and birth date. Then I wrote Girier's data on the second one and signed them both.

'I'm going up to Records,' I told Hidoine. 'If anyone asks for me . . .'

'I know,' he said. 'You're out.'

That's where every case begins, in Records. The section occupies the whole sixth floor of the Sûreté Nationale building, just above my head. It is really one vast room, surrounding the courtyard off the rue des Saussaies in which the cars of the force's higher echelons can always be seen waiting with their chauffeurs who have gone fat from inactivity. The room is intersected by long alleys running between flat hedges of cabinets where the file cards are kept, millions of them, classified alphabetically and phonetically. Anybody who might conceivably interest the authorities has a right to a card listing his civil status and the number of his administrative, personal or criminal dossier.

There are innocent people on file in Records, people who have applied for passports or identity cards or hunting licences. They are there because the police shrewdly believe that the innocent may one day become the guilty and that it is best to know all about them in advance. Data on the innocent are filed in administrative dossiers called DA. When they turn guilty, they win promotion to individual dossiers—DI—containing their biographies, photos, convictions, records of transfers from one prison to another. Their misdeeds and those of their accomplices swell the DC, criminal dossiers. The whole file is kept up to date by about a hundred detective-archivists draped in grey smocks. Their boss, Chief Inspector Roblin, a tall, skinny man, meticulous and polite, with greying temples, was both amused and annoyed by my enthusiasm. When we first met, three years earlier, he had asked me how old I was.

'I'm twenty-five, sir,' I told him.

'I see. I'm forty-two and to you I'm an old fart. But you'll get over that, you'll see. When you've slipped up on enough of the Maison's banana skins you'll have a wiser head on your shoulders to make up for the bruises.'

But, this afternoon, he glanced at my green slips and his jaw tightened. 'Buisson? A prize louse. His DC is monumental. I thought he was locked up.'

'He was. He broke out this morning with Girier.'

'Ah! And you're looking for him?'

I nodded. For a moment, Roblin stood motionless. Then he said: 'Don't let him shoot first, Borniche. Buisson's a wild animal.'

I watched him plunge into his labyrinth, clutching my two green slips. An irresistible feeling of doubt invaded me, a feeling almost of helplessness. I figured that, by this time, the whole Paris Prefecture must be at full boil. Superintendent Pinault, the boss of the Homicide Squad, would already have called in his top men, Courchamp and Poirier, and their teams and unleashed them on Buisson. Nearly 200 men there. The Flying Squad's chief, Clot, smiling under his pencil-stripe moustache, would have held a similar council of war with his assistant, Chief Inspector Morin, ending with the same battle order: bring in Buisson. Another 100 officers there added to the pack. Not to mention the street men, the mobile units, the Gendarmerie and God knew who else.

It was, you might say, discouraging. Aside from Fatso, who was happier in his chair than on the street, the Sûreté had two men on the case, Hidoine and me. And we were supposed to wade into a police war and come out with a man we'd never seen, described by everyone as dangerous and certainly as wary as a tiger on the prowl.

'Here you are,' Roblin said, dumping a stack of folders on the table. 'Monsieur Émile's exploits. You should have a ball with these. He's different, this guy.'

'Why?'

'Because he's intelligent, for God's sake, as well as being sullen, careful, suspicious. And brave. You know why everybody was scared stupid of him?'

'No.'

'Because, besides his gun, he went around with a grenade in his pocket so that he could blow himself up with the bull who arrested him. Are you going to read these here or will you take them out?'

'I'll take them with me.'

Roblin shot me a conspiratorial look. 'Smart boy,' he agreed. 'That way, if someone else wants to see them, you'll know who it is. That's always helpful.'

I went back to my office with the cardboard folders under my arm. Hidoine had left a note saying he was at the Santa Maria, a cocktail lounge on the rue des Saussaies. I opened the first folder.

2

21 December 1937. The thermometer was trying to reach a new low in the streets of Troyes (in the Champagne district of eastern France). Two people ducked into a shop off the rue du Colonel-Driand—a big man, walking hunched against the cold, his hands rammed into the pockets of a heavy, well-cut overcoat, and a woman bundled up to the ears in fur. The shop owner, Monsieur Nas, was waiting for them. The big man took off his hat, unbuttoned his coat and introduced his companion:

'Madame Felippe. I talked to you last week about her wanting to rent your shop.'

Nas eagerly greeted the young brunette. He was delighted. Madame Felippe planned to open a beauty salon and she charmingly handed him a deposit of 1,500 francs, promising more to come when the paperwork was completed. As she was about to leave, her gloved hand resting on the doorknob, she smiled prettily. 'I would like to bring the decorators in from Paris right away,' she told the owner. 'To avoid hotel bills, I'll put them up in the back room of the shop. Would you mind my installing some mattresses and a stove and a few pots there?'

Nas, enchanted by his new tenant's smile, readily consented.

The man and woman pushed out into the cold again. Walking fast, they left the rue du Colonel-Driand, passed the Crédit Lyonnais branch bank and turned into the boulevard Victor-Hugo. Too rigid with cold to talk, they pressed on for about five hundred yards, then turned into a side street where a car, a black Hotchkiss, was waiting for them, parked at the curb with its motor running. The man got in beside the driver; the woman took her place on the back seat. The car at once surged forward, heading towards Paris.

'Well?'

The question came from her neighbour on the back seat, a slight, dark-haired man with a prominent jaw who sat huddled in a corner with the collar of his grey overcoat turned up. His feet barely reached the floor. He might have been an obscure clerk. Only his black, piercing eyes, which he screwed up slightly when he looked hard at you, gave warning of danger. This was Émile Buisson.

'Everything went smoothly. You can move into the shop when you want to. And you?'

'Us?' Buisson echoed. 'We checked over the plan and re-checked the getaway route. Now let's drop the subject. I want quiet while I think.'

Buisson's voice was high-pitched, his accent still redolent of his native Burgundy. But the tone was curt, commanding.

Three Crédit Lyonnais bank messengers, Léon Forestier, Louis Chevalier and Louis Décombe, left the Troyes branch of the Bank of France after withdrawing 1,800,000 francs. On the street, Forestier fumbled his watch out of his waistcoat pocket, glanced at it and swore. 'Four-fifty! It's almost dark.'

'Stop complaining, Léon,' joked Chevalier, who was holding the money bag. 'At least we'll be invisible in the dark if a gangster tries to hold us up.'

Décombe was a worrier. The joke was enough to send his hand reaching into his overcoat pocket to grip the pistol there.

The three men started off, crossing the boulevard Victor-Hugo; walking abreast, they turned into the rue du Colonel-Driand. They were only a few steps from their bank when five men swarmed out of a street urinal and surrounded them. The messengers felt gun muzzles digging into their chests.

'The bag, quick!'

The little man's voice when he spat out the order was paralysing. It was thick with death. The messengers stood motionless. Forestier's arms hung loosely at his sides. Chevalier surrendered the bag. Décombe didn't dare move the hand clutching the gun in his pocket. All three were thrown savagely to the ground. As they fell, unable even to cry out, their assailants ran towards a black car which was moving slowly up the street to meet them. By the time the messengers could spring to their feet, the bandits had jumped into the Hotchkiss and were racing towards the boulevard Victor-Hugo. Forestier, Chevalier and Décombe drew their guns and fired. From the car flared an answering volley before the black bulk vanished into the darkness.

An alarm went out. The roads out of Troyes, especially the main highway to Paris, bristled with roadblocks thrown up with surprising speed. There was no moon that night. At dinner behind their barred shutters, residents in the neighbourhood failed to notice the five silhouettes slipping into Monsieur Nas's steel-shuttered shop.

When the little group had reassembled in the store's back room, stripped off overcoats and jackets and stacked their guns neatly within reach on a shelf, its members eyed each other with satisfaction. There was a flash of dazzling white teeth as Buisson smiled briefly. 'Milo,' he ordered, 'fetch the champagne.'

Milo was Courgibet, the gang's Émile No. 2. He was of average build and wore his hair brushed back flat, the way men did then. His eyes were green and mild. Women found him as adorable as Jean Gabin. The men called him 'The Escapee' because he had succeeded in breaking out of the Cayenne prison (part of the French Guiana penal colony, which included Devil's Island), where he had been sent for murdering the woman he loved. For six years now, Courgibet and Buisson had worked together. They were the nucleus, surrounding themselves as they needed them with reliable subordinates, daring, ruthless men on whom society had permanently turned its back. In only one respect did the two differ radically: Buisson was capable of snuffing out a man's life with total indifference, while Courgibet hated guns. 'Don't ever ask me to shoot,' he had warned, and Buisson had accepted the condition.

The Escapee returned with two bottles of champagne. Corks popped, bubbles frothed. The five men clinked glasses.

'We'll hole up here for a few days, give the cops time to wear themselves out combing the country for us,' Buisson said. 'Then we'll go back to Paris on the train. Separately.'

Schmull set his glass on the floor. 'And if somebody comes knocking at the door before then, what do we do, Mimile? Let him have it?'

Buisson glared at him, then shrugged. 'You really are incredibly stupid, Karl,' he said softly. 'This is a perfect hideout here, so just forget about the fireworks. What I've decided is this: during the day we'll wear the painters' overalls I brought and we'll pretend to be doing the place up. Now let's eat.'

While the five picnicked, sitting on the floor and gulping down champagne, the police searched frantically for a black Hotchkiss. Which explains why Abel Sauty, driving a cream-coloured Citroën and carrying a poodle on his lap, was waved through all seven roadblocks he stopped at. Shortly after ten p.m. he reached

Paris, got rid of the dog with a sharp kick and hauled the bank bag from under the driver's seat.

Detective Superintendent Belin was fed up. He'd had enough of the press' sarcasm, he was tired of the leaden pleasantries from his brother officers. It was Belin's chore to capture the Troyes bandits and, so far, he had not only failed to arrest them, he had not even identified them. And in the meanwhile, they were running up an impressive string of robberies.

On the Île-Saint-Denis one evening, a department store was surrounded by six armed men. After binding and gagging the watchman, one Péricard, they relieved the manager, Monsieur Cabane, and his wife of a large sum of money in cash and cheques.

Sometime later, six men in a stolen car blocked a bank truck near the Nogent bridge in Fontenay-sous-Bois. While one of them flattened the truck's tyres, a slight, dark-eyed man wrested a bag containing one million francs from the guard. Then another million was scooped up at the Rond-Point de l'Aigle, in La Garenne-Colombes, again by a gang of six armed men.

Belin, the man who had arrested Landru (the French super-Bluebeard), noticed with grudging admiration that every one of the gang's hold-ups was staged with chronometric precision based on meticulous planning. The technique never varied: they struck with stunning speed, then fled by car. In each case, witnesses reported the presence of a small man, about five feet three, slender, dressed in dark clothes, who leaped out at them with his gun in his hand. They all talked about his black glare, burning, as though with a feverish hatred that could freeze your blood.

'With a gangster of Buisson's class operating,' Belin had remarked, 'the country could become another Chicago.'

3

I closed the first folder and lit a cigarette. I sat staring into space, reflecting that with an animal like Monsieur Émile loose in the underbrush, the chances of someone getting hurt were high. But, at the same time, I was jubilant.

Buisson may have been a lion of the underworld, but I was a hunter. I like to search, ferret, question, sniff out a trail, find the hole that leads me to the lair. That's the way I am—a hunter who operates without gun or handcuffs. I prefer to work bare-handed. What really satisfies me is to fall on my quarry, grapple with him until I overcome him and carry him back to the Maison like a big, fat butterfly.

Yet nothing, at the beginning, had marked me for this kind of work. My overriding ambition, from my teens onward, had been to break into show-business. I had the call, the temperament, the presence; my gamut of facial expressions ranged from a seraphic smile to a villainous scowl; my voice was flexible enough to handle anything from a whisper to an oration, and my fingers agile enough to master a magician's card and scarf tricks. What's more, I had some famous friends, including the radio-television producers Jean Nohain and Pierre Louis, the actor Roger Nicolas, the operetta star Henri Genès and the great accordionist Jo Privat. I was made to be a pop singer. I even had a stage name: Roger Bor.

I had everything, in fact, except contracts. Theatre managers turned vague when they saw me. Some broke down under my constant pestering and gave me a chance, and compassionate audiences would give me a hand—not enough to raise blisters, but I was easy to please. At least I was onstage—not for long, mind you, but even those few minutes seemed like heaven to me. Oh, yes! I was a believer. I knew that fame would fold me in her arms someday and I was waiting for it.

The German Army came instead. My singing career retreated before them. From then on, trouble seemed to work overtime for me. Demobilized after thirty-six months in Marshal Pétain's rifle-less army, I lived in a shabby hotel on the hill in Montmartre. Hardly a day went by without a threat from the owner to throw me out unless I paid my back rent. I dragged around without a job, without a sou, constantly hungry. I was so stranded, so stripped, so miserable that I might very well have toppled into the underworld myself. These are the times when a man's fate is decided. I have never forgotten those months of heartbreak; I have particularly remembered them whenever I've had to make an arrest.

It was a dismal comedown for me, the potential king of the crooners, even to be tempted by a help-wanted ad in *Paris-Soir* announcing that the Printemps stores were looking for delivery men and salesmen. By that time, though, I was hungry enough to do anything, anything at all that would pay me the price of a square meal.

Because I was of average height and solidly built, I was hired for the security staff. In the time it took to sign a contract, I became a store detective.

My performance was lamentable. For the first few days, I had an old maid named Mademoiselle Kim as my instructor. I saw nothing, arrested nobody. I was keen as a sinusitic bloodhound. My eyes would swivel in my head like radar dishes, but I never managed to spot a thief in the act, which would have earned me a bonus. Mademoiselle Kim grumbled, goading me on with hints of impending dismissal. It was no use. I didn't have the flair.

There was one afternoon when I thought I had it made. I'd been watching a woman browsing at the glove counter. When I saw her slip a pair of gloves into her handbag, I began to bubble inside. Discreetly, relishing the capture in advance, I followed her to the door, waited until she got into the street and stopped her.

'Police, madame,' I crowed. 'Follow me. Don't deny it. I saw the whole thing. Give me the gloves.'

My triumph was short-lived. The woman drew the gloves out of her purse. They were worn; they were her own gloves.

As a reward for this achievement, I was bumped down to the night surveillance staff, watching the kilometres of stock stored in the cellars. 'At night,' I was warned by Fantomas, the security chief, 'the stocks are a beehive—full of carpenters, painters, electricians, firemen. Things disappear.'

So I spent my nights drifting among the crates and the ghostly, canvas-shrouded booths. I had just surprised a fireman stealing three dressing gowns when I learned from the personnel director that my name was on the list for the next batch of Forced Labour Conscripts due to be shipped into Germany.

I was desperate, ready to try anything to escape deportation. Even joining the police. The idea was planted in my mind by a friend I happened to meet in the street on the very day when, after my compulsory medical examination, a doctor with a soul like a compost heap had pronounced me fit for forced labour.

'Cops don't go to Germany,' the friend murmured.

The thought of cringing in the heart of the Third Reich while Allied planes aimed their bombs at me filled me with panic. I immediately applied to take a competitive exam as an inspector with the Sûreté Nationale. I subscribed to *Police-Revue*, a correspondence school for Grande Maison candidates. On 16 December 1943, I was summoned to the Sorbonne for the test. The first question in the written part of the exam—I'll never forget it—was: 'Tell what you know about the rise of the First Empire.' I knew everything about it. I passed. I was twenty-four years old.

On 1 May 1944, I was posted to the Fifth Security Police Brigade, 2 rue de la Bretonnerie, in Orléans. I was photographed, measured, given a new pair of handcuffs and assigned, like all greenhorns, to the political section. Mission: to hunt for members of the Resistance.

I was no sooner installed in my new job than I found myself standing at the door to my section with a machine gun in my hand, guarding a man who stood with one wrist fastened to the radiator. There wasn't much left of him but a battered face perched on a heap of wreckage; he was incapable even of drinking the broth I tried clumsily to feed him.

'He's a Communist,' my section chief said disgustedly. 'That makes him a bad Frenchman.'

At night, the prisoner was interrogated by the German police. During the day he was left in the custody of the French police. I would have liked to do something for him. I never found out what became of him.

Twice in succession my section was sent to beat the bushes for Resistance workers. The first foray was a fiasco. On the second, I helped two partisans to escape; the grateful family of one of them sent me a parcel containing a pound of butter and six eggs.

On 19 May 1944, I deserted. After two of my former associates searched my room, I was fired. Now it was my turn to be hunted by the police. I went to ground in Paris, adrift and broke. Then came the Allied landing in Normandy and the Liberation of Paris.

Once more, the stage beckoned. But, as a Charles Aznavour song says, although I could already see my name in lights, the contracts refused to come and relieve me of my obsessive hunger. On 2 September, a letter reached me:

'Monsieur: Under a decree dated 19 August 1944 you have been reinstated in your function as a detective trainee and posted in this capacity to the Police Judiciaire in Paris. You are requested to appear, with this notice, on 3 September 1944 at nine a.m. before the Divisional Superintendent in charge of the Regional Branch, who will assign you to your duties.'

I was punctual. I wore my cellulose fibre suit, the one that had been pressed a hundred times to keep the threads from puckering. For the second time, I joined the police.

At the First Mobile Brigade (a headquarters squad with no fixed territory, available for any assignment), 42 rue de Bassano (off the Champs-Élysées in Paris), I was given a revolver and seven bullets and a warning not to waste them. I also received a gilt tin police badge, a card decorated with a tricoloured strip and my photograph, another card, dated, which entitled me to ride free on buses and subways. Oh—and I forgot—a pair of hand-cuffs!

'Where's the key?' I asked Danse, the administrative officer. He didn't even bother to raise his nose out of his ledgers. 'The guy who had them before you waltzed off with it. You figure it out.'

I figured it out, army style. But I never needed his key or his handcuffs. My first case took me to Versailles to investigate an abortion ring. My superior then was a chief inspector, about as excitable as a garden slug. I wrote his reports, prepared cases for trial and, thanks to that veteran cop, I learned my trade. My time wasn't wasted. I was also able to observe my colleagues, whose sparkling Maison wit had nicknamed my group the 'speculum section'.

They were too right. My office looked like an abortionists' bazaar. Speculums, probes, contraceptive devices—I had dozens of them, confiscated during my investigation. In the attic room, lacking a closet or even a shelf, where I wrote my reports, they were spread out on the floor labelled and dusty, waiting for the court clerk's office to send for them.

The office next door to ours, on the other hand, was the fief of the brigade's hidalgos. Out of it worked a recently promoted chief inspector and a team of dynamic young detectives specializing in the suppression of 'anti-nationalist' plots. The setting hadn't changed since the Occupation. Neither had the methods.

I went in there one day. For a change, the door was unlocked. Hearing screams, I pushed it open just enough to reveal an ignoble sight. In the middle of the room, stark naked, his knees clamped inside a bicycle wheel, stood a man with his arms outstretched in a cross. In each hand he held a heavy phone book. Before him stood an inspector with his sleeves rolled up, forcing the poor devil to keep his arms raised by administering sharp whacks with a black-jack, which covered his forearms with purple smears. A detective kicked rhythmically at the edge of the bike wheel, sending shock waves through the man's kneecaps that made him shriek with pain.

'What the hell do you want here?' yelled the inspector, slamming the door in my face.

'You'll have to get used to it, Borniche,' my section chief counselled. 'He's a collaborator. That makes him a bad Frenchman.'

I didn't get used to it, not to the abortionists, not to their victims, not to the brutality. As my experience deepened, so did my repugnance towards some of my fellow officers. Their cruelty, their stupidity, their cowardice made me sick to my stomach. The police meant something else to me. Justice, for one thing. I was young, and still dumb enough to make a real pro weep. I had taken on all the dirty jobs in the 'speculum section', investigated the most sordid cases, checked out all the anonymous accusations. I was sinking deeper into filth every day. Soon it would choke me.

My letter of resignation was written. I was going to leave again, but this time it would be my own decision. It was late in 1945. I was just preparing to say good-bye to the police for good when the inside phone rang.

'Borniche? Come down to my office.'

'Yes, sir.'

It was Chief Inspector René Camard, a shy, gruff colossus of a Norman who wore heavy horn-rimmed glasses. When I entered his office, he stared speculatively at me for a long moment.

'The body of an unidentified woman has been found at Saint-Nom-la-Bretèche,' he told me. 'Take a photographer and a driver with you and show me what you can do.'

An hour later, accompanied by a couple of local gendarmes, I was examining the woman's body. It was sprawled in a wood, the bloody head lying in a pile of wet leaves. She had been pretty once.

I felt as though my stomach was stuck in my throat, and yet it was at that very moment that I felt the hunter's instinct stir in me. I hadn't a notion of how to go about identifying the murderer, but, suddenly, I had only one thought in my head: arrest him.

It was a hard case to sort out and it took a long time to solve. Carefully, patiently, I questioned, searched, getting more and more excited as I probed. I was going on nerve; I thought about nothing else, dreamed about it at night. At last, one morning, I got him. The killer was a twenty-year-old named Claude Careli. I had traced him to a small hotel on the rue Fontaine, in Pigalle. I had just started up the stairs to his room when he appeared in the doorway. A girl clung to him. They kissed and she left. Claude stood there a moment, sniffing the air like an animal scenting a trap. That moment was one moment too long for Claude. I was on him with a leap. My hand came down on his shoulder and I heard myself say in a loud, threatening voice: 'Police. Don't move!'

I quickly slipped the handcuffs on him. Christ, that was a great moment. Is it morbid, sick, to feel this way? I'm damned if I know. But feeling that man tremble under my fingers, seeing his look of panic, I experienced a sudden joy, vast, confused, one I had never felt before, as racking as an orgasm.

Claude was the first killer I unmasked. Because of him, I had discovered the exaltation of the hunt, had teetered between hope and despair, optimism and terror. I had stuck with it and I had won my first victory. Until then, I had been a bureaucrat. Now I was a cop.

I tore up my letter of resignation. A few days later, I was assigned to Chief Inspector Prioux's Homicide Squad. The chains were being taken off my imagination.

From the beginning, I knew that a cop is nothing, can never amount to anything without informers. So, in the evening, instead of sitting quietly down to dinner, I haunted the bars and the shady dance halls. I learned to act a part, I learned to speak

underworld slang like a professional. And all the while, my eyes
were snapping mental photographs of the crooks I saw, the
Corsicans and the Lyonnais, the Parisians and the Stéphanois
(from the industrial city of Saint-Étienne), studying them as they
yawned with boredom at their poker tables, their cigarettes
plastered to their underlips and their trilbys shoved back on their
heads.

From time to time, one of them would find himself in my office.
With great good nature, I would scatter small favours in exchange
for betrayals. So the pimps led me to the hold-up artists and the
robbers led me to the killers. It was slow, tedious work, and I had
to show my good faith. If a prostitute was picked up in a raid, her
'protector' would call me and announce funereally, 'Ah, Monsieur
Borniche, if the vice boys don't let her go, I'm ruined.' I'd get
the girl released if she wasn't in too deep. By way of thanks, the
pimp would tip me to a job in the works, or give me the names of
men who had already pulled one, or the address of some guy on
the run. My net gradually took shape. Sometimes, too, I would
pay for information by granting or extending authorization to
remain in Paris. Or a party sentenced in absentia on a minor
count might just become invisible to me. I even handed out a little
cash occasionally, which I fished out of Fatso's little black box
after he had me transferred to his section. There was a spirit of
give and take between police and underworld—on one condition:
that, in the long run, the police gave less than they got. Consider-
ably less. Almost nothing.

By going without sleep, by being understanding, I was able to
spin my web. I had my informers and my spies, shadowy pawns,
furtive and useful. Without them, there is no chance of bagging
the real prizes—the 'big heads' as we call them in police slang.

By the time the Buisson case fell on me, I had already hung
several dozen of these trophies on my wall. I had become Fatso's
blue-eyed boy, the youngster whose methods may not have been
strictly orthodox, but who, he was satisfied to note, got results:
I was filling the prisons.

Which is why the men on the Prefecture's Flying Squad and in
Homicide looked sourly at me. They accused me of sticking my
nose in where it had no business being. They had exclusive rights
over crimes committed in their bailiwick, the Seine Department—
which mostly meant Paris—and its immediate surroundings (since
divided into three administrative departments, Hauts-de-Seine,

Seine-Saint-Denis and Val-de-Marne). This was their living. Sûreté Nationale, please abstain. We had the rest of the country. Wasn't that enough for us?

But Fatso wouldn't see it that way. Ambition? An old score to settle? I never learned what his motive was, but one thing was certain: whenever Hidoine and I stole a march on the others, Fatso exulted, rubbed his hands, bought us a drink at the *bistrot*, sometimes even gave us a bonus. Anything went, so long as we came out ahead of the competition. So the police war raged. Superintendent Clot called us 'the head-stealers'. Jealousy on the part of the others, the ones Fatso called the 'phantom police', filled me with delight. Dazzled by my own brilliance, I stupidly forgot how tough life was—the long, dreary hours spent just watching and waiting, the financial acrobatics I had to perform to buy a Christmas gift for my mistress, Marlyse, my cramped three-room apartment on the rue Lepic, in Montmartre, where I washed in the kitchen sink.

I brought in the 'heads'. Fatso accumulated the medals, the official citations and the merits on the promotion schedule. Me, I got the interminable, grateful handshakes, an occasional wad of cash and always, like a carrot on a stick, the promise of a boost to chief inspector if I brought home a big winner. In spite of all this, I stuck it out. I like the work.

Now the big winner was in sight: Buisson.

The bastard had made progress since his Troyes days. I opened the second folder.

4

It was luck that put Detective Superintendent Belin on the track of the man with black eyes. Belin always went home on the bus. One evening, however, after a gloomy day at headquarters, he decided to walk to try to air out a headache. On his way, he ran into a smiling, slightly embarrassed small-time crook named Willy the Stéphanois. Belin had obtained a suspension of banishment for him in return for some choice bits of gossip. The two men turned into a bar for a quick one.

'Tell me,' the superintendent abruptly inquired as he rolled a cigarette, 'you wouldn't happen to know anything about the guys who are sticking up the bank messengers?'

His eyes suddenly all innocence, the Stéphanois shook his head. 'No.' Belin was sure he was lying.

'Too bad,' he sighed, draining his glass without releasing Willy from his icy blue stare. 'Too bad. Well, enjoy Paris. You won't be here for long . . .'

The Stéphanois choked on his drink. 'What exactly does that mean, Superintendent?'

'That means, Willy, that my boss doesn't see eye to eye with me. He doesn't approve of having you back in the capital. Why, only yesterday he said to me: "Belin, you're wrong to trust that man. In Paris he will be up to his old tricks. I am going to ask that he be sent back to his home territory. Believe me, it's in everybody's interest." '

'You're not going to let him do that, are you?' the Stéphanois bleated.

Belin raised a fatalistic eyebrow. 'But Willy, how am I supposed to show him I've got you on a leash? What proof can I give him of your good intentions? None!'

And, buttoning his grey raincoat, he added with a sigh, 'Of course, if I could give him a tip on that gang and tell him it came from you . . .'

'Okay, okay, don't overdo it, Inspector,' the Stéphanois cut him short in a resigned voice. 'Because of you I'm nothing, a fink. I've squealed on my pals. What does one friend more or less matter now, eh?'

'Well?' Belin's voice whipped at him with the impatience of a man who had spent eleven months chasing shadows.

'Check Desgrandschamps.'

Charles Desgrandschamps was as stupid as he was dangerous. You have to be uncommonly fat-headed to rent an apartment on the avenue Jeanne d'Arc, in Arcueil, in your own name—rent receipts, gas and electricity bills, everything—when you have been wanted for three years for trying to knock off some detectives in Lyons. It was so careless, so witless, in fact, that it simply never occurred to any cop to follow such a line. But it did to Belin. That's what distinguishes a conscientious policeman from a gifted one.

When Desgrandschamps left his apartment one morning a few days later, he had his usual two guns in his pockets, held firmly in his hands, ready to draw. A glance to the right, to the left. Nothing upsetting. Slowly he walked towards his car, which was also registered in his own name. He merely looked at the two mechanics fiddling with the motor of a broken-down Peugeot. That was a mistake. He was no sooner past them than they jumped him. There was nothing Charles could do. Before understanding could penetrate the fat around his brain, he was pinned, disarmed and handcuffed. The two mechanics, of course, were cops.

Brought before Belin, Desgrandschamps naturally denied everything. He had nothing to do with the Troyes mob, had never met the little man with the black eyes.

'Fine,' Belin said. 'That's fine.' Then he threw in the ritual phrase, the one that knots the criminal's guts, the phrase so full of menace that it turns a crook's mind blank with terror.

'A pity!'

Charles at once fell under the spell. 'What's a pity?' he brayed.

'Well, you see, little Charley,' Belin politely explained, 'I know you are part of the gang. Don't bother to deny it. I know. So what's going to happen? I'll tell you. By stupidly denying the evidence like a jackass, you're going to get everybody on your back —me, the examining magistrate,* the court, the jurors who are going to judge you. What will you get out of all this stubbornness? A stiff sentence. Very stiff, in fact. The consequences are obvious:

* An examining magistrate has the power to indict, conducts the preliminary investigation of a case and prepares it for the prosecuting attorney, who actually conducts the prosecution.

the longer you stay inside, the less chance you'll have of seeing your little girl friend again.'

'Keep your hands off her,' Desgrandschamps shouted furiously. 'She don't know nothing. She's clean.'

'Me? I won't touch her,' the policeman promised. 'But I know somebody else who is just waiting for you to be put away for a long stretch so that he can take your place in bed with her. And he's one of the gang you're covering up too.

The trap was crude, but it was subtle enough to catch Desgrandschamps' flea-sized brain. After long and laborious reflection which made the veins stand out in his temples, jealousy prevailed. He talked.

That was how Belin finally learned the names of Abel Sauty, Julien Berthoux, Lucien Gransard, Karl Schmull, Émile Courgibet and, above all, Émile Buisson. And their addresses.

Buisson was holed up in a quiet little hotel in the centre of Lille, working his way through his share of the spoils, some 400,000 francs. Co-operating in this enterprise, as she had been for the past four years, was a good-looking brunette named Yvonne Paindelet, part-time whore, shrewd, fearless and enormously greedy.

Belin got off the train in Lille at seven a.m., gulped down coffee and a *croissant* and, less than twenty minutes later, looking as fresh and pink-cheeked as though he had just left home, pushed through the hotel door. He had a ruddy, open face that inspired confidence, so when he asked where he could find Monsieur Émile, the desk clerk naturally told him: 'Second floor, number three.'

Oddly, for a man as careful as Buisson, the door was unlocked. The superintendent simply pushed it open. Émile and Yvonne were sound asleep, back to back. Belin tiptoed to the bedside table, appropriated the gangster's revolver and tapped him on the shoulder.

'Breakfast, Mimile,' he said.

Buisson grunted and turned over without waking.

'It's porridge, this morning.'

Émile sprang up, fumbling for the gun until he saw it in the policeman's hand.

'Come on, Mimile, on your feet,' Belin snapped. 'We're going back to Paris.'

As Yvonne looked on wordlessly, Buisson calmly dressed and

let himself be handcuffed. With no inkling of Desgrandschamps'
confession, he was confident that this case—like the thirteen
previous ones against him—would be thrown out of court for lack
of evidence. Puffing on his cigarette, he watched ironically as the
superintendent searched the room.

'Except for my toothbrush and Yvonne's panties, I don't think
you'll find much to interest you,' he said, smiling.

Neither, privately, did Belin. He was really just going through
the motions, for the sake of routine. He was sure no crook as
sharp as Buisson would leave anything incriminating lying around.
Suddenly, without even knowing why, he spun on his heel and
surprised Yvonne staring in panic at an umbrella standing in a
dark corner. He walked over to it, opened it. Both men were
astonished to see a shower of thousand-franc bills float gently to
the floor.

'Stupid bitch!' howled an enraged Émile, his customary polite-
ness gone. The fury was justified, too. Belin soon identified the
crackling new bills, bearing numbers in the X 50 500 series, as
part of the Troyes bank haul.

Yvonne cowered in a corner of the bed with her knees tucked
up under her chin, crying, the sobs shaking her whole body.
'Forgive me, Mimile,' she stammered, 'forgive me.'

Buisson, however, was not in a forgiving mood. Wholly out of
control, his face black with anger, he shook his manacled fists.
'When did you do that?' he screamed.

'At night, Mimile, while you were asleep'—she hiccuped. 'I
went through your pockets.'

So, despite all he had given her, including a café on the rue
Saint-Nicolas in Lille, it was Yvonne Paindelet's insatiable greed
that gave Superintendent Belin the irrefutable proof of the little
black-eyed man's guilt.

His arrest taught Buisson an important lesson: never trust anyone, man or woman. It also taught him to cover his tracks
ruthlessly.

Buisson was confined in the Troyes central prison, with Charles
Desgrandschamps as his cellmate, to await trial in the Aube
Department Criminal Court. In those days, the courts were stern
with criminals; Monsieur Émile's sentence was quite likely to be
hard labour for life.

And then came the war. For Monsieur Émile, the war was a

bonanza. It was during those years of agony that he perfected his
occupational skills. When, in June 1940, the green German wave
washed over France, the head guard at Troyes was ordered to
transfer his most dangerous charges to the prison in Nevers (in
the centre of the country). There were seventy of them, but only
twelve wore leg-irons; that was all the hardware the Prisons
Administration had. Buisson was one of the twelve. Escorted by
fifteen guards and seven mobile brigade officers, the little column
set out on foot to walk the 125 miles to Nevers.

The procession had no sooner reached the highway in a fracas
of chains and irons than the head guard knew he would never
bring his full consignment of convicts to their destination. The
wartime exodus was at full tide and the roads, clogged with fleeing
soldiers and civilians, were under ceaseless attack by the Reich's
Stukas.

At the entrance to the town of Breuilly, the German fighters and
bombers beat down on them with unaccustomed violence. When
silence returned—an anguished silence in which people stared at
one another, dumbfounded at finding themselves still alive—the
prison shepherd gathered his flock and counted heads. All the
prison guards reported present. The fifty-eight unchained
prisoners were there, the lot of them. The seven police officers,
who had orders to shoot any prisoners attempting to escape, had
vanished. Of the twelve men in irons, two were present and intact,
two more were wounded. The other eight had melted into the
forest. Émile Buisson was among them.

Eight months went by.

On the morning of 24 February 1941, two bank messengers from
the Crédit Industriel et Commercial withdrew 3,800,000 francs
from the Bank of France and started back towards their home
bank, pushing the money before them in a two-wheeled, box-
shaped pushcart. It was a risky method of transportation, but the
wartime petrol shortage had left the bank no choice.

The two men had just turned into the rue de la Victoire, in
Paris, when a Citroën pulled up alongside them. Three men
jumped out. Two held machine guns. The third, slight and dark-
eyed, waved a Mauser and barked: 'Hands up or I shoot.'

One of the messengers, named Guérin, reached for his gun.
Two shots split the air, their reverberation whining mournfully
through the streets. Guérin, his hands clutching his stomach,

staggered, took two steps, then collapsed. He had only moments to live. His mate bolted, taking refuge in the first building he could reach.

The little man's eyes narrowed for an instant. His body flooded with an almost sexual pleasure, he savoured the strange high that taking a life can arouse. Then he raised the lid of the cart, checked that the two canvas bags inside really were full of money. Stolidly, he helped his two accomplices load the little cart aboard the Citroën. The car started sedately off through streets emptied by the gunfire.

Paris had found a new killer: Émile Buisson.

5

The Toulouse–Paris express pulled away from the Vierzon station and picked up steam, heading for Orléans. In a first-class compartment, stifling in the July heat, three German SS officers read and smoked. From time to time, they cast veiled glances at the small man in shirt sleeves asleep in a tight ball near the door.

Buisson slept unconcerned. He had chosen his travelling companions carefully. He knew they would serve as shields for him, that their presence would discourage any police checks of the compartment. He had left Marseilles, left the hideout he'd found with some Corsican cronies, and, after a brief stop in Toulouse to pick up a set of false identification papers, he was now on his way back to Paris to look up his partners in the rue de la Victoire operation, Abel Danos, Jean-Baptiste Chave and Jean Rocca-Serra. Like him, they were men to whom human life meant nothing important.

An uncharacteristic sadness broke the surface of Buisson's sleep in a ripple of sighs: he was dreaming of his friend Courgibet, who had broken with him after the Troyes hold-up. At their last, stormy meeting, The Escapee had minced no words:

'With you, Émile, there'll be blood someday. You were only a breath away from it in Troyes. So I'm getting the hell out before it's too late. I don't want to wind up on the Widow (the guillotine). I've got my cut, enough to make a fresh start in America. *Ciao.*'

As Courgibet turned away, Buisson, his eyes sparkling with bitter anger, growled through clenched teeth: 'Milo, nobody has ever talked to me the way you just have, and nobody ever will again. I could put one right between your eyes . . .'

'Then why don't you, Émile?' Courgibet had dared him.

'Because you were my friend, because I loved you like a brother. All right, you've made your choice. Now blow. As far as I'm concerned you no longer exist. You're nothing but a cheap little blabbermouth. Afraid to dirty your little hands with blood? What crap! Perhaps you hope that society and the cops will lay off you because you've been nothing but a small-time thief because you have no stiffs on your conscience? Don't kid yourself— you'll be tracked, hunted down like the rest. Whether rats bite or not, society wants their hides. Go on, clear out, you poor stupid bugger.'

A series of jolting stops and starts woke Buisson from his brooding sleep. He sat up, blinking, then grabbed the jacket in the net over his seat, looking for his comb. Because the hand that reached for it was nervous, the jacket came down swinging. A nine-millimetre bullet fell to the seat and rolled on to the floor, followed by a second, a third—his 'cough drops', Buisson called them. Émile thought fast. If the Germans searched him, they would find the gun he had carefully hidden in the pocket he'd sewn into the belly of his trousers. There was nothing else to do. The compartment window was open. In a single sweep of his arm, he yanked the Mauser from its holster and hurled it as far as he could into the field through which the express was racing.

For a split second, the SS men sat frozen in surprise. Then the shouting started. Buisson guessed only too accurately what they were saying. One of them pulled the communication cord and the train came squealing to a halt.

Shoved, shaken and manhandled, Buisson was forced to climb down and look for the gun. A bizarre ballet developed along the track, the Germans looking for evidence of his guilt and Monsieur Émile, not yet handcuffed, praying to the villains' god to reach down and deliver him safely into a nearby wood. His prayer went unanswered. Two hours later, he was locked up at Gestapo headquarters in Orléans.

Unusually, for such organized, methodical men, the Gestapo agents' investigation was slipshod and half-hearted. On the day of his trial, Buisson, under the name inscribed on his false papers, Métadieu, appeared before German judges. After a brief, boring, depressing hearing, he was sentenced to a year in jail.

He didn't flinch, made no appeal. Émile had been let off lightly and he knew it. Ever since his arrest on the train he had lived in terror that the Germans would consult their French counterparts and discover his real identity. If that happened, he would be dealing with French courts. He had killed a man in the rue de la Victoire. It wasn't prison he risked now; his head was at stake. When Buisson returned to cell No. 12 in the Orléans prison, he was a relieved, almost cocky man.

Not for long. One afternoon, a visitor came to see him: Detective Superintendent Belin.

'Nice to see you again, Émile,' Belin said amiably.

The Gestapo's performance had been dispirited, but not so lax that they had neglected to relay Buisson's photo and fingerprints to the French police. It took no time at all for the PJ to identify the man they had been hunting for five months.

Émile was shipped back to the Troyes prison and placed in solitary confinement. In the bleak, silent cage, the beast began to learn dissimulation.

Buisson's conduct was irreproachable. To guard Louis Vincent, he was a docile, deferential prisoner, a little taciturn, who kept to himself, seemingly disdainful of the rest of his prison world. His faintly haughty manner and his obedience quickly earned him the acrid contempt of the other prisoners. Émile couldn't have cared less. Small-time thieves, down-and-outs—they didn't interest him. He preferred to be alone. On his cell door, the authorities had posted the regulation notice: '*Dangerous*—watch closely.'

Vincent watched closely. He knew Émile's record, knew his reputation for savagery. At first, he thought the man was faking submission to lull his guards' suspicions. Lots of guys before him had tried that stunt, but Vincent was too old a fox, too experienced, too familiar with all the old tricks to be easily hoodwinked.

Every prisoner and his guard play a long, patient waiting game, each trying to anticipate the other's intentions—an almost artful game of hide-and-seek. The slightest slip—a gleam of evil in a man's eye, the shadow of a sardonic smile, a clenched fist—is enough to show the wolf under the sheep's clothing.

Vincent had been through all that. He waited, stubbornly. This was his trade, this was what he was paid for. And, finally, he decided Buisson was sincere. So convinced of it was he that, one evening in the dining hall, he declared: 'If you ask me, this Buisson of theirs isn't anything to get worked up about. A thug, maybe, but you have to admit he's no terror. Never a sharp word, never a row. When I think that his cell is searched every day as though he was Al Capone when he's obviously nothing but a puny little runt, I reckon we're doing a lot of worrying for nothing on his account.'

On Saturday, 4 July 1942, Émile spent the morning groaning.

Sprawled on his bunk apparently unable to rise, he writhed in pain. His face twisted, he informed one of the day-shift screws that his 'stomach was on fire', that horrible, searing pains were tearing him in half.

'What do you want then?' the guard asked. 'Do you want to be sent to the infirmary?'

'Never mind, sir. I'll try to hold out. Just give me an extra water ration. Have a heart.'

The guard, sorry for him, brought him the water. Shortly after lunch, which he refused, Buisson fell to groaning again, so loudly and frequently that the sympathetic guard granted him still another water ration. 'Stay in bed,' he told the prisoner. 'I'll okay it.'

When Vincent made his first tour on the night shift, Buisson was whimpering in agony. The guard opened the little window in the cell door and talked to the man inside, trying to comfort him. But Émile writhed on his bed, clawing at the blanket. He was foaming at the mouth, unable to utter a word.

Ten past midnight on the cell-block clock. For some minutes, Buisson's moans had been howls. The men in the other cells, kept awake by the racket, shouted curses and called on him to knock it off. Émile's yelps were coming uninterruptedly now. Vincent, beginning his second round, tried unsuccessfully to quieten the uproar in the cells. With long, rapid strides he marched towards Buisson's cell. Turning the light on from the outside, he opened the peephole and saw Émile twisting on the bed, clutching his stomach; his hair was standing on end and there was a wild look in his eyes.

'Émile,' he called, 'do you want me to tell the head guard? He could send you to the hospital.'

His eyes shut against the pain, Buisson shook his head in refusal. 'Not worth it, sir. Don't bother him. Let him sleep.'

Suddenly, he fell silent. His eyes bulged. Then he let loose a long shriek of pain, which immediately triggered a storm of shouts and curses from the other cells. Uncertain, Vincent scratched his head. 'Calm down, Émile,' he said. 'Come on, buck up, man. What can I do for you?'

'Water,' Buisson panted. 'Water, just water. That's the only thing that stops the burning.'

'All right. Pass me your mug.'

'Fill the pitcher, please, sir. The mug only lasts a minute the way I am . . . I'm dying of thirst.'

Vincent was visibly annoyed. 'Impossible, Émile,' he said. 'The

jug won't fit through the window and you know as well as I do
that I'm not authorized to enter a cell alone at night.'

'Please,' Buisson moaned, 'I'm begging you. Have a heart. You
know I've never made any trouble for you. Give me a drink,
please.'

Vincent hesitated, peered again at the spectacle of suffering inside the cell. His charity proved stronger than the regulation. As
though trying to square the infraction with himself, he reasoned
that a strong, healthy man like him had nothing to fear from a
little weasel like Buisson.

He slipped the two bolts, turned the key twice in the lock,
opened the door and made for the pitcher near the bed. He was
leaning over to grasp it when Monsieur Émile struck with numbing speed. The day before, he had given another inmate a package
of tobacco in exchange for an empty half-litre bottle. Breaking
of the neck with a sharp crack, he had lovingly sharpened the
cutting edge on the iron hook that held his bunk folded against
the wall. Now the glass teeth bit into the left side of the guard's
throat. Blood spurted in dense, pulsing sprays. The blow was
driven in with such force that two of the glass teeth snapped off
in the victim's jaw. They saved Vincent's life, blocking the lower
cutting edges only five millimetres from the carotid artery.

Blood was already collecting in pools on the floor where the
warder lay, his throat rattling and his lips blowing pink bubbles
with a horrible, gurgling noise. Stepping coldly into the red
puddle, Buisson bent over to take his keys.

Vincent was still conscious. Despite his wound, he summoned
all his ebbing strength and yelled for help. At the far end of the
building, the other night guard heard him and immediately
triggered the alarm system. As he raced down the steps to the
prison office, where he guessed the keys to the main gate were
kept, Buisson saw doors suddenly open to disgorge pyjama-clad
guards, with guns in their hands, coming towards him at a
run. Glancing up, he saw Vincent's partner taking careful aim at
him.

It was all over. Émile stopped, raised his arms. Slowly he
climbed back up the steps. Slowly he turned back into his cell.
His dark eyes rested briefly on Vincent, now unconscious and
barely breathing. Then he crossed the cell, flattened himself
against the far wall and waited. When the guards burst in, their
guns trained on him, he was standing absolutely still; his face

wore a distant look, as though what was happening there no longer concerned him.

On 13 May 1943, Émile Buisson was sentenced in the Aube Department Criminal Court to hard labour for life. He was sent to Clairvaux prison, where he made another unsuccessful attempt to escape. In November 1946, he was transferred to the Santé prison in Paris. The examining magistrate handling the rue de la Victoire hold-up charged him with the murder of Guérin, the bank messenger.

Preparation of the prosecution's case promised to be long and slow. The machinery of post-war justice was so clogged up with denunciations as France purged itself of its Vichyites and its collaborators that ordinary criminal cases were viewed as mere nuisances.

Buisson was nevertheless questioned every week in the magistrate's office in the Palace of Justice. He knew he was fighting to hang on to his head. He had killed Guérin, but the judge still had to prove it. The duel was deadly, merciless. Émile, as always, denied the facts.

And luck was still with him. Abel Danos, arrested 20 July 1941, escaped soon afterwards and, to stay clear of the law, had enlisted in the French Gestapo under his pals Bony and Lafont. He disappeared when France was liberated and had not been seen since. Jean-Baptiste Chave, another Gestapo recruit, was arrested and executed in December 1944. The last of the bunch, Rocca-Serra, who had fled to Corsica to bury his pile, had been murdered in an underworld vendetta.

'Come now,' expostulated the judge, weary of running his head against Buisson's quietly obstinate denials. 'I know all about it.'

'That would surprise me,' Émile replied. 'There's only one who knows what I've done in my life, your honour, and that's the good Lord. But he'll never squeal. He's no louse.'

6

Night had fallen by the time I closed the last folder. For over four hours I had been plunged into Monsieur Émile's past. I knew what I had on my hands now. My mouth furry from too many cigarettes, I got up, collecting the folders. As I moved towards the door, I noticed Hidoine's rust-coloured suit hanging on the nail I had hammered into the wall because the Grande Maison, despite my repeated urging, declined to grant us a coat-rack. Absorbed in my reading, I hadn't even noticed Hidoine's return from the Santa Maria, hadn't seen him leave again. I could picture him now in the Metro, pirouetting to show off those booted calves to a row of thick-waisted women passengers, their make-up smudged and their varicose veins throbbing after a hard day's work. Annoyed, I went and knocked at Fatso's door, but he had deserted the Sûreté Nationale too; at that moment he was probably steaming towards the Deux Marches, Victor Marchetti's bar-restaurant on the rue Gît-le-Cœur.

I left too. With my hands rammed into my pockets, I stood on the pavement in front of the main entrance, undecided whether to go home or go and sip an aperitif at the Calanques, a bar on the rue Quentin-Bauchart (off the Champs-Élysées). I finally opted for the drink. I liked the Calanques. It was a posh bar, cushy, softly lit and snug, a gold-plated oasis where movie stars, executives, advertising men, reporters and the better class of bureaucrat congregate every evening to rub compulsions. Very heady. Not exactly in my price class, but I like to jostle the rich occasionally, to brush against the pretty, perfumed women in their mink armour. I get a kick out of other people's money.

Besides, I was in with the bar's owners. They knew I was a cop, of course, but they had accepted me as a regular. I would tuck myself discreetly in a corner of the bar and shoot dice with them, or chat. It relaxed me.

The owners were both Corsicans, but there the resemblance stopped. The customers called the older one Toto. His name was really Antoine Rossi and his brother was Tino Rossi, the famous crooner. Toto hid his bald spot under a brown wig, which he sometimes wore fitted to one side, like a cap. He was a roly-poly man, short, gentle and smiling, who liked to flit from table to table and natter with the paying guests.

His partner was a tall fellow, slim and muscular. He was twenty-eight—my age. My five feet nine inches barely reached up to his ears. He had wavy chestnut hair, which he brushed straight back, and blue eyes. There was something a little cruel in his rare smiles; women—especially the actresses Viviane Romance and Ginette Leclerc—ate him up. Professional habit had led me to do a little research on him in Records. All I found was one conviction, during the Occupation, for stealing cars for the Resistance. Since then, nothing, not a slip, not even a fine. The impeccable record of an irreproachable individual. The name of this upstanding citizen was François Marcantoni.

It was Marcantoni who greeted me when I entered the Calanques that evening. He stuck out his big, sinewy hand and offered me champagne. He filled my glass, thought about things for a moment, poured one for himself, raised it in a salutory 'Chin-chin' and drank it down, clicking his tongue. His calm, steady gaze searched my face. 'Everything going the way you like it, Inspector?'

'Yes,' I said, 'but it would be going a damn sight better if I had a line on Buisson.'

I was really hooked. I wanted to talk about Émile. I hadn't been able to get my mind off him since I finished reading his dossier. I tried to climb into his skin, to think as he would. I imagined him holed up somewhere in Paris, alert to the smallest alarm. Somewhere—but where? It would have helped to be able to talk about him to Hidoine or even to Fatso, but they were unavailable. I knew Marcantoni wasn't interested in my troubles. He never thought about anything but the take and the customers. But I had to talk to somebody about Monsieur Émile, about the little man with the black eyes who had erupted into my life.

Marcantoni's eyebrows slithered up on his forehead. 'Buisson. What's that?'

'A killer, chum. The worst kind. A thug who shoots by instinct. He broke out this morning.'

'Oh!' Marcantoni said, always polite. 'And he's roaming around loose?' He endowed me with a second glass of champagne and a sample of Corsican irony: 'I have a feeling you're going to wear out a lot of shoes trying to dig up someone hiding out in Paris. Luckily, you're not alone.'

Oh no, I wasn't alone. That's just what was bothering me. But then, all the competition had in its pockets was the same old 1937 police photo I had, showing Buisson in a prison jacket, with his head shaved.

'Come on, Inspector, don't let it get you down,' Marcantoni said. 'You'll find your Buisson. In the meantime, think about something else. Look at these lovely women all around us; they're as beautiful as a fat bankroll.'

I ran a distracted eye around the room, but not even women could push Émile out of my mind that evening. I bought my round, shook hands with Monsieur François and left. At that moment, somewhere in Paris, a little man was savouring his first evening as a fugitive. And at that moment, all over the city, the men from Homicide and the Flying Squad were searching for him with a fine-toothed comb.

Less than thirty minutes later I was at my place in Montmartre. I had hardly closed the front door when, as usual, Marlyse called out:

'That you?'

'It's me.'

She sailed out of the kitchen, wiping her hands on her apron and looking very put out indeed. She bestowed a mother-in-law's kiss upon me and, before I could take off my jacket, put on my slippers or even draw a breath, she announced in a strained voice: 'The cooker's at it again.'

I groaned. I was truly weary of that cooker. It was always on the blink. Always. If it wasn't the oven, it was the big burner that was blocked, or leaked. It wasn't a cooker, it was a scrap heap I spent hours stripping down, reassembling, patching up under the doubtful eye of my heart's delight. A new cooker was what we needed, but that cost 7,000 francs, which for us was ridiculous. I only made 11,000 a month, plus 2,000 francs in expenses that Fatso always haggled over. That was a little short of what I'd have needed to buy myself the Palace of Versailles *and* modernize the plumbing too.

This time it was the oven that had passed out. I twisted the key right, then left. The thing made a little gasping sound, more like a death rattle. Then it sank back into its lethargy. 'So how am I supposed to cook your dinner?' Marlyse challenged while, sitting on the floor with my tool kit beside me, I began unscrewing things, smearing myself with grease, already defeated by this Neanderthal gadget. I butchered an hour performing emergency surgery on it, but the pipe remained as lifeless as a plugged artery. I finally gave up. We ate in silence—tinned tuna, salad, cheese. As usual, after dinner, I washed the dishes. I enjoy it. Marlyse busied herself straightening up the apartment. She couldn't do it in the morning, because she had to rush off to the office at eight a.m. So I washed the glasses and the spoons and I thought, quietly.

If I can arrest Émile Buisson, I mused, my troubles are over. To begin with, it means promotion to chief inspector. That's the first ace. Second ace: my pay goes up to 13,000 francs a month and my expenses, however pained Fatso may look, go up accordingly. Third ace: I can buy Marlyse a new cooker with so much chrome on it she'll be too dazzled to nag at me.

If I did arrest Émile Buisson, though, I would have to be very careful not to be made a fool of. When I arrested the murderers of the Marly mystery man, who got the credit? The boss. When I arrested the four gunmen who plucked the Danish consul's friends, and Crazy Pierre's gang, when I identified the culprits in he Môme Moineau burglary, who got the promotions and the bonuses? The boss.

I washed the last glass and resolved that, if I got Buisson, I wasn't going to let Fatso take advantage again. The promotion list for inspectors was due to be drawn up soon. If I got to Buisson before then—and, naturally, before my colleagues at the Prefecture as well—I'd be on that list. I would try to keep Fatso in the dark about it as long as I could; I didn't want him calling press conferences in his office and preening for the photographers beside Public Enemy No. 1.

Marlyse came into the kitchen with the rubbish pail she'd just emptied in the courtyard. She dried the dishes, yawning. 'You know, Roger, I don't dare touch that oven. I'm too scared that one of these days it's going to blow up in my face. I'd be disfigured—do you realize that?'

She and her damned cooker were getting on my nerves. As though nothing else mattered. 'Don't worry,' I said, trying to pacify her, 'just don't use it.'

'That's no problem,' she retorted sourly. 'It's not as though I were always cooking expensive roasts and chickens. If that oven is falling apart, it's from lack of activity. We could fill it with water and put goldfish in it for all the good it does.'

The reproach brought me spinning around to face her, but I managed to keep my mouth shut. I was too preoccupied with Buisson, and too tired besides, to volunteer for a domestic scene. In my most conciliatory manner, I wound my arm around her shoulders and led her towards the bedroom. Lying there in the dark, I told her about Buisson and what he could mean to us. The more I talked, the giddier I felt. I described the new cooker I was going to give her—it would have an automatic pilot light, this one would—and the weekend at Le Touquet we could treat ourselves to with the bonus. I called up visions of oysters and swimming in the sea, of cold white wine and hot sand and lobsters and mayonnaise, of moonlight promenades. Positively lyrical, I was. I could see happiness beckoning and my romanticism sent me soaring into a kind of hysteria. I was a poet-cop, I could see myself on the beach, could feel the hot sun on my skin and the sea breeze brushing my hair.

'Well?' I chortled to Marlyse. 'What do you think?'

Total silence. My muse was asleep.

The next morning, in the local butcher's shop in the rue Lepic, I learned the details of the Buisson-Girier breakout. They were in my neighbour's newspaper, which I read every morning, leaning against the counter near the cash register before finishing the shopping. No saving is too small for economic midgets like me.

7

It did not take Buisson long to realize that if he still had any hope of escaping, however slight, the attempt had to be made while he was in the Santé. It was in Paris that his best chance lay, in transit to and from the interrogation sessions at the Palace of Justice, in Paris that he had family and friends to hide him. He was counting on the rue de la Victoire case being thrown out for lack of evidence. If it was, he planned to take the blame for robberies he had never committed, even to invent some if he had to. That would keep the investigation going indefinitely, avoiding his transfer away from Paris to somewhere in the provinces, to serve out the life term he was already under.

Émile didn't need much sleep. He spent his nights endlessly 'hitting the ten'—prison slang for pacing a cell—dreaming up wild, bold schemes to gain his freedom.

This shuffling of soles and pounding of heels on the cement floor finally got on the other prisoners' nerves. He was keeping them awake, and he paced to an explosive chorus of insults from the nearby cells. Buisson just kept pacing, concentrating, indifferent to the protests, hardly even hearing them; there was room in his mind for only one thought: how to break out.

Yet inspiration, when it came, was the product of an insult. One night, an irate voice in a nearby cell yelled, 'The guy's nuts; he ought to be locked up.' Émile stopped dead. *Nuts.* The word sliced through his mind, twisted his lips in a tight smile. What an idiot he'd been not to think of it before. 'That's the answer,' he exulted. 'I'll play loony and get myself locked up in a nuthouse. A breakout from there will be easy.'

Overnight, Monsieur Émile's behaviour became very odd indeed. He washed in his soup, played obscenely with his slop-pail, burst into wild laughter at the sight of a cloud during his exercise period, made grave speeches to the gravel and greedily licked the floor and walls of his cell. This was the gay period, the harmless-nut phase. This was followed by phase two: hallucinations of monsters, of horrible heads intent on hurting him. He began by moaning, then crying, yelling, finally rolling convulsively on the floor, yowling that they were choking him, biting him, killing him. He appealed pathetically for help and when the guards, their nerves scraped raw, pushed into his cell, he threw himself into their arms, hugged them and licked their faces.

One morning, two husky warders stalked in unexpectedly, grabbed him and led him, groaning, to the infirmary. There he grumbled, tried to bite the doctor, a young and very hygienic type, bayed, hugged a guard and wound up scrambling on all fours. The doctor, a specialist, gave a discreet signal. Émile was tucked gently into a straitjacket and carted off to the Villejuif mental hospital. The sky was a watery blue, the air a little chilly, as befits an early April day. His clothes were taken from him and replaced by a long, billowing smock. Then he was put to bed in a glass cage. The head nurse locked the door after him and hung a sign on it: 'Dangerous lunatic.'

Once again, Buisson began to study the place, its routine, its habits. He quickly noticed that the four guards assigned to watch the inmates during exercise periods—an hour in the morning, another in the afternoon—were nothing like numerous enough to put down a real disturbance. They waited until things settled down, then moved in to clean up and send the most battered combatants to the infirmary. Little riots like these blew up every day, out of the blue, for no reason, with diabolic suddenness.

Émile was small, puny, weak and entirely ungifted for brawling. He tried to keep to himself, to stay out of the mix-ups, avoid becoming involved, but the inmates were irritable, violent, vicious. And, above all, unpredictable. He learned that the first time he was taken to the shower room. This was a big room, its ceiling starred with shower heads that drizzled water—tepid or icy, depending on the attendant's whim—on some thirty naked, gesticulating, bawling fellows. Émile was peacefully soaping himself when he felt a warmer, stronger jet hit his leg. He spun on his heel and saw a man with pinched lips and a nasty expression urinating on him. Émile moved away, but made no protest. When the shower ended, the column of patients plodded back up the stairs to the glass cages. Émile, silent, studied the routine, his eye catching every detail that might fit into his escape plans. Suddenly, he felt pain lance through his thigh. He yelled, wheeling around. The fellow who had relieved himself against Émile's leg in the shower was now kneeling behind him, rabidly biting him. Émile jerked his leg away, but the madman, his mouth open, was poised to snap again. Émile, furious and terrified, kicked the man in the face. He heard something crack, saw blood spout. The man toppled over backward, sweeping those behind him down the steps in his fall. The staircase was a tunnel of howls, complaints, a hellish tumult. Then a collective wave of hatred washed over them. With guttural little cries, they charged. Buisson realized he would have to run for it or be torn apart. With the strength of despair, he charged the pack piling up the steps towards him, punching and kicking as he ploughed through, then raced down the steps at meteoric speed to the exercise yard.

There, his wind gone, he stopped, but the approaching pounding of feet told him he was still by no means safe. The first pursuit wave was already pouring through the door. Panicked, Émile looked wildly around for a refuge. He saw a tree, ran to it and clambered up, kicking wildly at the fingers digging into his calves. Then he was free and in the branches. Some of the inmates tried to follow. He discouraged them by flattening their faces with his heel.

Perched on his branch, he gazed in stunned contemplation at the crowd below him. They were making an appalling racket, shaking their fists at him, spitting up at him, shaking the tree in an effort to unseat him. From where he cowered, a disheartened Buisson could see the guards leaning against the wall with their arms crossed, waiting for the riot to end.

His arms wrapped desperately around the trunk, the branch under him bobbing like a runaway seesaw, Émile just managed to hang on. His feet were kept busy repelling the most stubborn of the wolves from climbing up after him. His face was white with fear. Then he had an idea. He raised an open hand over the rage-swollen faces below him. Silence fell. In a shaky voice, he called down:

'My friends, the time has come to talk politics.'

There was a rumble from below, then, gradually, silence again.

'One man saved France: General de Gaulle!' Émile chanted. '*Vive le Général!*'

In perfect chorus, the pack of patients howled, '*Vive le Général!*'

'One man thought of the people's happiness: Maurice Thorez (chairman of the French Communist Party, who died in 1964)! *Vive Maurice Thorez!*'

Again, the mob echoed him: '*Vive Maurice Thorez!*'

Clinging prudently to his branch, Émile kept them cheering— 'Long live the Pope', 'Long live Social Security', 'Long live Stalin . . . Churchill . . .' When he proposed the health of Hitler, however, the meeting went to pieces. Some of the inmates cheered loudly. Others protested. Discussion groups formed which quickly moved on to more violent contention. Within minutes, there was a full-scale free-for-all at the foot of the tree.

Émile jumped lightly to the ground and ran to his glass cage, where he had the nurse lock him in. Only then, his face shining with sweat, did he let himself be convulsed by a fit of trembling.

From that day on, exercise took only one form for Buisson: the instant he reached the yard, he took a few quick steps to get the blood moving in his legs, then practically flew up onto his branch, out of reach of blows and other assorted dirty tricks. From where he sat, he got a comprehensive view of the world below him. One inmate painstakingly gathered pebbles, examined them minutely, rubbed them on his sleeve and sucked them. If the flavour satisfied him, he would whisk the stone under his shirt, from where it would fall at once to the ground. Then he picked it up again and repeated his experiment. He kept this up until the end of the exercise period. Another inmate had his own routine, which he repeated exactly day after day, running from the building wall to the tree, spraying his companions with imaginary bursts of machine-gun fire to the accompaniment of a loud vocal 'tac-tac-tac'. Flattened against the tree trunk, he let loose a few more rounds, then looked up at Buisson. His eyes bulging, a flaccid smile on his lips, he would then pant: 'I got seven more this morning.' He shot his way tirelessly through every exercise period, under the mocking eyes of the guards. He was a young man with wavy fair hair and a fine-featured, romantic face. His name was René Girier, but the underworld had nicknamed him René the Exile.

A glum-faced Émile stared down from his branch at the mad-men milling around the exercise yard. He was in a bad mood that morning, too bad to hold it in. 'Christ, I'm sick of all these damned loonies', he muttered in an exasperated voice. 'Sick, sick, sick . . .'

Below him, Girier was blasting off his usual volleys of vocal machine-gun fire. The handsome face peered up at Buisson, the eyes perfectly lucid. In a steady voice, he declared, 'I'm just as sick of the buggers as you are, believe me.'

So Buisson and Girier discovered that one was no more mad than the other. From that moment, both men became the hospital's most fervent, most punctilious, most assiduous chapel-goers. They never missed a mass, never skipped vespers, developed insatiable appetites for taking communion. Guards and attendants saw them side by side, their heads bowed in contemplation, motionless, rigid with devotion. Only their lips moved—but not in prayer. They had found a perfect device for meeting to discuss escape plans.

Serious planning had begun during the visiting hour one Sunday. Shortly after one p.m. an attendant had informed Buisson that he was wanted in the visiting room. Surprised, wondering who the devil had come to see him, Émile walked into the room. A woman was waiting for him. He stared steadily at her . . . No, he'd never seen her before. She was short but nicely assembled, wore a shade too much make-up—'on the game', Émile thought—on a delicate, sensual face. She gazed at him, smiling. Her visitor's pass said she was Buisson's sister. Her real name was Yvonne Bernetou, a fact of which Buisson was unaware. In the usual Sunday confusion of the visiting room, she was able to whisper, 'I'm Screwball's girl; give me a kiss for show.'

Screwball! At the mention of the name, Émile felt his heart beating in his chest. Screwball was his elder brother, Jean-Baptiste, bigger than Émile, powerfully built, daring. When they were both teenagers, it was he who had taught Émile to pick locks, to steal, he who, later on, had trained him to crack safes and handle a gun. They had worked together for years, and the dangers they shared had brought them even closer together. Once, long before the war, they had sworn a pact: if one of them was captured by the police, the other would stop at nothing to free him.

Screwball was keeping his word.

Émile kissed the young woman, then they sat looking at each other, ill at ease. Yvonne didn't stay long, ten minutes at the most, but that was time enough for her to inform Émile that his brother and a group of reliable friends were working on the breakout. 'You'll have another visitor soon,' she told him, 'who will give you details.'

On the following Thursday, Buisson was led down to the visiting room again. A man was waiting for him this time. Émile almost exclaimed in surprise when he saw him. The man standing before him with his hands in his pockets wore a brown and white check cap that only a crook would affect—but a brand-new Legion of Honour rosette peeped from the lapel of his jacket.

His name was Roger Dekker. He was Émile's height, but strongly built, with a bull neck topped by a square face from which gleamed eyes like green marbles. They had known each other in Clairvaux, where Dekker was doing time for burglary, and for three years he had been Émile's only prison friend. Now they kept a routine conversation going, but, every time the guard turned away, even for a second, Dekker filled him in on Screwball's plans, talking in a scarcely audible voice, barely moving his lips, prison style. A hash of a dialogue—scraps of information interlarded with loudly announced family news:

'Your sister Jeanne is fine; the Hunchback is real good to her.'

'The Hunchback?'

'Yes, Paul Brutus. We call him that because he's got a deformed vertebra that gives him a funny walk, stiff, bent over— hunchbacked, what the hell! He can't even bend his neck. He's a big fat fellow, huge in fact, and funny as hell. Jeanne and him, they understand each other, it's nice to see a couple like that.' The voice dropped: 'Screwball has already cased this place. We get you out through the cemetery.' Then he carried on in a normal tone: 'Didn't you know about Jeanne? Didn't anybody tell you?'

'A little,' Buisson said, nodding.

'She's deaf as a post, pal, nothing will ever get through those ears again; they're plugged as a stiff's—we'll bring a ladder to get you over the moats.'

'How did it happen, to Jeanne?'

'It was in 1942, the sailors blew up their ships so as not to leave them for the Fritz. Made a hell of a noise, I can tell you, like a volcano going off for hours and hours. Jeanne was living in Toulon, near the Navy Yard, and her eardrums just couldn't take it.'

'Sailors! God, what stupid bastards!' Buisson yelped indignantly.

'Maybe they are, but that's how it is. Jeanne's peaceful. She lives in perpetual silence—we'll bring you guns and we've got a hideout; I'll let you know—it's for soon.'

Émile went back to his cell, thinking of Dekker.

Little Roger, as he was called, had kept his word too. They had had a serious talk in Clairvaux one day, he and Émile. 'If we're separated and you manage to get clear,' Buisson had told him, 'go to Paris and straight to my brother Jean-Baptiste. He lives at

10 Faubourg-Saint-Martin. He'll give you a hand.' On 16 June 1947, Dekker escaped from Caen Prison, where he had been sent on transfer. For over a month, he hid in the apartment of his mistress, Suzanne Fourreau, on the rue Bichat. Then, confident the heat was off, he went to see Screwball.

Émile's brother was not alone in his gloomy, two-room flat. In addition to his companion, Yvonne Bernetou, who worked the rue Blondel in the evening but who at that moment was frying cutlets, there was a man present, a snub-nosed individual with wary eyes who kept his mouth shut. One look at him reassured Dekker, however; 'jailbird' was written all over the man's pasty colour and shaved head.

'This is Francis Caillaud, a Breton and a very hard man indeed,' Screwball said by way of introduction. 'He's just broken out of Fresnes.'

Francis was not a big man, but he was known for his stubbornness—in this he was typical of the people from his region—and for his prodigious strength; he could lift a car by its bumper. More than any other quality, however, his insistence on 'paying his own way'—never betraying an accomplice—had earned him the respect of the underworld.

Dekker and Caillaud shook hands. Yvonne brought glasses, water and a bottle of *pastis*. Everyone took a glass. 'Good,' Screwball said briskly, as though there weren't a moment to lose, 'now we have to get my brother out of the booby hatch. You're both with me?'

His two guests nodded agreement.

'I saw the lawyer and he guaranteed me he'd get us passes for Villejuif,' Screwball said. 'Yvonne will go first, to sniff the wind. She's a woman, so there's no risk there. Then one of us will go and see Émile with a forged pass.'

'I'll go,' Dekker offered.

'What? Are you weak in the head?' Screwball snapped. 'You're on the run. A wanted man.'

'Exactly,' Dekker replied. 'The law would never think of looking for me in an asylum. I'll stick a Legion of Honour on me --that's bourgeois and respectable.'

'And what about that stubble on your skull?'

'A cap.'

And that was the beginning of post-war France's most spectacular jailbreak.

A black Citroën carrying Screwball, Dekker and Caillaud cruised slowly around the vast quadrilateral complex of sinister-looking buildings forming the Villejuif psychiatric hospital. The northern-most of the line of parallel blocks was reserved for the criminally insane. Deep, walled moats separated the building, named the Henri-Collin section, from a football stadium next to the town cemetery. On the south side, footbridges spanned the moats to link the section to the rest of the hospital complex.

Screwball passed his binoculars to Dekker. 'Complicated,' he growled.

To say the least. But the break had to be made. Screwball set the date: the morning of 3 September.

Dekker arrived at Screwball's apartment at eight o'clock on the morning of 2 September to find the elder Buisson in his pyjamas, sipping milky coffee with a friend, André Liotard, alias Dédé the Demon.

'Right,' Roger announced. 'I've pinched a car. It's a beauty; the owner was choosy. I've got it hidden in a yard round the back.' He eyed Screwball impatiently. 'Are you going to get dressed, or what? We've still got to look for a ladder.'

Jean-Baptiste was ready in no time. On their way out, Dekker looked Liotard up and down and asked him, 'Can you drive?'

'Can I drive! Why d'you think they call me Demon? Because I drive so fast!'

'Okay, you can come with us tomorrow, then. You can wait in the car.'

The three men found a nineteen-foot mason's ladder on a building site in the rue du Stade, in Villejuif, near the hospital. Unconcernedly, as though they owned it, they tied it to the roof of the stolen Alfa-Romeo. After a swing around the hospital, they dumped the ladder at the foot of the stadium wall. From there, they could see part of the Henri-Collin yard and, more important, the two nine-foot-deep moats around it. They could also see three men shuffling disconsolately around the yard. One of them was Émile. Depressed, the rescue team returned to Paris.

Just after lunch, Francis Caillaud went sick. His face turned olive green and he began to vomit convulsively, moaning softly. Screwball was frantic. He accused the delicatessen owner of selling them rotten pork and threatened to put a bullet through him. 'If there's one thing I can't stand it's a dishonest tradesman,' he fumed. 'They're poisoners, murderers, scum like that!'

Neither he nor Dekker were feeling all that perky; suspect rumblings could be heard in their stomachs. But they stayed on their feet, while Francis, sprawled on Screwball's bed, continued to complain despite the hot-water bottle and bicarbonate of soda with which Yvonne treated him.

'That's not the worst of it,' Screwball burst out. 'We got to find a replacement.'

That is how they came to recruit Henri Russac, a tall, dark, slender man they found draped over the bar at L'Étape sipping an aperitif. Russac had known Émile in the Santé.

At midnight, the black Alfa-Romeo whispered to a stop under the stadium wall. Screwball, Dekker and Russac got out. They raised the ladder against the wall. As quietly as cats, they climbed to the top, pulling the ladder up after them, then lowering it down on the other side. Now they were at the bottom of the first moat. Panting, but without wasting a movement, they set the ladder against the inner bank of the moat and scrambled up into the hospital grounds, again dragging the ladder after them as they slithered on their bellies to the second moat and climbing down into it. Still dragging their ladder, they advanced about thirty-five yards up the moat, to the cover of a footbridge. There, stretched out motionless in the grass, they waited for morning.

8

3 September 1947; ten a.m. Two attendants pushed a trolley loaded with mess tins across the footbridge over the moat. At that moment, Émile emerged into the yard. The attendants returned less than half an hour later. They no sooner opened the Henri-Collin gate than Dekker and Russac appeared over the edge of the moat and trained their guns on them. Screwball stood guard over the ladder below.

Their hands in the air, the attendants were catapulted into the yard. Émile raced to join his rescuers. 'Get a move on,' Dekker said, handing him a gun.

Buisson hesitated briefly. Two terrified guards were flattened against the wall, their arms over their heads. Émile glared at them, then registered that neither was the guard who had swiped a can of *foie gras* sent by his sister Jeanne; that one, Émile had sworn to knock off before he left.

'Well?' barked Dekker impatiently. 'Are you coming or staying?'

Wordlessly, Buisson ran towards the little door, followed by Girier and a third man, a bona-fide mental patient who had happened to fall into step with them that morning.

Russac double-locked the door behind them, while the others bounded down the ladder into the moat. In record time, they had all scrambled up the other side, brought up the ladder, and repeated the operation across the outer moat at Olympic speed, to the music of whistles screeching behind them. The six men and their ladder finally reached the stadium wall. Émile was the first up the ladder. At the top of the wall, he stopped to gaze at the yard, the building he had never thought to leave. Girier's nose smacking into his behind brought him out of his reverie. As soon as all six were astride the wall, the ladder was hauled up and set against the other side. Less than two minutes later, the group was inside the stadium.

'Shit!'

Screwball was furious. Only steps away from them, a dozen firemen were practicing with a fire hose. Alerted by the guards' whistles, they were ready to step in to block the break. Not a word was said, not a threat uttered. Nothing. Nothing but four revolvers pointing like a firing squad at those muscular young chests. The firemen froze. Without losing a second, the escapees and their accomplices, with Russac acting as rear guard, sprinted for the cemetery some thirty yards from the stadium.

'It can't be true,' panted Screwball, spotting a pair of grave-diggers at work. 'It's a bloody conspiracy!'

The two workmen might have thought fleetingly of intervening in the action. But, virtually simultaneously, came the idea that picks and shovels were no match for guns. One of them, impressed by the gallows look in the faces before him, even pointed to an opening in the cemetery wall, offering Buisson and company a short cut to the street.

As soon as he saw them boil out on to the pavement, Liotard brought the car up. Russac and Girier got in alongside him; Buisson, Screwball and Dekker piled into the rear. Left standing on the pavement, dismayed at losing such entertaining friends so soon, the madman who had docilely trailed them out watched helplessly as the doors slammed in his face.

'Back to your kennel, dog.' Russac yelled at him.

The car whipped forward, heading towards Ivry-sur-Seine, crossed the Seine at the Conflans bridge and careened into the avenue de la Liberté. There Buisson ordered Liotard to stop. 'You drop off here, René,' he said. 'From now on, every man goes his own way. Anytime you're up against it, go and see Screwball or the Hunchback.'

Girier took the 1,000-franc note Russac handed him, stuffed it in his pocket and, without looking back, strode off. The car continued on its way.

'Where are we going?' Buisson asked.

'To Roger's girlfriend's place, rue Bichat,' Screwball told him.

Place de la Nation, avenue Parmentier, rue du Faubourg-du-Temple. At last they reached the rue Bichat. His eyes glued to the rear window, Émile inspected the street until he was satisfied they had not been followed. The car slowed, cruising along the street as far as the Saint-Louis hospital.

'It's number fifty-seven,' Screwball said, 'third floor, last stair-way on the left at the back of the courtyard. We'll go in separately. I'll go first.'

He got out of the car and walked back to No. 57. Émile and Dekker watched him turn into the apartment building and disappear behind the grey, seedy façade. There was no trouble.

Émile, afloat inside the brown jacket his brother had given him, went next, followed a few seconds later by Dekker. He climbed the stairs, passing the dark mouths of unlit passage-ways. When he reached the third-floor landing, he looked through an open door to see Screwball waiting for him, smiling, near a woman who must have been a beauty in her time. 'Suzanne,' Screwball said. Her face was worn and resigned. Émile flashed a quick, tight smile and walked in. His glance took in the two-room railroad apartment where everything, walls and furniture, stank of poverty. Four mattresses were lying on the floor.

'The one with the clean sheets is yours,' Suzanne told him.

'The others are for Roger, Russac and me,' Screwball explained. 'I'm going to sleep here, just in case the cops take to haunting my neighbourhood.'

'And your mouse?' Buisson asked.

'Yvonne? No trouble. I sent her to the country, to her old man's in Auvergne.'

Émile nodded approval and strolled over to a table on which glasses and a bottle of *pastis* were lined up. 'Where are the other two?'

'They went to ditch the car. Don't worry, they won't be long.'

And, in fact, Liotard and Russac arrived within twenty minutes. Everybody drank to the success of the break. Liotard was the first to leave. He had helped out, as a pal, but he didn't want to know anything else about the gang. Then Suzanne went out to shop for food, buying at a number of stores to avoid attracting attention.

Émile spent his first day of freedom chattering with his friends, cleaning and oiling his gun. That evening, Francis Caillaud, his knees still feeling like used chewing gum, arrived at the rue Bichat hideout with Screwball, who had gone to fetch him.

Francis and Émile fell into each other's arms and hugged each other. Glasses were raised again, to the reunion, to freedom. At last, Émile got up. His hands behind his back, he paced up and down the room, his forehead wrinkled in thought. Then he said:

'Right.'

That one, short word was all it took to inform the others: he was the boss.

'Right.' Émile repeated, 'now it's time to get back to work.'

ROUND ONE

9

Hidoine was at a disadvantage that morning. Like me, he had learned the details of the Buisson-Girier breakout from the newspapers. Like me, he sported a strip of adhesive tape on his chin, where he had cut himself shaving. Like me, he had rushed to the Sûreté Nationale. There the resemblance ended, because I had all my teeth, whereas he in his haste had forgotten his upper plate. Which made him a little hard to understand. Hiding his mouth behind his hand to mask his deserted gums, he asked me in an awkward hiss:

'What are we going to do, eh, Roger? Any ideas?'

The phone rang before I could answer. Fatso wanted to see me and, from the sound of his voice, he was still in a sour mood. Today he was wearing a new grey flannel suit, very severe, that made him look like a cabinet minister, and his eternal maroon tie. He jumped to the attack:

'Well, how do you plan to go about it, Borniche? I presume you have an idea, at least one, or am I mistaken?'

'To tell the truth, Chief Inspector . . .'

'To tell what truth, Borniche? Do you have an idea or don't you?'

'There is only one way to begin this case,' I said prudently. 'Yesterday I went through the files on Buisson and his family and . . .'

'Well?' Fatso interrupted.

'Well, I'm thinking of checking on Émile Buisson's brother, Jean-Baptiste. Given his record, I think that Screwball certainly knows where Émile is holed up.'

Fatso pushed his heavy horn-rimmed glasses up on his forehead. 'Any idea where to find him?'

An idea, any idea. Was that the only word he could remember this morning?

'None,' I said, hastening to add before he could flare up: 'We have nothing recent on Jean-Baptiste Buisson ourselves. I thought

I would go and check the PP's records at the quai des Orfèvres.'

The fingers of Fatso's right hand drummed against his left palm. He thought about things for a few seconds. 'I guess you're right, Borniche,' he finally conceded. 'We have to start with the brother. And Girier?'

'I'm working on it.'

'Fine. Keep me informed.'

I walked to the Champs-Élysées and took a No. 73 bus to the Châtelet. From there I walked across the bridge and up the boulevard du Palais, turned right on the quay and entered No. 36. The door to the Prefecture's records room was at the bottom of the courtyard, under a vaulted entry on the left side. It is dismal, dark, dusty and depressing. And it smells. I handed my request form to a disagreeable librarian with a tic, then waited, thinking of those of my rivals who spent their lives in this overgrown lavatory. Being a flatfoot at the PP really takes faith.

'Sorry,' the librarian said, winking so hard it pulled up his mouth at one corner. 'The file has been out since yesterday.'

'Oh? Who has it?'

'Courchamp, Homicide.'

The rules of the game. Courchamp was hanging on to the dossier in order to find out who else was trying to pick up Screwball's track, just as I had done with Émile's file at the Sûreté Nationale. There was nothing I could do except to look up Courchamp and humbly request his permission to consult Screwball's honours list. I had no illusions about his reaction, though. I knew Courchamp too well. He's a stocky fellow with thick black hair, always dressed in a brown corduroy jacket and fawn trousers, his wallet bulging with the membership cards of about fifty different organizations. Identifying characteristics: always laughing, has a harmless look, but is really stubborn as a mule, a leech, nasty and tricky when he's on a case. Because of his eight children, I had nick-named him 'Prolific Freddy' and the word had got back to him. His appreciation of my sense of humour was moderate at most. 'Borniche?' he commented. 'The only prolific thing about him is his stupidity.'

The prospect of trying to pry information out of Courchamp really sent my morale flapping around my ankles. I could already see him throwing up his hands with impatience, already hear him asking me in his sourest voice: 'What are you sticking your

nose into this for, Borniche? The Buisson case is ours—mine.'
And he'd be right. Buisson broke out in the Paris region, the
PP's territory, where we had no business being. Once again, the
Sûreté Nationale was trampling the quai des Orfèvres' flower
beds. This was not the highroad to police co-operation.

Glumly, I climbed the 105 steps; they were hollowed out, time-
worn. When I reached the third floor, I headed towards the
office Courchamp shared with Ducourthial, an evil-tempered
citizen who could go without sleep for a week, and Poirier, who
brought Dr. Petiot* in after the Liberation of Paris and was
nicknamed 'Ten past Ten' because he was pigeon-toed. Courchamp was alone when I walked in; as soon as he saw me, he
slammed shut the file he was reading. For once, he withheld the
smile, sticking a suspicious hand out to shake mine.

'What are you doing here?' he asked before I could even get
my mouth open.

'Good morning,' I said, politely.

'Yes—good morning. What do you want, Borniche?'

'I would like to consult the file on Jean-Baptiste Buisson. I was
told you had it. So I came up for a look.'

'Well, well,' breathed Courchamp in amazement. 'You came
for a look! What for?'

'I need some information,' I said airily. 'Where he lives, for
example, who he sees—the routine stuff.'

'I am going to tell you something, Borniche,' Courchamp said,
carefully shaping each word, 'so listen closely: as far as the
Buisson case is concerned, you are going to stay the hell off, you
understand? Buisson is my case. It has been formally assigned to
me. So what are you sticking your nose in for?'

There it was, the line I'd been waiting for.

'Don't get excited,' I said. 'I just assume that when a killer is
on the loose, all police units should be looking for him. That
seems to me to be obvious, logical, human . . .'

---

* Dr. Marcel Petiot was alleged to have murdered between sixty and
seventy persons in his lifetime. Most of them were Jews who ended up
in a lime pit or the furnace in the cellar of his house near the Bois de
Boulogne, where they were lured in the hope of escape from Occupied
France via his apparently imaginary Resistance network. A brilliant,
incredibly daring, imaginative but obviously unbalanced miser, Petiot
was too vain to keep his exploits to himself; his arrest came about
largely through his own efforts. After a sensational trial, he was convicted of twenty-seven killings. He died on the guillotine 25 May 1946.

'Don't waste your time explaining to me, Borniche,' Courchamp retorted, his lively eyes trained on me, 'and don't worry about society. Because I can reassure you here and now, you and your boss. I'm taking care of Screwball. My men are already in position; a few hours from now we'll have Screwball and his brother too. In fact I'm about to go out on the job myself, just to make doubly sure. So take a word of advice, Borniche: keep your nose clean and don't come around here screwing up my operation. Got that?'

'Got it.'

Courchamp wasn't bluffing. I knew the bastard. He was perfectly capable of bringing Screwball in any moment. I could feel sweat running down my spine as I saw my bonus and my promotion receding into the distance. Not to mention the whipping I would take from Fatso.

By the time I got down to the Prefecture courtyard, my mind was made up. My only chance to find Screwball was to tail Courchamp. He was going out on the job himself, was he? Well, we would go together, one behind the other. I decided to wait for him behind a column in the shadows of an entryway leading off the courtyard.

Two hours later, I saw the unsuspecting Courchamp cross the courtyard, walk through the corridor connecting the quai des Orfèvres with the Palace of Justice, skirt the Sainte-Chapelle and pass through the gate into the boulevard du Palais.

We were never more than thirty-five yards apart and my eyes never left his broad back. Courchamp strolled at a leisurely pace towards the 38 bus stop and I began to worry. Obviously, I could not board the same bus he took. I had already begun a panicky search for a taxi when luck smiled. Two 38 buses pulled up, one behind the other. The first was as stuffed as an egg, the second almost empty. Naturally, Courchamp and the other people waiting at the stop piled, elbows flailing, into the first. Courchamp flashed his transport card and jumped on the open rear platform, which was already jammed to the legal limit. I boarded the second bus. At every stop, I practically unscrewed my head making sure Courchamp hadn't shaken me; keeping him in sight wasn't easy, because every time the bus stopped there was a minor free-for-all between the people trying to get off and those trying to push their way on.

I finally spotted him again at the Sébastopol-Strasbourg-Saint-Denis stop. He was pushing rapidly through the crowd on the opposite pavement. I had to wave my badge at the conductor to get the bus stopped. I hopped off. All this had taken only a few seconds, but that was time enough for me to lose sight of Courchamp. I spun like a weathercock in a hurricane and, finally, I saw him crossing the boulevard towards the rue du Faubourg-Saint-Martin. I got behind him again, determined that, this time, I wasn't going to lose him.

So, cop tailing cop, we covered a little over a hundred yards. I was feeling pleased with myself; my trick was working. And then, suddenly, he wasn't there any more. Courchamp had just disappeared. Anchored to the middle of the pavement, jostled by the passers-by, I swore between my teeth and tried to work out where he'd gone. He had not known I was following him, I was sure of that. Which meant he had not deliberately tried to shake me. So he had entered a building, but which one? I examined the near end of the street. There was only one entrance, plus a couple of shops. A truck with a canvas-covered back was parked at the curb in front of the shops. Courchamp could not have turned into the apartment building or the stores without my seeing him. Was he in the truck? The only thing I could do was wait. If he disappeared here, he had to reappear here sooner or later. I looked at my watch: just noon. In theory, I didn't have long to wait; I knew that lunchtime was a sacred hour for my colleague from the Prefecture.

I skulked in the shadow of a vaulted entryway, kicking out with my legs from time to time to keep the blood running. At one point, I could feel a wave of nausea rising from my stomach; my observation post was next to the dustbins and I was nearly dizzy with the stink. To mask the smell, I hauled out the pack of Philip Morris I had bought on the black market that very morning from a North African on the place Blanche. I lighted a cigarette.

Suddenly, I saw the truck's canvas slowly move. Courchamp's head emerged. He said something to the men hidden in the vehicle, jumped down and headed towards the porte Saint-Martin. I heaved a sigh of relief. First because I had found my rival again, second, because I knew where his ambush was. True, while I knew the street Screwball lived on, I still didn't know which actual building he was in. I stayed where I was for a few moments to make sure Courchamp had really left. Then I moved out.

There was a *bistrot* called L'Étape a few doors up on the same side of the street. I decided to go and treat myself to a *pastis*. I knew the place. I had spent long hours wtaching it, some months earlier, when I was chasing Crazy Pierre. I could still see the feline silhouette of Jo Attia arguing with the thicker shadow of Georges Boucheseiche on the doorstep while Mosquito, their driver, a gnome with a face as wrinkled as a withered apple, sat impatiently at the wheel of a stolen front-wheel-drive that shone like a gold ingot. I could still see Jeannot, the café owner, a big guy with brush-cut blond hair and flaring ears and arms as thick as winches. If Jeannot felt like talking . . . For the moment, his hands in his pockets, he was volunteering nothing but a suspicious stare from behind the bar. My cigarette stuck in a corner of my mouth, I strolled idly towards him. We were alone, but I don't think my patronage overwhelmed him with joy. He served the drink I ordered with obvious reluctance, and the glances he shot at me at frequent intervals were anything but friendly. Glumly, he slid a carafe of water towards me, then retreated wordlessly to his cash register.

I took a few sips of my drink and set the glass down. 'Strong smell of blue serge around here this morning,' I commented, jerking my head at the apparently empty lorryload of cops across the street. He fixed me with a blue-eyed stare. I was not playing straight with Courchamp, no indeed, but had he been square that morning, when he refused to show me the file? I made excuses for myself; all was fair in war, I reflected. In any case, what I said seemed to convey a world of meaning to Jeannot, because he brightened up and moved towards me, wiping a glass. He glanced at the street, smiling.

'You're not kidding!' he said in his thick Parisian accent. '*They* been there since last night. You can see them plain as a house.'

'Probably there for Screwball,' I commented casually.

I paid for my *pastis* and wandered towards the door. I had my hand on the knob when I turned back to the blond giant watching me. The frown of concentration on his face told me he was wondering who in blazes I was.

'In fact, I have a message for him,' I said with a wink. 'Do you expect to see him today?'

Jeannot shrugged in reply. He didn't know. 'Never mind,' I continued, 'I'll slip a note under his door if he's not there. It's number fourteen, right?'

The proprietor was not a man to get himself in trouble by giving away secrets. 'Or maybe it's ten', he said, 'or twelve.'

There was no point in insisting. I gave Jeannot a friendly wave and walked out. I lit a cigarette while scanning the street. I walked slowly by the truck, but no sound reached my practiced ear.

A smell of cabbage or wet socks had soaked into the walls of No. 10 rue du Faubourg-Saint-Martin. Sporadic gusts of juvenile howls, the bawling of exasperated mothers echoed through the halls, followed by savage barking. It was probably to blot out the racket that the concierge drank. She was corked to the eyes when she opened her door, barely able to stay on her feet. She was about forty, with a chalky complexion and moist eyes, like a frog's; she wore plus fours and a man's shirt, too large for her, which gave ample room for her breasts to lie in quiet decline. 'If you're a salesman or a cop, buzz off,' she mumbled, swaying with each word.

'I'm looking for Screwball,' I said, retreating out of range of her breath.

'Whozzat?'

'Screwball. Jean-Baptiste Buisson.'

Her eyelids drooped and I wondered if she was going to sleep it off on her feet, but her eyes finally managed to pull themselves open again. Drooling a little, she brayed: ''S not here . . . He ought to be too; his dogs keep on yapping, day and night.'

'He has dogs?'

'Mmm. Two boxers. Nice animals, usually, but he's wormed them, so naturally they want to go out.'

'When was the last time he was here?'

'Last night . . . or night before . . . I don't know. He walked his dogs, brought 'em back and left.'

'He didn't say when he'd be back? I have a message for him, an urgent message, you understand . . .'

'He never says anything.'

At this point, the concierge began giving me the once-over, narrowing her eyes, puckering her face with a come-hither smile and shaking her shoulders, which sent her breasts flying under her armpits. 'I go for cute, dark types like you,' she hiccuped. 'How about coming in for a bit of fun, eh?'

I turned the offer down politely and beat a quick retreat. Out
on the street, I was briefly pursued by her voice shouting 'faggot'
and 'eunuch' and similar compliments designed to relieve her
spite. Incredible! I realize that a good-looking chap like me,
hazel eyes, wavy hair, angelic smile, good build, fine health and
lots of ambition, might tempt her, but there are limits, even to
dreams.

I mounted guard on Screwball's lair until nightfall, when
Hidoine arrived to relieve me. He was feeling put-upon because
he had promised his wife he'd take her to the pictures and she
had received the news of the change in the evening's plans with
minimum grace. Before I left, he told me: 'Fatso's waiting for
you at the Deux Marches. He wants to see you to get things in
focus. Absolutely necessary, it seems.'

The Deux Marches was the café-restaurant on the rue Gît-le-
Cœur where the Paris Homicide men, the Flying Squad and we of
the Sûreté Nationale gathered almost every evening to drink, roll
dice and give each other phony tips as loudly as possible. These
informal briefings were also attended by various crooks who were
temporarily clean and who passed the word to their chums on the
run waiting in the bars in the Saint-Michel district.

It was a long room with beige walls decorated with copper
pots, portraits of the Emperor Napoleon, blunderbusses and old
hunting rifles. Against the left-hand wall, a heavy coal range was
laden with endlessly simmering pots. We all coagulated around a
big table that faced the entrance and served as a bar.

The owner's name was Victor Marchetti, a Corsican with a lock
of black hair curling down over his forehead. His *pastis* was the
best in Paris, for the simple reason that he made it himself,
illegally, in the little courtyard behind the restaurant. It was delicate work, an alchemical miracle which Marchetti only once
messed up. That was in one of his early experiments: there was an
explosion, just one, but loud enough to wake the whole neighbourhood and bring a police emergency truck to the scene. Naturally,
every man in the force with any influence stepped in to protect
Marchetti and he went right on producing his delicious brew in
his clandestine still. Between the rounds he so freely offered
and those bought for him, Marchetti drank an average of sixty to
eighty glasses of *pastis* every evening without ever feeling even
slightly pissed.

'It's a Corsican gimmick,' he explained to me one night while I was trying to keep my eyelids propped up. 'If you want to drink without getting stoned or sick, all you have to do is swallow a generous tablespoonful of olive oil before you start in on the booze. That way the alcohol floats on the oil and doesn't get absorbed into the blood.'

I never could follow his advice. I always remembered the olive oil when it was too late.

When I arrived at Victor's place that evening the room was foggy with cigarette and pipe smoke and the air was saturated with the aroma of aniseed. Vieuchêne was sitting with his rival, Clot. Both were purple in the face and they were trading nasty cracks before an audience of detectives and mugs. As I entered the Deux Marches, I heard Clot's indignant voice blanketing the noise: 'And besides, if you people at the Sûreté Nationale have any success, it's not because of your professional skills—it's because of all the manpower and equipment you have at your disposal.'

'The manpower?' echoed Fatso, nonplussed.

'That's right, the manpower. There must be close to a thousand of you at the rue des Saussaies.'

Fatso, whose composure is usually as smooth as marble even when he's got a stomach full of *pastis*, couldn't help loosing a wild whoop of laughter this time. He laughed so hard he cried, he gasped, he wiped his eyes with his handkerchief. All he could say, over and over, each time pounding on the table so hard the glasses jumped, was, 'If I told you how many of us there were, you wouldn't believe me.'

My appearance calmed him instantly. He stared at me and, as the others looked me over, immediately inquired:

'Everything all right?'

'Everything's all right.'

That was it. That was what Hidoine called getting things in focus.

Victor served me a *pastis*, which I drained at a gulp. He served me a second. Glass in hand, I drifted over to the range to see what Dolores, the owner's girlfriend, had cooking. Small, lively and pretty, she bestowed noisy kisses on me, then made the tour of the casseroles, lifting the lids and announcing the day's specials: 'Corsican-style tripe this evening, and pot roast and chicken in red wine.'

'Save me some tripe,' I told her, chucking her under the chin, 'a man-sized portion.'

While she caressed the sauce with her ladle, Dolores winked at me. 'Not to worry, Roger,' she told me. 'You know you're my pet.' Then, pointing with her chin at the others, she whispered, 'Say, they don't sound very chummy, your bosses . . .'

I set a record that night: *pastis*, heavy red wine, rough but full-bodied cognac; by three a.m. the faces of Fatso and Clot were melting into one head with four eyes, three noses and three mouths. It occurred to me that I was thoroughly drunk. From time to time, the ceiling began to come down on me, and I closed my eyes, waiting to feel the shock on my skull; or the floor and the table would rear up and plaster me angrily to my chair. The time had come to go home. Slowly, heavily, my movements blurred, I managed to get free of the table, stammering apologies. Affectionate and maternal, Dolores helped me leave.

'Do you want me to call you a taxi?'

I shook my head and staggered off, covering the whole pavement as I aimed myself towards the place Saint-Michel. But it was three o'clock in the morning, and the Metro had stopped running. So I decided to walk home, to Montmartre. The walk, I told myself, would sober me up.

It's a long way from Saint-Michel to the rue Lepic. A very long way. Especially since the last lap of the journey is almost vertically uphill. God, I wished I hadn't drunk so much. And, as though I had not already been punished enough, I knew that my calvary would end at a cross named Marlyse. I suddenly remembered about Marlyse. I could see her already standing there, looking sexy in a transparent pink nightgown, her hair awry, peering furiously at me, burying me in an avalanche of reproach, spitting out her contempt. The scene would go on and on and it would certainly end in shouts, threats, tears. A flash of enlightenment brought the bitter reflection that life is an absurd game of musical chairs: I scared criminals and Marlyse scared me. Grumbling irritably to myself, I plodded up towards the rue Lepic. Marlyse had suddenly become an obsession. Fatso, Buisson, all my other worries were wiped out by the image of that exciting blond body asleep in my bed, recharging her batteries the better to push me around. Hugging the house fronts—which occasionally rejected my advances—I built up my stock of Dutch courage by repeating aloud: 'And anyway, if she doesn't like it, she can just pack up and go. I wouldn't lift a finger to stop her.' That's what I said . . . and I was fooling myself. How could I live without those blond locks, without those green eyes, those pink lips? I needed all those soft colours. I stopped dead and proclaimed loudly to the silent street: 'She's beautiful but she's a bitch!' That made me feel better. I lowered my head and slogged onwards. At the entrance to my building, panic swept over me again. I took off my shoes, conscious of my own cowardice. I wiggled my toes in my socks for a moment, then crept up the stairs. When I reached my landing, I realized with despair that I had lost my shoes. Anyway, I made it to the door of my flat. There I took a deep breath and, in a low voice, gave myself my final instructions: 'No noise now, Roger, take your time, don't wake her.' The key was a little cranky getting into the lock at first, but I finally got the door open. I was home. On tiptoe, I sneaked like a thief towards my bedroom. Everything was quiet, peaceful. Marlyse was asleep. Then a noise shattered my eardrums: the damned telephone was ringing.

'Roger? Raymond. Sorry to wake you, but there's a guy walking some boxers here.'

Painfully, I tried to make my mind function, to resurface, be decisive. But Hidoine was talking again: 'Listen, I don't have much time. I had to run all the way to Strasbourg-Saint-Denis to find a phone booth, but I warn you that my man doesn't look anything like Screwball. He's a big guy with an enormous gut and stiff neck.'

'That doesn't mean anything,' I maundered. 'Maybe Screwball's put on weight.'

'No, no, it doesn't look like him,' Hidoine insisted, 'I'm sure of it. According to the police photo, Screwball has a rectangular face whereas this twisty-necked guy has a round head—moon-faced type. But he is walking Screwball's dogs, that's for sure. There can't be that many boxers in the building.'

'You're right,' I agreed, yawning.

'So what do I do, Roger? If I tail him and Screwball comes back in the meantime, I'm a chump. If I don't tail him and Screwball doesn't show up, I'm still a chump. You listening?'

'I'm all ears, friend. Okay, tail the dog-walker. I'm on my way. I'll take your place watching the door.'

Marlyse, awake by now, appeared in the hall, well rested, ready for a row. But I was no longer available. I had to get moving. I stopped in the doorway and gave her a glassy smile. 'Duty calls,'

I bleated. She called me a bastard, but the rest of her tirade missed me. As I edged gingerly down the steps I reasoned that, with luck she'd calm down by evening.

On the pavement in front of the house, I found them. Side by side, neatly aligned and all ready to go, my shoes were waiting for me.

My head buzzing and my stomach in flames, I ran down the rue Lepic to a taxi stand. Well, not exactly ran—the shape I was in, I could only run a few steps before everything began to spin around me, including my innards, and I had to stop and rest, breathing raucously. I finally reached the place Blanche and poured myself into a taxi. I must really have looked like death warmed up, because the driver gave me a long, worried look before we drove off.

I stopped him at the porte Saint-Martin, paid him and got out. He was already pulling away when I remembered I hadn't asked him for a receipt, which meant I was going to have to argue to be reimbursed. I turned into the deserted rue du Faubourg-Saint-Martin, staying close to the walls, walking softly so as not to wake my colleagues snuggled in their truck.

It was still dark, so I simply slipped into the inky shadow of the doorway opposite Screwball's building. Then I waited. It was five a.m. Marlyse was probably back in bed. Fatso would just be waking up. And I was fighting to stay awake. I had been there about half an hour when a sound of footsteps made me jump and I realized I'd been dozing. It was Hidoine returning. He walked right by me without seeing me. I called to him in a whisper. At that point he wasn't so hot to look at either; his eyes were sunk deep in his head, he needed a shave and his face was as pasty as unbaked dough.

He dived in alongside me. I squeezed out a faint 'Well?'

'He screwed me. Nothing I could do about it. He was smooth, faultless. Perfect.'

'Oh? How's that?'

'Why, he took the dogs home, came back downstairs and walked towards the boulevard Sébastopol. I was about fifty yards behind him—he never spotted me. I was being tailed in turn by a guy from the PP, who stayed well back. Suddenly, in front of a cinema, my client entered a parked car. Hey, you reek of alcohol.'

I stepped back a bit. 'What then?' I asked.

'Hell . . . There was another fellow already at the wheel and they took off. Since I'm just a detective, I didn't have a car and there weren't any taxis. I was just left standing there like an idiot. Same for my shadow. I was too far away to see the licence number of the car.'

I could understand Hidoine's disappointment. It was not the first time he or I had been handicapped by our service's lack of manpower and means. When the newspapers and radio talk about us, when they compare us to the prestigious American FBI—so powerful, well organized and unimaginably rich—we feel ridiculous and poverty-stricken. This explains the police philosophy outlined to us in a bar one night by Fatso, who despite his faults and his avidity for honours is a fine cop.

'At full strength, there are three of us,' he said. 'Three to watch over the country's safety. Which is as much as saying we amount to zero. If we are to fit effectively into the overall fight French police forces are waging against crime, we have to work in a different way from them. The Prefecture's Homicide Squad and the Flying Squad are rich in men and equipment that make it easy for them to shadow, to bait their traps, to carry on an investigation. That's not our situation and you know it. So I see only one solution for us: we have to replace their numbers and equipment by something the others don't have.'

'Like what?' I asked.

'Informers, Borniche. Among the three of us, we have to organize a network of informers—paid or not, voluntary or forced, I don't give a damn which—bigger and more reliable than anybody else's. Believe me, one good informer is worth more than twenty cops.'

I had remembered this speech of Fatso's, word for word. Since that evening, I had extended my ring of informers but, until now, none of them had shown themselves and I hadn't had the time to look them up. Besides, Buisson was a prewar mobster, unknown to the young wolf packs that formed after the Liberation.

Hidoine and I worked in relays around the clock for five days on the rue du Faubourg-Saint-Martin, sleeping only a few hours a day, dragging ourselves around like sleepwalkers, functioning in a thickening daze. We were maintaining surveillance, Hidoine and I, mostly to watch our colleagues from the Prefecture, who were probably atrophying in their truck even though they worked no more than an eight-hour shift. Besides, Screwball might very well turn up. But Hidoine and I were also convinced that, in that neighbourhood, we had already been spotted, tagged and catalogued and that we were wasting our time.

On 10 September, I was sleeping, plastered up against Marlyse. Our love life was non-existent, because all I could do when I got home was to fall into bed and sleep. I was so tired I snored. Marlyse wasn't sore at me. She knew my fatigue was purely occupational and she enveloped me in an almost maternal affection.

There were moments when she gave vent to her frustration, making bitter remarks about Fatso because he worked me so hard, exploited me, because he was wasting the best years of my youth. Women are like that: kill yourself working and they are ready to knit your shroud.

I was deep in a stultifying sleep when, just before seven a.m., the phone rang. 'Borniche? Vieuchêne. Be at the shop at eight sharp. There's news.' He hung up before I could even get my eyes open.

10

The Auberge d'Arbois was one of the most elegant restaurants in the chic district around the Arc de Triomphe. The decorative style was luxury composite, a mixture of hangings, colonnades, stucco, gilt, statues and carpets. Attentive and silent, the waiters moved among tables occupied by a clientele drawn from international high society. As the women moved, their jewellery sparkled in the light from the crystal chandeliers.

This was the restaurant in which Émile Buisson chose to celebrate his escape, like a solitary lordling, over a sumptuous supper. The navy blue suit he had bought the day after the break had been altered to fit him perfectly, and he wore it with easy distinction. His whole outfit was faultless: black shoes and socks, white shirt, dark blue silk tie and a black homburg hat.

On the evening of 8 September, he walked into the Auberge d'Arbois looking as dignified as a prosperous notary. A headwaiter greeted him and shepherded him with proper ceremony to a table at the far end of the room. His questions and remarks showed the headwaiter and the wine steward that they were dealing with a connoisseur. He ate slowly, savouring his first feast as a free man. No one paid much attention to him. Everyone took him for a wealthy provincial visitor treating himself to some high life. Nor did anyone notice that this polite little man spent part of his time scribbling notes in a notebook in a tight, precise hand.

Buisson awoke in excellent spirits the next morning. While Suzanne Fourreau made his bed, turning the men's mattresses, folding sheets and blankets, Émile languidly joined Screwball, Dekker and Russac in the kitchen, where they were having breakfast. His eyes still puffy with sleep, he sat down at the head of the table. Even at meals, Émile presided. Suzanne left her chores to serve him a breakfast of sausage, pâté, an onion, a clove of garlic, cheese, a bottle of claret and a cup of coffee. Émile surveyed this wealth with a gluttonous eye, then fell to, eating slowly, spearing the morsels on his knife. He preferred these peasant repasts, tasty and comforting to the stomach, to the breakfasts of city folk, whose idea of eating was to smear a little jam on their bread.

He was digging into the cheese when Screwball, after lighting a Gauloise, broke the silence. 'Émile,' he said, 'we're broke. We're going to be back living off the women pretty soon.'

Still chewing, Buisson told him wryly: 'I hear they're hiring at the Renault plant. You ought to go and see.'

The three men grinned. They knew Émile well enough to realize that when he joked, it meant there was an idea playing in his head.

'I bought myself a sensational feed last night,' he went on. 'You'd have sworn the oysters came straight out of the sea; my mouth waters when I think of the steak in pepper sauce. As for the cheeses, take it from me, they were perfect. I would have liked to eat more, but, unfortunately, my stomach has shrunk from all that porridge.'

'Ah, how sad,' said Dekker. 'You're going to have us crying.'

With a little smile, Buisson rose wordlessly, disappeared into his bedroom and reappeared moments later with a notebook, which he placed on the table.

'There it is,' he said. 'While I fed my face like a bourgeois, I cased the joint. I've noted'—he tapped the notebook as he spoke—'the layout of the tables, the number of flunkeys. I asked questions and found out that the emergency exit is alongside the kitchen, far enough away so that we don't have to worry about it.'

He fell silent, lit a cigarette, blew out the smoke; his eyes swept the faces of the three men, who had been listening attentively and who, he knew, were calculating the risks involved in the adventure.

'It's dangerous,' Screwball finally volunteered. 'You realize what it means, a job like this near the Étoile, in a district crawling with cops?'

'Exactly. It's because it's dangerous that it ought to work. Nobody would expect villains on the run to stick their heads in the lion's mouth like that. Nobody has to come in on it with me, but my mind is made up. I'm going back to the *Auberge* tonight, but not to eat—to stick up the customers. Believe me, it's worth it. The people who eat there are loaded with dough, jewels, rings and necklaces; you'd think they were walking safes.'

'I'm with you,' said Dekker.

'Me too,' said Screwball.

'Likewise,' Russac chimed in.

'Good,' Buisson said, rising. 'We'll wander down to the rue Lesueur this afternoon to give the place a final once-over and time the operation. Roger, you go and warn Francis this morning.'

'You think he'll go for it?' Russac asked.

'Positive. And you can give him a hand swiping a heap.'

Ten p.m. Four men walked quietly into the crowded restaurant. A headwaiter slithered obsequiously towards them. 'Do you gentlemen have a reservation?'

For a second, his smile froze, then it vanished completely and his face crumpled in fear. With perfect co-ordination, the four 'clients' opened their raincoats and drew their guns. The head-waiter's eyes roamed from the little man who seemed vaguely familiar and who was holding a Police .38 in his hand, to the other three. Slowly he backed off, unable to control his painful quaking.

'On your feet,' Émile barked loudly, taking two steps forward. 'Everybody line up against the walls.'

A suffocating silence fell over the room. Astonished at first, the diners one by one obeyed the order, never taking their eyes off the four intruders. They realized that the slightest false move would start the guns talking, and they ranged themselves meekly around the walls, already resigned to being robbed. All these men and their women hid their weakness behind the conviction that it would be extremely stupid, unpardonable even, to risk death when one was rich and healthy.

Every man in the gang knew his job. Dekker had remained at the wheel of the car, keeping the engine turning over. Caillaud, holding a machine gun, stood guard near the front entrance. Screwball watched the kitchen to keep any over-eager skivvies from trying to sound the alarm. Russac's revolver covered customers and staff while an icily calm Buisson, his gun held firmly in his left hand, began the collection.

The men didn't attempt any heroics. The situation was humiliating for them, especially with their women looking on, and they were anxious to get it over with quickly. So, unprotestingly, they relinquished their wallets, their watches, even emptied their pockets of change. The women were terrified, but at the same time they were thrilled to take part in so exciting, so heart-stoppingly dangerous an incident. With feigned indifference they stripped themselves of bracelets, rings, necklaces, earrings. The mob's pockets were soon bulging with loot.

When he reached his last victim, Buisson saw that, despite her efforts, the poor woman had not managed to rid her finger of a diamond as big as an olive. 'You're going to hurt yourself tugging like that, madame,' he said politely. 'Come to the toilets with me —it will come off with a little soap.'

Grabbing her by the arm, he led her off. Less than two minutes later he was back, looking pleased with himself. He pushed the woman towards the wall and strode to the till, where he filled his pockets from the drawer. He glanced around the room to make sure he had not overlooked anyone.

'Let's go,' he ordered. He had to say it again for Russac, who had spotted a jar of caviar and, unable to resist, was standing there licking it up greedily. Émile's look hardened and his P.38 swung towards Russac, who tossed away the pot and ran for the door. Screwball was already outside. As he went through the door, Russac passed Caillaud, who was covering the getaway.

'Get a move on, Francis!' he said. 'We're blowing.'

He never suspected how much trouble those words would cause him.

At the Ministry of the Interior in the place Beauvau, word of the Auberge d'Arbois hold-up fell like a bombshell. The principal private secretary summoned officials of all police units to voice the minister's lively displeasure on learning of this latest gangland victory.

The first statements collected by the local force indicated that the chief of the gang was a small man with very black hair and eyes. Although the bandits had wasted no time, they had spent nearly ten minutes in the restaurant and their victims were able to describe them in detail. Not only were the police supplied with accurate descriptions, but the first name of one of the men, Francis, had been overheard.

Fatso gave us a precise account of the hold-up from the telex message the PP had sent to the Ministry. He had arranged— without the Prefecture knowing about it, of course—to get duplicates of all the daily reports our Paris colleagues filed with the place Beauvau. This kept us abreast at the rue des Saussaies of all the cases our competitors were handling.

At eight in the morning, Hidoine and I were in Vieuchêne's office, watching him exude satisfaction at knowing that Clot, Pinault and company were tearing their hair. He went over the details of the hold-up like an old woman telling her beads. When he finished, he lit a cigarette and, his eyes half shut, sat silently for a while blowing smoke rings at the ceiling. At last he focused on us again.

'The job was certainly Buisson's. The description fits him and it was his way of operating. If he weren't a killer, I'd admit to a certain admiration for him. Here's a guy who broke out only six days ago and he's already formed a gang and gone back to work. And what work, gentlemen! We still don't know for sure how much loot he got, but it's already safe to put the figure in the tens of millions.

'The witnesses spoke of one Francis. I'm counting on you to identify him. As I see it, he has to be a former prison contact of Buisson's from Troyes, Clairvaux or the Santé. There can't be that many ex-jailbirds called Francis. And if he's working with Émile, it must mean he's tough. And who were the others? We'll try to find out, but I'd bet anything that Screwball is one of them. It stands to reason: he is Buisson's brother, a villain in his own right, and as hard as Émile. Since the little guy's escape, Screwball has dropped out of sight. So you see, we do have something to work with. I'm sure we'll get there in the end.'

His forehead puckered in thought, Fatso fell silent long enough to stamp out his cigarette. Then, fingering the notes spread out on his desk, he went on:

'These are dangerous criminals, the Buissons, absolutely pitiless, willing to go to any extreme. In their situation, that's understandable. They have no hope of judicial leniency. Émile, in any case, is headed straight for the guillotine. So the only way he can stay alive and free is to block his trail with corpses.'

Fatso's tone suddenly went serious. He bent over his notes, read them under his breath and then looked up. 'I'll tell you what happened after the hold-up,' he said sombrely. 'It will prove to you just how dangerous these men are.'

11

The gang's car spurted up the avenue de Wagram, along the boulevard de Courcelles, up the rue de Rome and into the rue Cardinet. Traffic was light at that time of night. It was there that the car came nose to nose with a blockade of police cars drawn up in a herringbone pattern across the street.

Tyres screamed as Dekker stomped on the brakes; the car swerved, shot forward. Dekker's technique was dazzling. He crashed through the blockade at what seemed to be suicidal speed; when the rear of the car skidded, he played a virtuoso duet on brakes and accelerator, scattering policemen as he went.

A motorcycle cop named Deroo roared after the car. Another bike man, Loren, delayed by a balky engine, followed more than a hundred yards behind him.

Buisson, on the car's rear seat with Russac on his right and Caillaud on his left, peered anxiously at the motorcycle headlight growing bigger and bigger. Furiously, he grabbed the P.38 Screwball had given him during the breakout (after an admiring inspection, Buisson had poured champagne over the barrel with the words 'I baptize you *Saviour*'), smashed out the rear window with the butt, aimed at the motorcycle tyres and emptied the cylinder. 'One down,' he said happily as Deroo hit the asphalt.

Monsieur Émile's pleasure was short-lived. The second bike man, Loren, was now closing in rapidly. When he was only a few yards from the rear bumper, Buisson shouted to Dekker, 'Brake!'

Dekker obeyed. Loren, surprised, tried to stop, but he knew he could not avoid a collision. He swerved desperately to the right, his motorcycle skidded, the rear wheel breaking away on the cobblestones. Then the bike came down on top of him with a crash. A violent shaft of pain stabbed along his knee, hip and elbow, wrenching a groan from him as he felt the machine's weight press down on him, lacerating his flesh. He tried to free himself, but there was no time left. Frantically, he watched a man leap from the car, which had stopped about twenty-five yards away, and run towards him. It was Buisson.

The little man was foaming at the mouth with rage. As he threw open the car door, he yelled to his accomplices, 'I'm going to cut him in half, that lousy cop.' His P.38 was empty. So what? He grabbed the English-made sub-machine gun from the rear seat and, joyfully, approached the fallen policeman. He saw the cop unholster his 7.65 Police Special, but luck seemed to have abandoned the poor devil: as he straightened his arm to aim, the gun snagged on a bike cable and went flying out of reach.

His eyes wide with panic, Loren watched the dark silhouette, now only six feet away. Buisson's eyes, black and smouldering, were trained on his victim. Loren watched the black hole of the muzzle approach to within inches of his head; he had no strength left to cry out, to duck. He felt himself only seconds away from death.

Buisson's finger squeezed the trigger. Nothing. His weapon failed to go off. Buisson was rattled. He shook the gun, clamped the trigger back again and again. The gun remained mute.

'Come on, for God's sake!' yelled Dekker, his head poked out of the car window. Once more, Buisson's finger pressed the trigger. Same result. Livid with frustration, he ran towards the car and dived in.

'Stupid bastard,' Dekker fumed as his foot hit the accelerator. 'What the hell were you messing around at?'

Émile's voice shook with anger and vexation: 'What kind of crap are these machine guns made of? I squeezed and squeezed; the damn thing refused to work.'

'You just forgot to cock it,' Russac said, examining the Sten. 'You have to pull back on the breech.'

'I don't understand these modern gadgets,' Buisson grumbled. 'These didn't exist before the war, and there were no evening classes in gun-handling inside.'

'You see, you have to move with the times,' Russac said slily.

Buisson, reloading his *saviour*, shot a withering glance at him, but said nothing.

The car was racing towards the porte de Clichy when Émile spotted the first motorcycle patrolman, who had returned to the chase. Deroo's skid had not been serious, and he had been able to get under way again almost at once, but he had lost precious seconds helping Loren, who was still lying in the middle of the avenue. A passerby reassured him that the police emergency service had already been summoned. As Deroo prepared to leave, Loren warned him: 'Be careful! As soon as you pull up close to them they'll brake hard; that's how I got wrapped up in this lot . . .'

The gang's car reached the porte de Clichy and Dekker tried to repeat the manoeuvre that had already succeeded so well. He let the motorbike get within twenty yards, braked hard, then pulled broadside across the road. But Deroo was watching for the trick. He managed to stop, Keystone Cop fashion, jumped off, lay down behind his machine, drew his gun and opened fire.

Caillaud and Buisson jumped out of the car. Francis sprayed the street with machine-gun bursts to cover Buisson, who raced for the opposite pavement, trying to come up behind the policeman. He got within fifteen yards. At that distance, he couldn't miss. The P.38 in his hand rose. He aimed.

Suddenly, a shot rang out behind him. He jumped with surprise. At the same instant, he felt something sear his chin.

'Take cover! They're trying to plug you in the back!'

It was Screwball who shouted. He had burst out of the car, firing at a shadow he could just make out shooting down from a window. The concealed marksman was a police officer who happened to live in the building and who, hearing the sound of gunfire and seeing the motorcycle cop lying on his stomach, had joined in the fight. He kept up a steady, deadly fire, sending bullets wailing all around Émile, whom he had singled out as his prime target.

Buisson realized that he had lost this match, that neither he nor his friends could get Deroo, much less the guy popping at them from the window. He also realized that if they hung around there much longer, they would soon be surrounded by enough upholders of law and order to start a convention. Monsieur Émile continued firing at random to cover his retreat until his gun was empty.

'Let's get the hell out of here,' he yelled.

The gang fell back towards the car and catapulted themselves into it. There was an anguished shriek of gears as Dekker rammed the car into first, sending the vehicle rocketing into the darkness.

Nobody spoke. The only sound was the panting of men winded by flight and fear. Tyres screeching, the car flicked across the exterior boulevard into the long, straight, deserted avenue running towards the northern suburbs. Buisson touched the burning spot on his chin; his hand came away bloody. He was reaching for his handkerchief when Russac warned:

'Shit, he's back again, the bastard!'

Émile turned around and a cruel light flickered in his eyes. He was swept with a murderous rage. He was going to finish off that pig-headed cop once and for all. 'Son of a bitch,' he growled. 'I'm going to make pulp out of him.'

'What do you want me to do?' Dekker asked coolly.

Buisson thought fast. It was vital that they get rid of the motor-cycle cop on their tail before the road-blocks went up all over the city. 'Skirt the Batignolles cemetery and pick up the outer boule-vard again—dodge in and out of the little side streets on the way; maybe we can shake him.'

The car whipped along under the high cemetery wall, followed the rue du Bois-des-Caures, turned at right angles into the rue Toulouse-Lautrec and swept into an unlighted alley, throwing its passengers heavily against each other. Suddenly, the headlights picked out a wall rearing up before them.

'Christ!' breathed Screwball. 'A dead end!'

Émile turned round and saw the motorcycle's headlight entering the alley. Dekker saw it too, in the rear-view mirror. Wasting no time, he leaned on the brakes in a groaning of tyres, reversed and swung around. The car's muzzle was now facing the exit.

Some fifty yards away, Deroo realized what was happening. He stopped to draw his gun when the car's high beams suddenly blinded him, growing rapidly bigger as the Citroën rushed to-wards him with a roar. The policeman had no time to manoeuvre. The car was already on him. A desperate reflex sent him plunging to the ground, bike and all, firing at random. There was a sound of tearing steel as the car hit the motorcycle. A hail of bullets rained on him from both doors.

'Back up,' Buisson ordered. 'Grind the bastard into the road.'

The car plunged backward, gears grinding, and crushed the bike's front wheel. Screwball and Caillaud sprayed the alley, hoping to hit the cop. The shots made a single protracted, dismal echo through the empty streets.

At last Buisson gave the order to move on. After a final salvo, the car slid out of the alley and headed back towards Mont-martre. Deroo picked himself up, amazed that he was still alive.

Buisson's rage subsided abruptly. He dabbed at his chin to

staunch the flow of blood which continued to trickle down on to his shirt. 'That cop,' he said. 'You got to hand it to him. Fucking society doesn't deserve protectors like that. He's either nuts or he's a hero . . .'

'What about us? Where are we heading?' asked Dekker.

'To La Paillote,' Buisson decided. 'We're going to have a little champagne and clean up a little. We look as if we'd just fought the battle of Verdun.'

La Paillote is a tiny, softly lit bar on the rue Burq run by Frédo, a man who never asks questions but who is always willing to do a favour. His clientele is made up of regulars, mostly pimps. Unfamiliar faces are turned away with no special diplomacy.

The five men went there separately. It was nearly midnight when the last of them, Dekker, walked in; he had taken the time to ditch the car near the place des Abbesses. The gang gathered at the far end of the room, waiting for their champagne, filing back to the washroom to straighten their clothes and comb their hair. The money and jewellery they had scooped up at the restaurant was laid out on the sink while the men shook out their jackets and brushed them down. One after another, they beamed at themselves in the mirror and returned to their table. Monsieur Émile was the first to beautify himself. He washed his blood-stained hands and face, took off his shirt and put on another lent him by the owner. Russac was the last man back. As he took his seat, he crowed jovially, 'Boys, I think we got something to celebrate.'

Russac was tall and dark, a good head taller than the other four men. He had regular features and velvety eyes, was self-assured and articulate. But he lacked a sense of psychology. If he had possessed one, he might have noticed, while he went briskly about uncorking the first bottle, that Buisson was looking coldly at him, a veiled hostility in his eyes. Émile did not like Russac; he had classified him as one of the small-timers of the underworld, one of those weaklings who begin singing the moment a cop so much as raises a hand to them. 'He's got too pretty a face,' Émile thought; 'women go for it, and he's afraid somebody will spoil it for him.'

By two a.m. they were on their fifth bottle of Krüg. Screwball was beginning to yawn and his eyelids were drooping. Sprawled in his chair, he said in a husky voice: 'I think we can move now. They must have lifted their road-blocks by this time.'

Buisson agreed. He paid the bill and rose, followed immediately by the others. Caillaud's legs were a little wobbly. They stumped slowly down the hill to the place Blanche, piled into a taxi and rode to within a moment's walk of the rue Bichat. Climbing the stairs was hard work. Aside from the champagne, the nervous tension they had been under all evening, fatigue and lack of sleep had filled their legs with lead, and they stopped frequently for breath on their way up.

Once inside the apartment, they sank down on chairs around the kitchen table. They were alone, undisturbed. Suzanne had not returned from her beat on the rue Blondel.

'Okay,' said Buisson. 'Let's see what we've got.'

Each man emptied his pockets, piling his hoard of stolen money and gems on the table before him. 'Beautiful!' Caillaud kept saying. 'Christ, how beautiful . . .' Little Francis' eyes bulged so gluttonously that the others burst out laughing. All of them, that is, except Émile. His glance had stopped at Russac's pile and he examined attentively every item the tall man pulled out of his pockets. There was a diamond missing. Émile's memory was infallible. He had a clear recollection of Russac weighing a ring in his hand with an admiring little whistle at the *Auberge* and stuffing it into his pocket. But the ring set with diamonds was not on the table. That could only mean one thing: the big guy who towered so infuriatingly over him was holding out on them. Émile shot a quick look at Russac, who was still laughing, but he didn't say a word. He just scooped up the bank notes before him and began dealing them out.

'There's 103,000 francs,' he announced. 'That makes 20,000 each. The other 3,000 goes to Suzanne. Screwball will take the hardware to a fence tomorrow. Now, everbody to bed.'

12

Seventeen days had gone by since the Étoile hold-up, and the Prefecture was still marking time. The only consolation was the capture of René Girier. Detectives Courchamp—Homicide—and Morin—Flying Squad—had questioned him and had even shaken him up a bit, but Girier insisted he did not know the names of Buisson's accomplices. Then he was sent back to the Santé, where he was given ninety days in solitary. All that the gun battle through the streets of Paris had produced so far was a collection of empty shells, which were turned over to the police laboratory for examination.

Fatso rubbed his hands. The way he looked at it, time was on his side. The longer his colleagues at the Prefecture floundered, the better the chances of his two beasts of burden, Hidoine and Borniche, turning up a lead on Buisson.

One morning, he called me into his office. Fatso's coat was open, his belly ballooning like a barge prow going through a lock.

'Borniche,' he said, 'one of these days you should pay a visit to Golléty, the examining magistrate assigned to the prison break. Ask him for a pass to the Santé so that you can talk to Girier. Maybe you'll have better luck than your friends across the way. In the meantime, I have an urgent job for you. It'll be a change from Buisson. Read this.'

He handed me a message from the local police at Conflans-Sainte-Honorine:

> *Body of unidentified man, without identity papers, discovered today, Sept. 26, in the La Faye Forest in Andrésy. Send investigators. Gendarmes Petit and Herproteau awaiting your arrival.*

Fatso looked at me with irony in his eyes. 'I hope you'll show more flair on this case than you have with Buisson. Take Cocagne and Crocbois with you and keep in touch.'

Not at all unhappy at the idea of getting a whiff of fresh air and a vacation from the Buisson file, I returned to my office. Quickly, I filled Hidoine in on the case I had just been saddled with. He was so engrossed in the sports page of his newspaper that he hardly heard me. I struggled into the khaki raincoat I had bought at a U.S. Army surplus store. 'You coming with me?' I asked him.

'Where?'

'To the La Faye Forest. Air out your lungs.'

'Some air. Around a corpse.'

'Don't be a chump, Raymond. We'll be there by eleven o'clock. We show 'em how it's done for an hour, and at noon on the dot we will be sitting like lords in the Pêcheurs restaurant in Conflans. I know the owner—the chow's good and the prices are low.'

'Fried whitebait?'

'Obviously.'

'That's it. I'm with you.'

I phoned Cocagne and Crocbois to prepare to travel. Cocagne is the Maison's photographer, forty-five years old, six feet one, nicknamed 'the Mast'. A heart of gold and a stomach ruined by routine. Without a sign of repugnance, he photographs cadavers from every angle, turns them over, examines them, backs off, comes closer, snaps his pictures with his bellows camera and takes the corpse's fingerprints. However decomposed the bodies, however sickening the stench, Cocagne remains the iron man. Sometimes, when the victim is nothing more than a stinking mush, he even manages to joke about it. I do not usually hear these pleasantries—I'm too far away, too busy trying to steer my stomach back to its moorings. I never could get used to corpses.

Crocbois is our driver. Wavy hair, lovingly dressed. He is slim, clean-cut, the motor-pool Lochinvar. Absolutely nothing interests him but women. A sex fiend. When Hidoine and I climbed into the car, he was already at the wheel, with Cocagne beside him. The engine was running.

'Well, now, happy to be going out where the grass grows?' I asked.

'I'll say! Nothing like oxygen for recharging the glands,' Crocbois conceded.

The body was sprawled in a muddy hollow. It was dressed in a well-cut dark blue suit, white shirt, blue and red striped club tie. It was lying face up, the eyes open in a wide stare, one eyelid half eaten away. Rigor mortis had not yet worn off, and the fact that one leg was bent back under the right buttock indicated that death had surprised him from behind. The arms were outflung in a cross.

Gendarme Petit walked over. 'We've gone through his pockets, Chief Inspector.'

'Just Inspector,' I said. 'Find anything interesting?'

'Nothing. Not a thing.'

I turned to Cocagne.

'Your turn, my friend.'

He had already screwed his camera on to its wooden tripod. Now he hid himself under the black cloth, stooped to the viewfinder and adjusted for distance. Then he slipped a plate into the camera. 'Nobody move,' he smirked, squeezing the bulb. There was a click. Cocagne emerged, giggling like a second-rate comic at his own jokes, changed the angle and went through it all again. Then, satisfied, he bent over the corpse and flipped it over like a mattress. Wet leaves were stuck in the hair, mud caked the jacket; the shirt collar was speckled with brownish spots.

'He took one in the back of the head,' Hidoine said, squatting over the skull.

He had to separate the locks of hair hardened by coagulated blood to uncover the hole the bullet had made going in. He stood up, brushing himself and shaking his trouser legs. Cocagne, after getting a close-up of the back of the head, busied himself with his tailor's tape, measuring the length of the deceased's arms, legs and torso, jotting down the figures in a little black notebook. Kneeling in the moist grass, he drew his bag to him and took out a wad of cottonwool, which he soaked in alcohol. With this he cleaned the corpse's fingers and hands, tugging at them as he did so. Then he calmly dried them.

'I won't be much longer, children,' he said to no one in particular. 'Then we can go and eat. What would you say to a nice lamb stew?'

I gazed at him in disgust. Dexterously, Cocagne blackened each of the dead man's fingers with ink-soaked paper. Then he rolled them, one by one, on a sheet of white paper, getting clear prints of each fingertip. The palms of the hands were next. Cocagne inspected his work, whistling, then packed his equipment and the print sheets back into his bag.

While our photographer was at work, the Pontoise procurator, the examining magistrate, his clerk and a police doctor arrived on the scene. Together, we poked through the grass and dead leaves and broken branches for clues. A waste of time. The gendarmes carted the body off to the hospital in Conflans for an autopsy.

'What do you think?' the magistrate asked me.

'The fact that the body was relieved of all its papers to prevent identification suggests a gang killing.'

'Just what I thought,' he muttered, handing me a slip of paper officially assigning my section to the investigation. 'In view of proceedings instituted against X . . . on a charge of murder,' it read, 'we hereby commission one of Messieurs the Inspectors attached to the Police Judiciaire in Paris to proceed to any hearings, searches and seizures that may help to reveal the truth.'

The judge nodded in farewell and walked off towards his car.

'Are we going?' Cocagne groaned. 'I'm hungry as a wolf.'

I wasn't. In fact I was feeling sick; moving the body had released a pestilential stench. But the others' appetites were intact. So we wedged ourselves back into the Citroën and drove to the Pecheurs. A few *pastis*, some fried whitebait, a chicken in cream and mushrooms, a bit of cheese, a fruit tart and a number of bottles of Beaujolais gradually cleared my nose of the sweetish death smell. Crocbois had disappeared with the waitress. I daydreamed about the coat I was going to buy to face the winter in, the one I had seen in Max Evzeline's window. (Max was the stars' tailor.) I wanted it in dark grey, the all-purpose colour; Marlyse preferred beige—she thought it would make me look like a singer. But it was expensive, too expensive for me. So I would probably end up at the Samaritaine instead.

We were in the throes of digestion when a gendarme appeared. He took an envelope out of his pocket and emptied it over the table. A brass slug rolled out, apparently in good condition.

'It was found in the dead man's head,' he told me. 'According to the doctor, it was fired from below, about twenty inches from the guy's head. The victim was standing up at the time. Which means the killer was a lot shorter than the victim. Must be a very cool customer.'

Early next morning, I charged over to the Palace of Justice. In my briefcase were the slug and the sheets bearing the dead man's prints. I hurried along the Chief Justice's gallery, mounted stairway T to the second floor, then continued on to the police laboratory in the attic, between the Sainte-Chapelle gallery and the new Appeals Court section. Four million fingerprints are on file in the dactyloscopy-anthropometry section and I would have been very surprised had my corpse's not been among them. I was also counting on the ballistics experts giving me a quick answer on the type of gun that had fired the fatal bullet.

I was winded by the time I reached the top of the spiral staircase that ended at the small laboratory door. I knocked. A peephole opened in the door.

'Maison,' I said.

The peephole slid shut and the door opened. I showed my badge, a clerk wrote my name in a register and waved me on. I made first for the fingerprint room, knocked at a glass-panelled door and walked in. A bald inspector looked up from his microscope and examined me instead.

'Morning,' I said, sticking out my hand. 'Borniche of the SN. I have a corpse to identify.'

The man in the white smock pivoted on his chair, grasped the sheets of paper I handed him, studied them and nodded his head. 'No smears. You do these?'

'No. It was Cocagne, a pro. He took them on the spot.'

The man didn't reply. He slipped the left-hand prints under the microscope lens, adjusted the focus and immediately jotted a figure under the print of each finger.

'What are the numbers for?' I asked.

Still trying to wedge his eye into the tube, he explained:

'It's a code. Each print is classified by form: left whorl, right whorl, vertical arch and double whorl. I translate all that into figures and I get number 22–225.3833. That means double whorls on both thumbs, left whorls on all the fingers of the left hand, right whorls on all the fingers of the right hand. You understand?'

'Yes,' I said without conviction. 'Then what?'

'Then I should find a card bearing the same numbers from the corresponding series of files up there above your head. Assuming the card is there. Your chap may not be on record.'

As he talked, he pulled over a sliding ladder, climbed up to the third rung and, after a brief search, took a rectangular card from the cabinet.

'Here's your cold cut,' he said as he descended. 'It's him all right. Name of Russac, Henri, born 5 December 1905, at Charenton; several convictions; recently discharged from the Santé.'

I looked at the front-view and profile photos pasted on the card. It was him, all right. 'You wouldn't have a spare picture?' I asked.

'No, but Records will have what you need.'

He turned back to his microscope and I trotted to ballistics, where I hoped I could get as rapid a finding on the bullet as I had on the fingerprints. No such luck. 'Come back tomorrow,' they told me in the front office.

So I left the Palace and walked across the boulevard. There was a phone booth in the Commercial Court building and, after two false starts, I succeeded in getting through to my office.

'Raymond?' I said. 'Chase up to Records and get me the Russac Henri file. Yes, I've identified him. I'll be there in half an hour.'

I hung up, dropped another token in the box and called the Santé. At that point, I reckoned that the La Faye Forest case was a cinch; the information I had just obtained, added to what I was going to collect, should, I thought, put me on the murderer's trail in no time.

For what seemed the better part of the morning, I sat there with the receiver pressed against my ear while the prison clerk pawed at his files. He resurfaced, finally. 'There's not much, you know,' he told me. 'He had no visitors; he kept a low profile. On the soft side, he was.'

'Still, he must have talked to somebody.'

'No doubt. But the guards who knew him don't come on duty until tomorrow morning. All I can tell you is that he was in cell number 2.51. He shared it with Émile Buisson, among others.'

'What? Repeat that, please.'

'Buisson. The guy who broke out of the nuthouse not long ago. I couldn't tell you if they were mates or not. You'll have to call back for that. When he was sprung, he gave his address as 10 rue du Faubourg-Saint-Martin. Well, that's it.'

I hung up. Mechanically, I lit a cigarette while I wondered what connected the corpse to Buisson and Screwball. I knew the criminal world too well to consider it mere coincidence. If Russac gave the turnkey Screwball's address, he could only have been given it by Émile. Now, I had been convinced from the first that it had certainly been Screwball who organized his brother's escape. Might not Russac have been in on it too?

I was out of the phone booth and running for the rue des Saussaies. Hidoine had left the file on my desk, complete with an ID photo of Russac. I hesitated about filling Fatso in on developments; better to pull it all together a little more before talking to him. I phoned Marlyse to tell her I would probably be home late, then I called the garage to ask Crocbois to be ready to leave with the car.

'Damn!' he said. 'It's almost lunchtime.'

As I ran for the lift, I jostled men from other sections, heard doors open and close, was conscious of the almost continuous rattling of typewriters. The operator let me ring several times before revealing that the machine was out of order again. I went down the stairs like water over a cliff.

'Where to?' asked Crocbois, stowing his comb in his pocket.

'Villejuif, the psychiatric hospital.'

All the way out there, I prayed heaven that a guard or an attendant who had witnessed the break would be on duty that day. Luck was with me: the two surveillants and an attendant at whom Buisson had waved his revolver were there. As soon as they saw Russac's photo, they formally identified him: he was unquestionably one of Buisson's accomplices. He was the rear-guard man in the escape.

I had just scored a point over my rivals at the Prefecture.

13

'Chief Inspector? Borniche.'

'Yes. Where are you this time?'

'In front of the Palace, chief. I wanted to warn you I'd be late; I have to go back to ballistics to get the report on the bullet.'

'What bullet?'

'You know what bullet—the one they took out of Russac's head.'

'Oh . . . of course. Well, don't be too long, my boy.'

Fatso hung up. I went back to the bar of the Café du Palais, where, as I read the newspaper, I treated myself to coffee and two *croissants*, which sat in my stomach like bricks. Twenty minutes later I was at ballistics.

A technician in a white smock rose and walked in crepe-soled silence to a long table. He rummaged among a pile of folders, plucked one out of the pile and returned. 'The official report isn't ready yet,' he drawled. 'Won't be for another two weeks. We're swamped.'

He laid the folder on the counter, opened it and continued:

'Your bullet was fired from a P.38. It came from the same gun as the bullets and shells found after the Auberge d'Arbois shootings. The photo enlargements leave no doubt of it; the rifling marks are identical.'

Looking at the pictures, even I could see that the number, size and angle of the scratches were similar.

'Got it,' I said 'The man who fired the fatal shot is the same one who fired at the motorcycle cop.'

'Easy, easy, not so fast,' the man in the white smock cautioned. 'I didn't say that. All I'm telling you is that it was the same gun. It's up to you to find the hand it fits in. And that, my friend, is your worry.'

I don't understand the government. It would be easy to pull all the various police records departments together under a single roof, yet the administration seems to look for ways to scatter them all over the landscape, in distant buildings, in the most out-of-the-way places.

This explains why the rooming-house-and-hotel section, which keeps an eye on the Paris region's floating population, wound up on the fourth floor of the Île de la Cité headquarters building, stairway D (well removed from the other records sections).

Naturally, because of the heavy traffic to and from these files, two lifts are reserved for fourth-floor use. And, just as naturally, these lifts are usually out of service for repairs. So, that morning, along with everyone else, I had to give my well-developed adductor muscles a work-out.

I had brought a stack of blank Sûreté Nationale research cards with me, all stamped with the name of my section. I wrote Russac's name and particulars clearly on all of them and handed them to the lout with fanglike canine teeth lording it like a jack-in-the-box over a caged-in shelf on which sat two archaic telephones. He glanced at the cards and unsheathed the fangs. 'This urgent?'

'Yes. I've got one in the current and two others in the six-months-and-one-year. Can do? I'm on a murder . . .'

'I couldn't care less. Come on.'

The records clerk bent over, drew the bolt on the cage door; I practically walked on his heels following him into the grey light of his cavern.

The 'current' is just what it says: the up-to-date file, often consultable by phone but sometimes only in writing, of the registration forms travellers fill out in hotels; these are filed in three-month blocks as they come in and enable the police to get hold of interesting transients. The six-months-and-one-year file is a backlog contained in two to four cabinets full of white file cards speckled with green observation chips.

The records clerk flipped through the file with the dexterity of a magician. 'Nothing here,' he remarked laconically. 'Are you sure of the spelling?'

He bent over my cards, squinting, then slid the drawer shut. 'We'll have a look at the others.' A few minutes of poking through older records turned up two cards on Russac, both apparently out of place. 'Here's your man,' he said, ramming the cards under my nose. Both had been filled out in childish hand-writing with an illegible signature and the 'profession' space left blank. I noted the addresses, 10 rue des Prêcheurs and 17 rue Saint-Denis, as well as the dates, which would enable me later on to check on whether Russac was alone when he stayed at those addresses.

'Whorehouses,' the clerk sniffed disdainfully, replacing the cards in the file. 'I'd be surprised if this got you anywhere.' He stepped over to a third drawer, which he slammed back on its rails. 'What a mess,' he muttered. 'It's a good thing we've had a bit of a purge recently.'

I looked blankly at him as we returned to his cage. 'Yes,' he explained, 'one day somebody noticed there were scraps of cards scattered around the toilets. So the chief had them watched. And we caught one of our own fellows red-handed; he was the one who used to complain regularly that his stomach hurt; to save having to file the cards he was allotted he took to flushing them down the bog in packs of ten. But what can you expect? As long as they go on staffing records with other departments' rejects there'll always be trouble.'

Checks at the two hotels produced nothing. With Hidoine, I spent part of the afternoon trying to find out whom Russac might have been shacked up with. Seated opposite one another at a table, we had drawn up a list of old addresses lifted from his file. We split them, each going down his list questioning concierges. It's depressing, exhausting work. And it got us nowhere. It was routine, but it had to be done.

That evening, while Marlyse got dinner ready and fought with the cooker, I sat wordlessly on a chair with my swollen feet in a basin of hot water. And I tortured my brain trying to decide who it was who had used the P.38. Buisson? One of his boys? And why was Russac liquidated anyway? Lots of questions. And no answers at all.

14

Breasts high and firm, hips with a life of their own, legs long and supple, the face of an angel—framed by short blonde hair—that was Maguy. She had been apprenticed to a milliner until she got sick of working, sick of wasting her health and beauty for a pittance. Where she landed instead—it was the old, old story—was the rue Blondel. She had met a fellow at the Sunday afternoon dance. Very handsome, he was. He had soft hands, not at all cracked or work-roughened. A pimp. Maguy's life changed. She passed through the hands of a chain of 'protectors' until, having mastered her trade, she went into business for herself.

Of course, she would sometimes give up part of her income when she found a new heart interest, but she never lost sight of sound business procedure.

Maguy was one of my informers. I calculated that a whore was the only kind of woman Russac could have had. Maguy might know who she was. Worth trying, anyway. So I went looking for a spot of gossip with my friendly neighbourhood tart.

It was a little past two p.m. when I got there. The blue sky had brought the rue Blondel to life. It was full of leisurely prowlers attentively examining the clusters of girls displayed for immediate consumption.

Maguy was there on the pavement. The first thing about her that caught my eye was her skirt, short, slit up the side, of a green that made your eyes water. My gaze travelled up to her form-fitting blouse, red with white polka dots, open for vast distances down the front. She stood there smoking, her eyes provocative, hips arched, sure of her appeal. As soon as she saw me, she winked and yelled her battle cry: 'In Maguy's arms you're safe from harm. Coming up?'

I nodded, fell in behind her through the door of the hotel run by Lulu the Shrimp. We climbed the narrow, winding stairs and the third step gave under my foot so that I staggered slightly.

'Your staircase is rotten,' I told her.

'I'll explain that later my darling little constable.'

Up we went. Before me, a foot and a half away at eye level, moved the curve of her hips. I speculated on the round, muscular buttocks straining at the light cloth. It was unnerving, upsetting;

I swallowed hard. Maguy could sense what was happening, because the bitch immediately accentuated the movement, rolling her hips furiously like a sweet little caravel rolling in a storm. She turned to me and laughed. 'Like it?' she asked.

'Very much.'

A chambermaid opened a door for us, uncovered the bed and placed a towel on the washbasin. As she left the room, I stopped her. 'Bring us two cognacs,' I told her. 'Doubles.'

We looked at each other as we waited for the drinks to come, Maguy sitting on the bed, me standing in front of her. From time to time she crossed her legs, giving me a glimpse of lingerie, while her eyes held mine firmly. It went on that way. Maguy trying to draw me into her web, me fighting down temptation, until the maid returned. I paid her, not enough, apparently, because I didn't even get the beginnings of a smile. As far as she was concerned, I was just another sucker, and broke at that. She walked out, closing the door behind her; I could hear her footsteps receding down the corridor.

I inspected the green wallpaper, a meadow splashed with faded red roses.

'Are you going to contemplate the landscape for long?' Maguy asked.

I turned round. She had unhooked her blouse and was lying back on the bed, her hands clasped under her head.

'I came to talk,' I told her.

'So I imagined. But we can talk lying down. Come over here next to me. I'm not going to rape you.'

I picked up the two glasses, handed her one and sat down on the edge of the bed. We sipped at the cognac.

'What do you want to know, my darling detective?'

I stared at her, as I drank my cognac. 'Listen,' I said, putting the glass on the bedside table, 'I'm looking for information about a guy whose name was Russac. Henri Russac.'

'Was?'

'Yes. Past tense. He's dead. But before he died, when he was still a good-looking kid, there must have been a little woman in his life. I've got one chance in a thousand of finding her in a hurry, but I can try. The object of my visit is simple: I'd like to know if any of your girlfriends hung around with him.'

Maguy raised herself on one elbow to reach for her drink. The movement uncovered one of her breasts, a fact she ignored as she took a big gulp of cognac. In the yellowish light of the room, her face had suddenly turned grim. 'I know the girl who was with Henri. It was me.'

Her voice was serious, almost sad, and I was annoyed with myself for having referred to the defunct so flippantly. Maguy closed her blouse. 'I hadn't seen anything of him for several weeks,' she went on. 'I learned recently that he helped one or maybe two guys break out of a hospital or something. And then he was in on a big hold-up in a restaurant. There was a lot of shooting. You must have read all about it in the newspapers like everybody else.'

I nodded agreement. 'Yes,' I said.

'Well, that's it. That's all I can tell you.'

She raised the glass to her lips. 'But . . . how did you learn all this?' I asked her. 'Did Russac tell you?'

Maguy took another slug of brandy, put the glass down. 'I told you I hadn't seen him since the beginning of the month. No, it was a girlfriend of mine who told me. She works the street with me but she disappeared for a while. When she turned up again, just a few days ago, I asked her, like that, as a gag, if she'd inherited a fortune. She told me she had been given some money by four guys who were holed up at her place. Two brothers, real thugs, plus a friend of hers who is on the run, and Henri.'

'What's her name, your chum?'

'Suzy. Suzanne Fourreau, if you prefer.'

'She got a guy running her?'

'Now you're asking too much. She talked to me about somebody named Roger, but I don't know if that's her sweetie. That all you wanted to know?'

'One last question. A stupid one. What about that loose step? You said you'd explain it.'

Maguy smiled. She drained her glass before answering. 'When you come down on the third step, it sets off a bell in the office where Lulu keeps her accounts. She opens a peephole the sucker can't see so that she can see which girl is going up. That way, Lulu can jot down in her book how many times each of us has operated. It's for her cut, you see?'

'I see. A Madam Superior.'

'If you like. But everybody has to live.'

'Great,' I said, getting up and putting on my jacket. 'I'm going back to the shop. Thanks for the information, Maguy. If you hit any snags that aren't too nasty, you know my phone number.'

'Okay, constable. I won't forget.'

I bent over the bed and kissed her. Maguy's voice stopped me as I went through the door: 'Did he suffer—Henri?'

'No, Maguy. He never knew what killed him.'

Tracing Suzanne Fourreau was child's play—a check with the Vice Squad files told me she lived at 57 rue Bichat.

But later, in front of the building itself, with its cracked walls and its labyrinth of intertwined corridors, I realized that I would never accomplish anything here alone. There were courtyards, recesses, all steeped in shadow; at night it would be a lethal trap. Standing at the bus stop almost directly in front of the building entrance, I reflected that if I hung around for long I would attract attention. So I went back to the Maison.

By the time I finished briefing Fatso on what I'd learned, he was jubilant. 'Tomorrow, Borniche, you'll have everything you need to keep that place under constant surveillance. I'm going to ask the superintendent for a nice van, just like the one your friends at the PP have. We'll all go together, Hidoine, you and I. This time we've got them. If we don't we might as well retire.'

The next morning, at my butcher's, I learned from reading the *Parisien libéré* that I might as well retire.

15

Screwball was becoming very unhappy. He was annoyed by the discomfort of the rue Bichat; at his age, sleeping on a mattress on the floor was like being broken on the rack. Naturally, he was happy to have Émile back, but he was worried. Not about his mistress Yvonne, hiding out in Auvergne, but about his two dogs. He missed his boxers. He paced the cramped flat on the rue Bichat, obviously lost, wondering obsessively what was happening to them. Yes, of course, Émile's 'brother-in-law', the Hunchback, swore he was looking after them, bringing them food and walking them. But Screwball knew the Hunchback could never lavish on them the total affection his dogs so desperately needed.

'You give me the shits, with those hounds of yours slobbering all over the place,' the exasperated Hunchback had grumbled as he threw his cards on the table.

'You can't understand, Paul,' Screwball said. 'With dogs, the bigger they are, the more loving they need.'

They were sitting in a far corner of the *bistrot* adjoining No. 57, playing poker. Dekker was with them.

'You know, you're making a fool of yourself over the dogs don't you?' the Hunchback insisted. 'I buy meat for them, no fat on it; I cook macaroni and vegetables for them; I serve them bottled water; I waltz around with them for an hour every night. What more do you want me to do? Take them to the movies and cuddle them up in the balcony?'

'You don't give them love,' Screwball sighed. 'And a dog without love is a flower without water.'

'Right,' the Hunchback said. 'Next time I'll water them.'

'If only I could see them for a moment. I'd pay anything just to stroke them.'

'Are you off your head? With all the cops there are roaming around . . .'

Love triumphed over fear in Screwball's heart. For the sake of his animals, he committed a grave imprudence. He checked to make sure the truckful of cops the Hunchback had told him about was gone. Then, all alone, having bought some prime beef and sweet biscuits, he went back to his flat.

He wasn't alone any more when he left. A man was following

him, staying well behind him, a Flying Squad inspector who happened to be passing by and who recognized him. When the shadow saw his quarry enter the rue Bichat building, he tipped off his boss, Superintendent Clot.

In no time, a van crammed with armed police slid to the curb near No. 57.

Night had fallen. In her kitchen, Suzanne Fourreau was getting dinner ready. Dekker, Screwball and Émile Buisson sat at the table sipping silently at their *pastis*. A dangerous tension, a barely repressed animosity had developed between Roger and Émile in the previous few days. Since 22 September, in fact, when Caillaud had arrived, wreathed in smiles, at the rue Bichat. He had opened his raincoat, plunged his hand into his trousers pocket and pulled out a ring set with diamonds which he placed on the table as carefully as though it were an egg.

'Where'd you get that?' asked Buisson, suspicious.

'You'd never guess,' Francis replied, dropping into a chair. 'What do you think? I dropped into La Paillote a while ago for a drink and the owner called me over and handed me the ring. "Here," he told me, "you forgot this in the toilet the other night." Can you imagine? And to think we thought Henri palmed it.'

Dekker had blanched. Buisson still sat there as though he'd been carved out of marble. The previous evening, on the pretext of stealing some paintings from a château, he had led Russac out to the La Faye Forest and Dekker had witnessed the execution.

After Francis left, Roger told Émile exactly what he thought of him; Screwball had to step in to keep the peace. Since that day, the two men had looked coldly at each other.

Suzanne opened the window and stuck the salad basket out to dry the lettuce. Suddenly, she spotted narrow flashlight beams darting through the darkness in the courtyard. She wheeled abruptly. 'Get out, all of you!' she yelled. 'Cops.'

Screwball and Dekker jumped for the door, but footsteps could already be heard thudding on the landing. Émile ran to the open window, threw a leg over the sill and hauled himself to his feet. Then he hesitated. Some fifteen feet below him he could see the dull gleam of the rainspout on the next building. For an instant, he recoiled before the danger of missing his hold and crashing down to the pavement below. A fist pounded twice on the door and a voice bawled, 'Police. Open up.'

So Émile jumped. The split second in which he dived through space seemed endless to him. Brutally, his fingers slammed against the gutter. Despite the agony of the impact, they closed over its lip with superhuman strength. The shock was so violent he thought his arms were tearing loose from his shoulders. But he hung on. Horrified, he felt the gutter sag under his weight. Then it stopped bending. In the silent darkness, he could hear shouts and the noise of fighting coming from Suzanne's flat. Only at that point did Émile cautiously drag himself up until his torso was sprawled flat against the sloping roof.

His forehead dripping sweat, he caught his breath, then, slowly, brought first one leg, then the other up over the gutter. Lithe as a cat, he scrambled up the roof incline and crouched behind a high chimney. He no sooner reached it than a beam of light swept the tiles to which he had been clinging. 'Shit!' a disappointed voice growled furiously in the darkness. 'He was here a little while ago. I don't see how he could have jumped, though.'

The police spent all night searching for him, ransacking every flat, every hidden corner, shredding the shadows with their flashlights. It was dawn when they finally gave up.

Still squatting behind his chimney, Émile let another hour go by. Then he went over the roofs to an adjoining building which had an entrance on the quai de Jemmapes. Breaking a skylight, he dropped down into an attic room, forced the lock on the door, walked downstairs and went out into the street. An angler was watching his float in the Saint-Martin canal. Buisson walked calmly to the place de la République, where he disappeared into the underground.

Monsieur Émile had been saved by the bell.

ROUND TWO

16

'Something wrong, Monsieur Borniche?' the butcher asked.

I must have looked pretty sick if he noticed it. I folded the newspaper which told me of the hectic arrests in the rue Bichat and of Émile's escape, and laid it gently on his cash desk.

'A low blow,' I said. 'Look, I haven't the time to take the meat upstairs. You give it to Marlyse if you see her. I've got to run.'

Funny how we run even when we know we are running towards a reprimand. The prospect should slow us down, but all it does is spur us on. I'm not the only one who reacts that way: factory hands, office workers, minor civil servants, they all do it. A good lashing at the end of a brisk canter draws us like the grand prize in a lottery. And the more extensive we know it is going to be, the faster we drive ourselves. Which is why, that morning, despite my end-of-the-month deficit, I took a taxi to the office.

All the way there, I kept telling myself, 'Fatso is going to tear me apart.' And I was right. His usual calm self-possession gone, he literally roared at me the instant I set foot in his office.

'Ah! Nice work, Borniche!' he thundered. 'Bravo! You have certainly outdone yourself this time. Keep it up, my boy, keep it up and you'll make chief inspector in no time.'

I tried to defend myself: 'But, last night, Chief Inspector, when I gave you my report . . .'

'Did you report that our friends from the Prefecture were already at the rue Bichat?'

'But they weren't there.'

'How do you know? They were not going to cluck "cuckoo" at you from their van.'

Fatso was getting on my nerves. 'Listen, chief,' I said, 'according to the newspaper there were more than twenty of them on the raid, backed up by a detachment of uniformed men to cordon off the street. What was I supposed to do all alone? And despite their numbers, they let Buisson get away.'

'That is true,' said Fatso, suddenly calm, 'and that is the only thing that really consoles me. What are you going to do now? We've got to begin all over again.'

I had thought about this on the way there, and I had my answer ready:

'I'm going to see Examining Magistrate Gollety and ask his permission to question Dekker and Screwball.'

He was almost a friend, the judge. Squat, round, blond and smiling. We sometimes met in the bar of the Hôtel Terminus, at the Saint-Lazare Station, where he caught his bus for Neuilly. Whenever we did, we drank a *pastis*, then he took me by the arm and hustled me outside to begin what seemed an interminable walk. I'm a talker, but it was hard for me to get a word in when I was with him. He would go on uninterruptedly talking about pending cases, about crime, about the mystery stories he was so crazy about. I knew that, in spite of himself, he had a weakness for the Sûreté Nationale, to the detriment of the PP. He was an able, tenacious magistrate; it was his work that finally brought Dr. Petiot to the scaffold.

When I entered his office on the third floor of the Palace of Justice, half a dozen lawyers formed a wall before his desk, requesting visitors' permits, requesting bail for the clients, seeking authorization to consult official files.

'My respects, your honour.'

'Ah, Borniche. Take a seat, my friend.'

With a curt gesture, Gollety dismissed the lawyers, locked his office door and dropped back into his swivel chair.

'Well?'

'I need a permit, your honour. I would like to interrogate Dekker and the elder Buisson, whom the Prefecture has placed in your custody.'

'But, Borniche, your section has nothing to do with the rue Bichat arrests. They are out of your territory. What's more, they've been formally charged.'

'I know it, but I've been instructed by your colleague in Pontoise to look into the murder of another criminal called Henri Russac.'

'What do Dekker and Screwball have to do with that?' Gollety asked, taking a pack of Gauloises from his desk drawer and offering me one.

'No, thanks. I always stick to Philip Morris, your honour.'

'Well, well, prosperity is rife at the rue des Saussaies.'

'I buy them on the black market, your honour—and I pay less for them than I would for Gauloises.'

'Fantastic. Could you get me a carton?'

'Certainly. But, with your permission, your honour, getting back to my case, Russac was killed by a nine-millimetre bullet. And that bullet was fired from a P.38—the same one used in the Paris shooting spree after the hold-up at the Auberge d'Arbois, which is one of your cases. So the murderer must be one of Russac's accomplices in the hold-up.'

'Seems likely, Borniche; in any case, your reasoning is sound.'

'I have been all the more convinced since a prostitute told me that Russac was being put up by Suzanne Fourreau. It looks like an open-and-shut proposition to me; if I can succeed in getting Dekker or the elder Buisson to talk, my case is solved.'

Ferdinand Gollety knocked the ash from his cigarette, reflectively. 'Borniche,' he said at last, 'I'm perfectly willing to give you your permit. But I doubt whether Dekker or Buisson major will talk. They're both old hands you know. Your colleagues at the PP have questioned them—somewhat forcefully, I think: the prisoners' faces were a little puffy when they were brought to me. But neither of them talked. The only time Buisson opened his mouth was to the effect that his brother had never been at the rue Bichat and that they hadn't seen each other for years. As for Suzanne Fourreau, all she would admit to was being Dekker's mistress.'

Suddenly, an idea hit me.

'I read in the paper,' I said, 'that a regular little arsenal was found at the rue Bichat, machine guns, revolvers, lots of ammunition. The Flying Squad presumably sent it all to the laboratory for examination.'

'So they did,' Gollety said, 'but the ballistics report hasn't come in yet, probably won't for several more days. Which means that, for the moment, I'm stuck. I won't be able to lay a solid charge of attempted murder of police officers against the prisoners until I've seen the results of the tests.'

'Do you know, your honour, if there was a P.38 among the weapons found?'

'Let me think . . . Yes, it seems to me there was.'

I heaved a sigh of relief. I wouldn't wait for the results of the tests to question Dekker and Screwball. I would try to bluff.

It was after three p.m. when I left Gollety's office with my permit in my pocket. Half an hour later I rang the bell at the big Santé prison gate. A starred kepi appeared behind the judas window.

'Inspector Borniche, of the SN.'

The gate opened. I walked along the short corridor to a glass door, where I showed my badge to the duty officer. He turned his key twice in the lock and the door swung open. I crossed the paved courtyard to a stone staircase straight ahead of me. I couldn't help shuddering as I climbed the three steps; it is at the foot of those steps that the scaffold is raised in the shadowy dawn light of an execution day. The closely guarded glass door ahead of me opened on to death's antechamber. When the condemned man, his neck bared, his hands bound behind his back, escorted by guards and black-clad men, walks through that door, he comes up against a plank set up in the doorway. The plank falls away. Two of the executioner's assistants grab the man's arms, place his neck under the lunette. The ninety-pound blade drops, slices. The head rolls, blood spurts in floods, which are washed away at once by hoses in the guards' hands. The corpse ends its twitching in a wicker trunk filled with reddening sawdust.

I have often gone to the Santé prison to interrogate inmates. Every time I climb those three steps, I feel a shock. My memory carries me inexorably back to the only time in my life—I was a young inspector then—when I had to witness an execution.

The condemned man was a young gypsy. I was the one who had arrested him. I saw that man scream and cry as they dragged him to the scaffold. I shall never forget the limitless terror in his eyes. Paralysed with horror, I watched him pass me. He looked at me, imploringly. 'I didn't kill him,' he cried out to me, 'it was my brother! It wasn't me!' He was telling the truth, the gypsy. He was innocent.

The real killer had been his older brother, who had murdered an old man with despicable refinement. Bowing to the rights of seniority, the younger brother had agreed to sacrifice himself for the older. He claimed responsibility for the murder. During the trial, he stuck to his story, supporting it with a profusion of sickening detail. His brother, in the defendant's box, listened impassively. When the verdict was announced, the younger man's passion for life submerged him; he begged his brother, adjured him to tell the truth at last, to admit his guilt. The brother, who had been sentenced to life imprisonment, simply turned his head away. When the guards led the two men off, chained together, I knew that justice had been deceived. But the gypsy had done everything he could to deceive it.

It may have been curiosity that led me to accept the invitation to witness the execution. I had never dreamed of how horrible it would be. I never accepted again. And, since that day, I have been a fierce opponent of capital punishment. I am a hunter, not a killer.

Going though a barred gate beyond the door, I showed my permit to a guard seated behind a counter. He examined it, laid it down in front of him, stamped it, wrote my last name, first name, rank and section in a huge visitors' ledger. I headed for the lawyers' visiting room with its double row of glass doors. I chose booth No. 3. A guard opened it, rattling his keys; I walked in and sat down at a wooden table. 'They're bringing you Dekker,' he told me. 'He's in solitary for the moment.'

For some minutes I stared at the grey walls of the little room, until my wandering gaze fell on a young woman lawyer, blonde, slender and pretty, in the booth opposite. She was waiting for her client, too. 'Nice, eh?' the guard murmured, giving me a knowing wink. I had my mouth open to answer him when Roger Dekker appeared. Short and stocky, his hair was rumpled, his lips were thick and his eyes bulged. The left side of his face was bruised. Judge Gollety had been right: the Flying Squad boys had not gone about it light-handedly. The guard shut and locked the door behind him.

'Sit down.'

Dekker sat, slowly. We examined each other. I took note of his tough, stubborn manner, his shifty look. I wondered how to approach this man who was on his guard and determined to keep his mouth shut. In any case, force was no solution. With him it would get me nowhere.

'Dekker,' I said, 'I don't belong to the Prefecture of Police, so I won't be talking to you about the hold-up of the Auberge d'Arbois. It doesn't concern me. I've come about something a lot more serious.'

He didn't flinch. On the contrary, he showed the ghost of an ironic smile. And he waited.

'Do you know what I'm talking about?'

No answer. He stared at me, his smile now lifting the corners of his mouth. That annoyed me, but I knew I would need patience if I wanted to pierce his shell of feigned indifference.

'All right, you don't want to say anything, and that's your right,' I said, digging into my briefcase and taking out some printed forms. 'So I'm going to write out a statement. I'll ask questions and I'll note that you refuse to reply. I'll ask you to sign it, I'll note that you refuse to sign and that will be the end of it. I'm no fool, you know, and I'm not in the habit of talking to myself.'

He didn't move. Then I took a pair of statement blanks, slipped a sheet of carbon paper between them, took out my fountain pen and wrote, repeating aloud as I went:

'We, Roger Borniche, police inspector of the Police Judiciaire, Paris headquarters, acting on the instructions of Monsieur the examining magistrate of Pontoise . . .'

I stopped and looked up. 'You notice, the judge is in Pontoise. Does that say anything to you?'

He shook his head. He hadn't moved, but his gaze grew more intent.

'Your name is Roger Dekker, born 2 October 1915 in Paris, 20th arrondissement?'

He nodded. I went on:

'You admit you were sentenced to seven years' imprisonment by the Seine Department Criminal Court for theft, then to four months for fraud, later to another fifteen months for theft before you escaped from Clairvaux gaol?'

He blinked agreement. We were still staring at each other. He was tense, watchful. I was smiling, pretending to be relaxed. Without taking my eyes from his, I fumbled in my briefcase and brought out Cocagne's photos of Russac. Slowly, deliberately, I spread them out on the table, turned towards Dekker. The first one was a close-up of the wound in Russac's skull; the second showed Russac's body sprawled in the weeds; the third was a portrait of Russac, the eyes wide open and dirt-spattered, the mouth open in a rictus.

Dekker still said nothing. But this time I saw his nostrils tremble.

'Was he your friend?'

He looked away.

'You see, Dekker, you owe the privilege of my visit to Russac. There's no connection with the Buisson escape, the rue Bichat hideout, the restaurant hold-up and the little war with the motor-cycle cops. I don't bother with anything but the really serious stuff: murders. And everything leads me to believe that it's you who will take the rap for Russac's murder.'

His eyes opened wide, his mouth gaped. At last he spoke:
'Me?'

'Yes, you. Because the bullet they took out of Russac's skull was fired from the same gun from which we found bullets at the rue Bichat and others recovered after the gunfight with the motor-bike cops. Two of the bunch were almost intact, one embedded in the headlight and the other in a tyre. Now, the gun is a P.38, nine-millimetre, and it belongs to you.'

'Is this some kind of a joke?' Dekker roared in a voice gone suddenly hoarse. 'If you've come here to fuck me up just say so and I'll get back where I come from.'

He spun round abruptly and began drumming on the glass door to attract the warder's attention. Fortunately, the screw was absorbed in contemplation of the blonde lawyer. I stood up.

'As you like, Roger,' I said, deliberately using his first name, 'I don't give a shit either. You can straighten it out with the Pontoise judge, and I can assure you that he's not exactly soft. Neither is the Versailles Criminal Court, you ought to know that. Well, if you want to drag Suzanne into it with you . . .'

Dekker whirled to face me, furious.

'What do you mean, Suzanne . . . ?' he demanded.

'No way out. She'll have to confront you. She'll be transferred to Pontoise when Golletty is finished with her, which means in four to six months, maybe more. She'll repeat what she told me—that the P.38 was yours—and Screwball will confirm it . . .'

'That would surprise me!'

'What would surprise you?'

'That Suzanne said anything. She's my woman. She'd never shop me. And anyway she knows fuck-all about guns.'

'Have it your way, but the Police Lab are one hundred per cent certain. They're your prints on the gun. So you see, the shells, the bullets, the prints, Suzanne, Screwball—that's a lot of evidence against one man.'

'True,' Dekker admitted. 'But what proves the gun's mine? It could just as well have belonged to Screwball or his kid brother. And nothing proves I was with them over Russac.'

'And the prints?'

'I could have left them when I was just handling it. I love handling guns.'

'Okay, okay. I'll write down what you're telling me. So you admit handling the gun that killed Russac?'

'Whoa! Not so fast.'

'Come on, Roger, use your nut. You know I can't really write that in a statement. Look, I've seen your sheet in Records. I'm certain it wasn't you who shot Russac. But don't kid yourself: the Buissons would be only too happy to stick you with it, because of the prints. And Screwball isn't the man to cross his brother.'

'Naturally.'

'You know the story about the car?'

Dekker shook his head, his bulging eyes round with curiosity.

'Listen. One day, Mimile was in le Rat Mort, a bar on the place Pigalle that no longer exists. He was shooting dice with the owner. A stranger called to him from the end of the bar.

'"That your car in front of the door?" the guy asked.

'"Yes," said Mimile.

'"It's a nice piece of work! Wouldn't want to sell it, would you?"

'"I hadn't thought about it," Mimile said, "but if you like it, it's yours."

'"How much?"

'"Ten thousand."

'The following day, the two men met by agreement in the same place. The buyer was weighted down with hard cash; Buisson's right arm was in a sling. "I fell downstairs last night," he grumbled. "I've got to have it put in plaster."

'"How about the car?" the other asked.

'"Here are the keys."

'"Will you make out a receipt for me?"

'Émile pointed to his injured arm. "I'm perfectly willing," he said, "but look at my arm. You write it out, I'll sign it."

'The other man did so. When it came time to sign, Émile, after two false starts, scribbled a vague, completely undecipherable scrawl with his left hand. The other guy drove happily off at the wheel of his new purchase.

'Two months later he was in the office of an examining magistrate. The car had been stolen. Buisson was brought in between two guards.

'"That's the man, your honour," the buyer exclaimed, pointing his finger at Émile.

'"Me? I don't even know this man," Émile said calmly. "If I had sold him a car, I'd have given him a receipt."

'"Exactly," the judge said. "I have the receipt here, and it will prove your undoing, Buisson."

'"Well, your honour, have the handwriting analysed and you'll see if it's mine."

'Buisson was discharged and the buyer, whose record was not exactly shining, got a year in prison for theft and receiving. That's Buisson for you.'

Dekker listened with interest, but he didn't say a word. I continued:

'You see, Dekker, you're a regular guy, but it won't do any good to insist in front of a jury that "it wasn't me, it was the other guy". And if you don't help yourself, you are going to find yourself with your head under your arm, believe me.'

'But what do you want me to tell you?' he cried.

'What happened. You tell me the whole thing, calmly, methodically, in detail. I write your statement down on the form, you sign it and I leave.'

'Christ!' he groaned. 'You cops never give up, do you? Do you realize that you're trying to get me to hang myself?'

For a long moment, Dekker thought, his eyes lowered. He knew Buisson was on the run and that it might be a long time before the police caught up with him, if they got him alive at all. I could guess what he was thinking; so, to encourage him to talk, I spelled it out:

'Suppose your case comes up before Émile is picked up. What's going to happen? They'll load everything on your back. Suppose they find Émile—dead. What happens then? If you accuse him, they'll say it's easy to accuse a corpse and that you're acting like a louse.'

There was a pause. 'Give me a cigarette,' Dekker said.

I handed him a packet of Philip Morris and a box of matches. He took one, lit it, drew on it and coughed. 'Women's cigarettes,' he grumbled disgustedly. 'Women or queers . . .'—he stopped, but I was careful to say nothing—'Okay, this is how it was. Émile couldn't stomach Russac. For three reasons. The first, pretty stupid, was because he was tall, young, good-looking, just the opposite of Émile. Second, because when he left the Auberge d'Arbois, Russac tossed out the name Francis. Third, Russac, who was a skirt-chaser, was making sheep's eyes at Suzanne.'

'Your woman?'

'That's right. He helped her with the shopping and the dishes, he'd pat her ass when she walked past him. He was itching to make her. Émile didn't like that at all. It drove him crazy.'

'And you?'

'Me? I didn't give a shit. I learned a long time ago that if a man wants to keep his head and his freedom, the first thing he has to avoid is falling in love. Love is where all the foul-ups begin. I like Suzanne. I give her what she likes in bed. She feeds me, houses me, brings in some dough when I need it; I keep my nose out of the rest. Sometimes, when Émile pestered me about Russac hanging round Suzanne, I'd tell him, "Look, she's a whore; dozens of suckers get up her every day—so what difference does it make if it's Russac or somebody else?"'

'Okay. One morning, 21 September, Émile came to me and Russac with a really good proposition: twenty million francs in paintings in a château near Andrésy. All three of us went out there in a stolen car. When we reached the La Faye Forest, Émile told me to stop. We got out. Émile headed for a wall that had fallen down at one point, and climbed over. Russac and me, we followed him, not worried. The job looked easy. Buisson walked through the underbrush. Without any warning, he stopped near a tree and opened his fly. So did Russac. It was a trap. With a leap, Émile got behind him, his gun in his hand. He pushed the barrel against the back of Russac's head and fired; the flame lit up Russac's hair and he fell with a dull thud, his eyes open and his prick still hanging out in the sunlight.

'I'm not saying this to defend myself, but, frankly, it made me sick. I knew Émile had a killer's nature, but I never would have thought he'd knock off a pal who'd helped him get out of Villejuif. He blew down his gun barrel, stuffed the gun back in his pocket, looked at Russac and said to me:

' "Did you see that jet of blood? It spurted like when you cut a pig's throat. Even jumping behind him like that, I got it all over the bottom of my trousers."

'It was Suzanne who washed it off when we got back. She was terrified.'

Dekker fell silent for a moment. He ground his cigarette out underfoot. 'You see,' he went on, 'Suzanne is my best witness.

If I had killed Russac, the blood would have spurted on me. The trousers are probably still at her place. I don't understand about the fingerprints; I must have touched the gun without noticing. Naturally all the hardware was piled together.'

'One last question, Roger, and I'll get out of your hair. Who is Francis?'

He shrugged, and put on his stubborn look. It was pointless to press him. I knew the criminal mind too well not to sense that a man like Dekker had said all he was going to say. I handed him the statement and my pen. He signed without even reading it. I tucked everything into my briefcase and got up. Before knocking at the booth door to summon the guard, I turned to Dekker.

'Not too tough, in solitary?' I asked him.

'Aah!' he grimaced.

'Listen, if you want to tell me anything, let me know. I'll have you brought to the rue des Saussaies.'

An odd light flushed in Dekker's eyes. It was easy to read his mind. From now on, in the darkness of his solitary cell, his imagination would be concentrated on figuring out how to profit by this offered trip outside the Santé to make his break, as he had done so effectively from Clairvaux.

I left the Santé. Tomorrow I would go to Fresnes to interrogate Screwball. Russac's murder was cleared up, but there were still two men roaming free: Émile Buisson, whom I had never set eyes on—but then, neither had any of the other police now hunting him—and Francis, whom I had to identify, because I knew he could lead me to the killer.

17

I like Fresnes Prison. It is light, airy, peaceful. A whole different world from the Santé, which is a glorified latrine trench. And getting to Fresnes was like going on an outing in the country. In those days, you climbed on to the open rear platform of a 187 bus, crossed your arms comfortably on the railing, anchored your brief-case snugly between your ankles and watched the landscape flow by. The bus goes through Montrouge, then Cachan, L'Haÿ-les-Roses to the avenue de la Liberté, where I got off. A long, tree-lined walk runs alongside the prison complex to the central gate, where a smiling guard lets you through without any fuss. Between gate and main building is a courtyard where the prison vans load and unload. Then you are inside, in a corridor with a parquet floor that gleams like a mirror; on the right a hearing room the size of a cathedral. A line of chairs leads to a green baize-covered table and, behind it, a directorial armchair. I sat down and waited until the friendly guard brought Screwball to me.

I was feeling exuberant that morning. I had gone to bed early the previous night. I had slept well. Marlyse had smothered me in affection and I thanked her on waking by serving her breakfast in bed.

I tried to anticipate how my interrogation of Screwball was going to go. I planned to use the fingerprint gimmick that had worked so well with Dekker. There was one hitch, of course: Émile was his brother, and Screwball would try to shift the blame from him to Dekker. Too bad; they could settle it between them in front of the examining magistrate.

A door opened and Jean-Baptiste Buisson, accompanied by a screw, appeared at the far end of the room. He stopped for a moment, spotted me and, his espadrilles shuffling along the wooden floor, came and sat down opposite me. Of average height, powerfully built, he was really a fine figure of a man. His nose was straight, thin, almost distinguished and his mouth was beautifully sculptured, sensual. But his eyes, hard or ironic by turns, and his square jaw hinted at uncommon energy. He looked, by and large, more like an engineer or a retired army officer than a thief.

The contrast with Roger Dekker was striking. Where Dekker

had been suspicious, glum and taciturn, Screwball was relaxed, airy, mocking.

I had already spread the statement blanks and carbon on the table and uncapped my pen, but now I suddenly wondered if any of it would be useful. The unusually severe discipline to which Screwball was being subjected did not seem to have had the slightest effect on his determination or his self-assurance. The fact is that he was almost cheerful and he scrutinized me with a derisive look, not insolent, just utterly self-possessed. He placed his hands flat on the table, cleared his throat and, by God, moved straight into the attack.

'You're from the Sûreté, I'm told. Right?' he opened, addressing me in the familiar 'thou'. 'What's your name?'

'Why do you ask?' I blustered, a little taken aback.

'Because I like to know who I'm dealing with. Either people are straight with me and we get along, or I don't take to them, and, in that case, so long, my friend.'

My astonishment grew at this reversal of roles; I couldn't help answering: 'Borniche.'

'Funny name,' Screwball observed through pursed lips. 'Well, now, young Borniche, what's on your mind?'

I don't know why, but I couldn't bring myself to use the 'thou' with him, as I habitually do with criminals. It was as though he had forced me to respect him. 'I've come to talk to you about Russac's murder,' I said. 'You know what I mean. Besides, it would be a waste of time to deny it; Dekker has told me all about it. I'm really just here for the form.'

'Got a fag, Borniche?' Screwball asked, stretching out his hand.

I offered him my pack of Philip Morris. With a sly smile, he took three cigarettes, slipped two in his jacket pocket, tapped the third on the table and glued it to his lip. 'They're to smoke later, while thinking of you,' he said. 'Got a light?'

I struck a match. Screwball pushed his wrinkled face towards the flame, puffed at it a few times with his eyes closed, blew smoke up towards the ceiling.

'Dekker?' he grunted. 'Who's that?'

He saw that his question had got my back up and that I was about to lose my temper; he hurried on before I could say anything.

'Listen, Borniche,' he said, 'You seem a decent enough guy and not too much of a fool, so I'm going to level with you. I'm fifty-two years old and if I had a thousand-franc bill for every time I've been questioned by the fuzz I could live on the interest. I don't know Dekker, I don't know Russac, I don't know anybody. You can knock my eye out or hang me from the ceiling by the balls, but I'm not going to tell you any more. Now then, you ought to know what the statute of limitation means, eh?'

Obviously I knew what it meant. I had to answer the question on my exam for entry into the Sûreté Nationale. The law stipulates: 'In a murder case, the courts may no longer act after ten full years from the date of commission if no indictment or formal criminal proceeding has been initiated in that time. For lesser felonies, the period of limitation is three full years.'

'Why do you ask?' I said.

'So as to make you understand, my boy, that I can talk myself blue in the face to you about anything I might have done up to 1937. After that—my memory's a blank.'

He gazed ironically at me and I realized it was useless to try to lean on him. If we started playing cat and mouse, I would be the mouse. The 'interrogation' was over; Screwball was not going to say anything about the Russac killing, or about the Villejuif escape, still less about the Auberge d'Arbois. I did, nevertheless, try one more gambit as I stowed my pen and statement blanks in my brief-case.

'You're making a mistake behaving this way,' I ventured. 'You are implicating your brother.'

Screwball gave a shout of laughter. 'If you think Émile can't defend himself without anybody's help,' he retorted, 'you are very green, young Borniche.'

I glanced at my watch. It was nine-forty a.m. We had been skirmishing for less than five minutes, and already it was over. I felt badly let down. I had an impulse to let it rest there—to send Screwball back to his guard and his solitary cell, but the man intrigued me. I almost liked him. I decided to stay and chat with him.

'I read in your file that you've been around the world,' I said. 'Before 1937, naturally.'

'Correct, sonny,' Screwball agreed as he stubbed his cigarette out on the green baize. 'Right after my escape from Mulhouse. It was a phony rap, as usual. Émile was free. He gave me a hand getting out.'

'So you were just returning the favour at Villejuif?'

'Borniche,' warned Screwball, glowering at me, 'don't start being clever. We are talking about before 1937. Period.'

'All right. You were convicted in the Seine Criminal Court of robbery and attempted murder and you got eight years. Right?'

'Right. But I was innocent, like I told you. Okay, to get back to my breakout. Émile came to see me in the visitors' room. While the screw on patrol was out of earshot, he whispered to me to get myself taken to the hospital. Him and Courgibet would be there with a car one night to pick me up.

'The date was set for 21 November 1934. I don't have to tell you that I was worried that day. I had tried everything I could think of to get into the hospital, but it was no go. And, that night, Émile and Courgibet were going to be waiting for me with a fake passport to get me out of the country.

'You know, when you are all alone in a cell, you stir your stumps, you go around in circles, you think non-stop. No matter how hard I tried, I could only see one way to get myself transferred: break a leg.

'You know, it takes a lot of guts to bust your own leg. We've always had guts in the Buisson family. I stood in a corner of my cell with my right leg stuck straight out over the bed. I raised my stool as high as I could and, wham! I came down hard on my shin-bone. I thought I was going to pass out from the pain, but it hadn't worked—the damned bone wouldn't break. So I did it a second time, and a third time, whacking at the same spot. Christ, I was dripping with sweat, almost out cold with the pain. Finally, on the sixth try, I heard a nice, sharp crack; there was a wave of pain that made me sick to my stomach. Then I blacked out. When I came to, I was in the hospital with my leg in a plaster. I'd made it.'

'A nurse came with a knockout pill. I pretended to swallow it, then asked her what time it was. Eleven-fifty. At midnight, in ten minutes, Émile would be at the hospital door.

'I was lucky. The cop on duty went to take a piss. He just got up and walked out. I forgot to tell you that there were four of us in the room. I got up too, but the plaster weighed a ton. Hopping on my good pin, I reached a pair of crutches lying against my neighbour's bed. They were too big for me, but I swiped them. The stupid bastard was getting ready to yowl—I could have brained him with his water carafe. But he shut his trap when he saw me reach for it. I hobbled out into the corridor on my crutches, in my pyjamas. A duty nurse flashed a smile at me as she went by and told me the lavatory was straight ahead. I went on without seeing anybody else until I was through the door. Émile was there, gassing with the night porter to distract him. My crutches had rubber tips, so I didn't make any noise leaving. The car was purring in front of the door. Courgibet left the wheel to come around and help me in. Émile got back soon after that, and we beat it. Got a fag, Borniche?'

I handed him the pack. He extracted a cigarette, lit it, drew softly on it, his gaze lost in his past.

'We ditched the car in Grenoble. That's where they lost our trail. They looked for us in Switzerland, in Germany, in Austria, in Italy. We were at sea. Émile, with his bird, Yvonne Paindelet, Courgibet and me, my leg still in plaster. We'd boarded in Genoa and there we were bounding through the waves, headed for Shanghai.

'You know, Borniche, China was paradise in those days, it was Eldorado, Mecca, the works. A guy with enough push could make his fortune there. And we had enough of it for ten guys. So in we went. All the way, with everything we had. It's true, nothing could stand up to us. We had the hearts of conquerors. And we didn't waste any time. Émile bought a bar-hotel, the Fantasio. He installed Yvonne behind the till, set up a gambling room in the lobby and a cathouse upstairs. And it went like a steam engine, Borniche my boy, twenty-four hours a day it snorted away. A hive, a factory. All anyone wanted to do there, white or yellow, was to have a ball. You see, the Japanese were being greedy at that time and they were hot to take over the provinces. Manchuria was down the drain and they were already infiltrating Peking, Canton, Shanghai, Nanking—you name it.

'As usual in set-ups like that, there were the rotten ones; there were lousy Chinks who played the Nips' game and they were crazy for guns at any price. Émile was on to that one right away. "We've got to get into the gun-running trade, chaps," he told us.'

'How did you go about it?' I asked.

'Simple, Borniche, simple. We bought them from Chiang Kai-shek's regulars—they sold them right out of the arsenals. Émile loaded them aboard an old plane he bought, flown by an American pilot, and delivered his merchandise in it.

'We were raking in the dough. Nothing but dollars. Then, one day, the plane took a nose dive into the brush. The pilot was killed and Émile walked back alone, a long, long walk, with the American's ring, his wad and his silver ID bracelet.

'So guns were out. "There's dope," Émile said. 'So dope it was. Only, that's a trickier racket than guns.'

'Oh? Why?'

'Why? Why? Think, Borniche! You can't get done with guns. They bring in the cases, you check the merchandise and you deliver it. But drugs! You really need to know what you're doing. You pay for cocaine and they slip you flour. And there's nothing you can do with it except bake cakes.'

He burst out laughing. 'In fact, that happened to us once,' he went on. 'Just once. An American wanted to buy, a Chinese wanted to sell. Émile and me were the lucky middle-men. Good, so the deal goes through. The American forked out his dollars, the Chinese sent us the stuff and we collected our commission. Life was beautiful.

'Then came the disaster. A little while later, the American turned up again, yelling his head off that the stuff was phony. He started throwing his weight around. An hour later, the Chinese showed up shrieking that the dollars were fake. He began threatening us too.

'Émile was annoyed. He don't like that sort of thing, Émile. He's always been straight. I asked him if he needed a hand, but he shook his head no. I knew that black look of his; it meant he was furious, foaming at the mouth, that he wanted to settle this business his own way, all by himself.

'I never knew exactly what happened. All I know is that they found the Chinese drifting down the river a few days later, his head held underwater by one of his own flour sacks weighted down with a lead pipe. The day before, they'd found the American hanging from a tree; in each of his eyes there was a counterfeit dollar rolled up like an arrow and planted in the socket.

'People suspected it was Émile's work. Even in a rotten town like Shanghai, you couldn't go too far in those days. Everybody ganged up on us, the hoodlums, the smugglers, the whores and the fuzz. We had to leave in a hurry.

'Émile shipped Yvonne to Paris to sniff the wind there. Courgibet hotfooted it to Spain. Émile sailed for Fusan, in South Korea. He was accused of slugging a silk merchant for his roll. So he took a freighter to Hakidate, in Japan. He had ants in his pants round about that time, Émile did. While I was still stuck in

Shanghai trying to sell the Fantasio—hell, trying to save something out of the wreck—Émile ran into a buddy in Canada, stuck up some trappers to keep himself in groceries and got himself hunted by the Mounties. The atmosphere was getting very nasty, Borniche. There was only one thing my brother could do: blow.'

'Where did he wind up?'

'In Barcelona, in the middle of the Civil War. And a bloody, crazy merry-go-round that was. Puddles of blood everywhere, executions non-stop. Émile was happy. He could go back into the gun business.

'I said before that Courgibet had gone to Spain from China. I was wrong. He was in Genoa, Courgibet. That's where Émile joined him and asked him to restock us in hardware for both sides.

'Business was good, except that Émile didn't trust pesetas. He wanted dollars, he kicked up a ruckus, threatened to suspend deliveries. One day a bunch of locals, all armed, tried to arrest him. He let go with his machine gun, mowed down seven of them and then he was denounced. They were Franco men.

'He was thrown into the nearest jail. His cellmate was a communist, a French deputy, name of André Marty. Very impressive man, he was. He taught Émile to read and write. All my brother knew before then was numbers, figures. He didn't worry much about the rest.

'The Spanish weren't sure what to do with Émile, so they finally turned him over to the French cops at the border. That's where he learned that the time limit had expired on his conviction in absentia for complicity in my breakout; he was free, with nothing hanging over him. So he went back to Paris, met up with Courgibet and his pals, and there we are, in 1937.'

Jean-Baptiste fell silent. His black eyes, shining, were fixed on me, but I sensed that his mind was far away, far behind him. The only sound audible in the room was the ticking of the seconds fluttering by on the big clock over the door. It was eleven o'clock. I could have listened to this strange man indefinitely, but I had to get on to the Palace of Justice in Versailles, where I was due to testify early that afternoon in an abortion case which had been dragging on since the year before. I'd come back and see Screwball some other time.

'And Courgibet?' I asked suddenly.

Jean-Baptiste came back to earth with a thud. With a slow shrug, he explained: 'Oh, he burned his bridges with us. He wanted to start again, go straight. Straight, with his record! He went to the United States and that's the last we heard of him. Maybe he made it, got a wife, kids, a job. Who knows? Courgibet wasn't a real lawbreaker. Not of the faith. He always felt guilty ...'

I was in an unsettled mood when I left Fresnes. I had spent an instructive morning, but I hadn't learned anything.

18

Micheline Borgeot was a mess. A real mess. A fat, flabby, fortyish creature with heavy eyelids the colour of a fresh bruise, an inverted ladder of chins that rippled like small waves every time she opened a mouth surprising for its lack of lip. She did have all her own teeth, arranged in a neat, white line. But this display of bone china did not begin to compensate all the other injustices Nature had heaped on her, crowning its work with a tangle of yellow hair as stiff as sauerkraut. She was built close to the ground, strong, with short legs that made her prance like a dachshund when she walked. Her grandfather, Auguste, was guillotined for killing a policeman. Her father and uncle died of illness during an extended stay in a prison colony.

Micheline would have liked to have been a hooker, but even as a girl her ugliness was so aggressive it scared the customers away. So she resigned herself to selling flowers near the fountain at the porte de Saint-Cloud.

Doubtless out of remorse, Nature gave Micheline a lovely, delicate daughter, Chantal, whose slender figure and oval face in its frame of chestnut hair kept the young gents in the neighbourhood in a constant state of nerves. Chantal was twenty years old.

Every morning, Micheline left her apartment at 140 rue de Paris, in Boulogne (on the capital's western rim), with her basket of flowers under her arm. Antoine, her husband, a massive, mild-mannered man, stayed in bed, not troubling even to open an eye to watch her go. He did a little shoplifting, a little fiddling with the serial numbers of stolen cars, which he also rejuvenated a little with his paint gun. Nothing serious, in short, but it brought him the price of a few nightly *pastis* at his old pal Victor's bar, the Deux Marches.

Micheline, Antoine and Chantal lived on the ground floor of a low, four-storey building, a grey cube, filthy and malodorous. They occupied a three-room-and-toilet apartment giving on the far end of the courtyard. The little furniture they had was much repaired and rickety, bespeaking its owners' attenuated interest in the goods of this world.

The couple had a friend, Dédé Quarteron, a villain of the Roaring Twenties and the Throbbing Thirties. A fine-looking man, Dédé was, solid, brave, elegant, who always had money in his pocket. There was only one flaw in the old armour—a heart which had begun to weaken in its forty-sixth year.

It was Dédé whom Émile Buisson contacted after his flight from the rue Bichat. Dédé was reading his newspaper in his usual *bistrot* on the rue de Montreuil when the owner informed him he was wanted on the telephone. It was Émile, his old pal Émile, in need of a bit of help; in his curt, authoritative voice, he now assigned Dédé to find him a hideout.

'Call me back in twenty minutes,' Émile was told.

Dédé hung up, then dialled a number. At that time of the morning, Antoine Borgeot was having coffee and *croissants* at the café across the street from his apartment building. After Antoine had been briefed on the situation, he let himself be coaxed a little. 'You're a good guy, Dédé, but I'm not your boy,' he cooed. 'Hiding someone like that on the run is too risky.'

Quarteron wheedled: 'Just two or three days, long enough to find him a flop of his own. If my house in Bagneux was heated, I'd have gladly taken him in there. Besides, fifty thousand francs a month in pocket money's nice to have.'

Antoine weakened. So, on the stroke of eleven, Émile Buisson, in his shirt sleeves despite the chill in the air, arrived at the rue de Paris in Boulogne, where a mattress awaited him on the floor.

'I'm going to get some sleep,' Émile told Antoine while his host prepared to park his car. 'Phone Dédé and tell him I want to see him at five o'clock.'

When Buisson awoke, late in the afternoon, a man was sitting on a chair a yard away from him, smoking while he waited. It was Quarteron.

Buisson was not feeling expansive. He tossed off a brief 'Hi! Everything all right?' Then he got to his feet, fresh and cheerful.

'Listen,' he said, pulling on his clothes. 'I want you to warn Francis I'm here and tell him to come and see me.'

'That's very funny, Émile. And where am I supposed to dig him up, your Francis?'

Buisson suppressed his irritation. 'It'll take you two seconds, for Christ's sake! You go to Gaston's, rue Léon-Frot. He's the guy who found him his hideout; he'll know where to reach him.'

'Okay,' Quarteron said, surprised to see his friend treating him like a doormat. 'It's not far from my place. Do you need anything else?'

'Yes. A gun.'

It took only three days to organize the reunion between Caillaud and Buisson. When Dédé arrived one evening at the rue de Paris, Émile, Antoine, Micheline and Chantal were at table, tucking into a plate of stew. Dédé quickly noticed the attentions Chantal lavished on Émile, but he took his cue from Antoine and Micheline and said nothing.

'Well?' Buisson asked.

'You have a date with Francis tomorrow afternoon at two o'clock. At the Botanical Gardens zoo, in front of the bear pit.'

'Good,' said Buisson, his mouth full of food. 'And the other?'

Twisting in his chair, Quarteron opened his overcoat and jacket, unbuttoned his waistcoat, plunged his hand into his trousers waistband, digging cautiously around almost to his genitals, and came up with a Colt automatic and a spare clip. These he handed to Émile.

Buisson shoved his plate away. He took the gun, weighed it in his hand, aimed it. Then he stripped it down rapidly and reassembled it, finally placed it on the table. He was so intent on the chore that no one else dared make a sound.

'Okay?' asked Quarteron.

'Perfect,' Buisson said, reaching for his plate.

Superintendent Clot had still not digested his setback in the rue Bichat. No matter how rich a harvest of murders, thefts, holdups each day produced, or how many dozens of lawbreakers his detectives brought in, Clot was consumed with an obsessive grief: he wanted Émile Buisson. Whatever the cost. Dead or alive. Sometimes, in the course of his day, he would leave his desk and move to the window. He would contemplate the Seine, the white front of the Rôtisserie Périgourdine restaurant on the opposite bank, and wonder, as he stroked his slender moustache, just where the hell in all that scenery Public Enemy No. 1 could be.

And when he heard an informer's voice one morning on the telephone telling him: 'This is the Lawyer; Buisson and Caillaud have a date by and by at the Botanical Gardens,' Superintendent Clot thought his bird was in the net. He placed men at every entrance, hidden in cars and trucks. And the wait began. The informer had told him the two men were due to meet at two p.m.

At four, there was still no sign of them. So, bitterness again flooding his policeman's soul, Clot ordered a search of the gardens before dark.

For over an hour, in the biting cold, the police explored the Buffon and Cuvier pathways, the central alley, the Orangerie walk and the Ménagerie walk. A waste of time. 'All right,' Clot finally announced, his face almost invisible in the twilight, 'call it off. They're not here. The Lawyer will hear from me about this . . .'

The Prefecture's hunters retired in defeat. Night had shrouded the city and, in the blackness of the gardens, there was no sound but the far-off rumbling of traffic. Two heads slowly emerged from the bear pit. 'They've gone,' one of them whispered. 'You go right; I'll go this way.'

Invisible in the night, the two men scaled the protecting wall and, bent double, raced for the deeper shadow of a tree. One of them was dressed in mechanic's coveralls and a lumber jacket; that was Caillaud. The other, Monsieur Émile, was elegantly got up in a dark blue overcoat and suit and a black trilby. Both held guns. They scanned the quay through the grille. 'What do we do?' Francis asked.

'We climb,' Buisson said, nodding towards the gate.

Francis, his back to the boulevard, legs splayed for maximum balance, made a hand ladder, almost hurling Émile to the top of the gate. Once down on the other side, Buisson stuck his hands through the bars and clasped them to make a step for Francis. The two men were quickly reunited on the pavement. 'Let's cross the street,' Buisson ordered.

They ran down the slope to the Seine, stopping briefly behind a pile of barrels at the Port-aux-Vins to catch their breath. They felt safe now.

As they separated, Caillaud muttered:

'I wonder who the shit was who put them on to us. It's not as though everybody in Paris knew where we were meeting.'

'Forget it,' said Buisson. 'He won't do it a second time.'

Émile did not go directly back to Boulogne-Billancourt. As he walked towards the gare d'Austerlitz, where he could take the Métro, he reviewed his recent conversation with Quarteron. When Dédé had told him the time and place of the meeting, Émile had asked him suspiciously:

'Who knows about this?'

'Nobody,' Quarteron had assured him. 'When I got to Gaston's Michel the Lawyer was there. But I'll vouch for him; he's a sound kid, Michel.'

'That remains to be seen,' Buisson had objected.

Now, walking fast, Émile reasoned it out. Gaston was in the clear; he could be trusted—he had proved that time and again. Émile didn't know Michel. Despite Quarteron's confidence in him he was clearly a worm, a squealer only too eager to tell the cops anything he knew. He was nicknamed 'the Lawyer' because he had spent some time at law school. No doubt about it: he was the leak. He had either reported directly to the cops or he had talked too much to an informer or some tart. As far as Émile was concerned, the result was the same.

'That's one Lawyer who won't be practicing much longer,' Buisson murmured to himself.

The lights of the gare d'Austerlitz glittered ahead of him. He hailed a taxi. 'Twenty-five rue de Montreuil,' he told the driver.

This was Dédé Quarteron's headquarters, the café near his home where he spent his days playing an endless poker game. When he saw Émile in the doorway, he jumped up. 'Are you crazy? What are you doing here?'

'I need the Lawyer's address,' Buisson said casually. 'I have a job for him.'

Three quarters of an hour later, Inspector Bouygues walked into the Lawyer's hotel room and found his half-naked body with a bullet hole between the eyes. The inspector had been sent by Superintendent Clot to invite him along next day 'to help the police with their inquiries.'

19

Buisson had to be found.

From the Prefecture's reports to the Interior Ministry, from newspaper accounts and the victims' testimony emerged a recurrent image: a small man with dark eyes and a big gun who perpetrated a series of armed robberies at the rate of at least one a week.

Émile had collected a new gang together after Screwball and Dekker were captured and he was back on the warpath. Despite the intensity of the police hunt, he remained undiscoverable, elusive. And the Lawyer's murder had produced its logical consequence: informers generally had grown discreet and cautious.

After my colleagues from the Prefecture got through with it, I made my own cellar-to-attic examination of the building on the rue Bichat, spending days questioning the inhabitants. Nobody knew anything, nobody wanted to know anything. I had finished and I was standing grumpily on the pavement with my hands in my pockets when my attention was attracted by the lighted front of the little *bistrot* near the block of flats. Another light suddenly snapped on—in my mind: Suzanne Fourreau, Dekker's girl, didn't have a telephone in her flat. So Buisson must have received his calls at the café. I headed for it.

The owner, a bald, ruddy man in shirt sleeves, wiped away at the zinc counter with a wet sponge.

'You know, *monsieur l'inspecteur*,' he told me, 'that Suzanne, she didn't get calls very often, and when she phoned, she did her own dialling. As for Buisson, *primo*, nobody knew who he was, *secundo*, he didn't do much telephoning and he didn't say who he was calling.'

'And you never heard anything, a name, even a first name ...?'

He retreated, shaking his head, scooped up two glasses in one fist and a bottle of *pastis* in the other. 'No, Inspector, honest,' he insisted, pouring out the drinks. 'Hard as I try, I can't think of a thing. People phone from here all day long, you know. My wife and me, we wait on people, we talk, we keep an eye on the cash drawer and we don't listen.'

'And your wife?'

'I'll call her. You take your *pastis* straight or with water?'

'With water, of course.'

'Me, never; pure, straight, neat. Like in the Legion.'

He tossed off his drink in one swallow, poured himself another and yelled, 'Germaine.' I heard Germaine's impatient 'Coming!' from the kitchen. Then she appeared, her hair in curlers covered by a net.

'This gentleman is from the police,' the owner said. 'He wants to know if we heard anything when Suzanne or the little dark guy telephoned.'

Germaine concentrated, her low forehead disappearing with the effort, caught in the squeeze between her rising eyebrows and descending hairline. The suction it set up in her brain made her screw up her eyes.

'Wait . . . one afternoon . . . no, morning, it was . . . no, no, afternoon—a man asked for Suzanne. I remember that I didn't catch the name at first and I had to ask him to repeat it.'

'Do you remember what it was?'

'Yes. Because I remember my father, who was out in the Colonies, telling me once that out there that's what they call the mixed breeds: Quarteron. That struck me. Suzanne went to call Buisson. He came down to talk to the guy and, just before he hung up, he said to him, "See you, Dédé." '

'Have you told my colleagues about this, madame?'

'Well, no. It only came back to me, just now.'

Back at the rue des Saussaies, I began by putting a tap on the café's phone. Then I climbed up to Records. Inspector Roblin took my slip and, at his usual slow, solemn pace, disappeared into his network of alleys. He was back soon, with a slender folder containing nothing more than the subject's civil status: André QUARTERON, alias Dédé the Stéphanois, born 24 June 1901, in Saint-Étienne; no known occupation. There was a note on the back of the sheet concerning his only brush with the law: 'Person of doubtful morality. Questioned in connection with identity check at L'Étape bar, rue du Faubourg-Saint-Martin. Released after verification.'

Just reading that gave me fresh hope. If Quarteron hung around L'Étape, which had been the haunt of Screwball and Russac, that could mean he was also in touch with Émile Buisson.

*

The address Quarteron gave in the identity check was 32 passage de la Bonne-Graine, in the 11th arrondissement. It was late in the day by this time, but I went there anyway. No. 32 doesn't exist; the street numbers stop at 20. Once again, I thought I was following a dead trail, especially when the concierge of the last house on the block, to whom I showed Quarteron's photo, failed to recognize him. She advised me to inquire at the café next door.

'Does he own a Citroën?'

I shrugged. 'Maybe. I don't know. He's certainly a guy who is not fond of work; must live off feminine charm.'

'Christ!' exclaimed the owner, clapping his hand to his brow. 'I've got it now—he's the one who hung around with Lucienne, the bird on the fifth floor. He came to see her almost every day.'

'Doesn't he come any more?'

'No, not since Lucienne . . . hold on . . . Lucienne Herbin, that's it, that's her name—she moved about a year ago, without leaving an address.'

So there I was, back in the blind alley. What drove me up the wall in this Buisson business was that every time I felt I was nearing the end, it turned out to be a dead end.

'Let me have a phone token, and pour us both a *pastis*.'

The phone booth stank of burned fat from the kitchen. I called Leloup, a friend on the Vice Squad, and asked him whether Lucienne Herbin appeared on his love list. He didn't keep me waiting long, and he did give me an address: Quarteron's mistress, an old customer of the Vice boys, lived in a house on the rue du Maréchal-Foch, in Bagneux (on the eastern edge of Paris).

A good tail should, obviously, remain invisible. But watching without being watched in daylight in a quiet, virtually traffic-free suburban street is just about impossible. From the moment I began going from house to house, questioning the residents, I could feel the eyes pasted to front-room windows, following my progress with fascination.

'We're just going to make idiots of ourselves like this,' I complained to Hidoine. 'Perhaps I'd better try the old fancy-dress.'

Hidoine agreed. So I resigned myself to wearing a disguise. Sitting on a folding stool at the entrance to the street, muffled in a beat-up old hat, an oversized old coat borrowed from my concierge, shapeless trousers of equal antiquity and dark glasses, I set a beggar's bowl at my feet and made like the blind accordionist.

The day oozed by that way. By evening, my teeth were chattering, my fingers were stiff, I was sniffling and I was exhausted. And I hadn't seen a soul. Disgustedly, I scooped up the coins passers-by had dropped in my bowl: thirty-two francs. I wasn't going to buy any gold bars with that.

For three days I kept watch near the villa. Hidoine came by occasionally and led me to a nearby café to get me something hot to drink, then guided me back to my stool. The villa seemed uninhabited. It was heartbreaking.

'I wonder if you're on the right track,' Fatso groused one morning. 'In any case, you're no damn good around here. I never see you any more, you're letting your other cases slide. This can't go on. Instead of clowning around, Borniche, you are going to have to organize yourself some other way—and seriously.'

Ungrateful bastard! I was reduced to watching the house at night, without telling him. I bicycled to Bagneux, sometimes posing as a house painter, or a gas company employee, but the villa remained plunged in darkness. By poking my hand through the bars of the gate, I managed to open the mailbox: no mail. I was ready to give up, but there was one more trick I hadn't tried.

In an envelope I bought in a stationer's, I put a circular I had picked up in a local council block and mailed it to Quarteron. I could feel the envelope in the box the following evening, but it was gone the night after that. Some one had come and taken it.

I wanted to be sure. I took two tiny balls of wax, each no bigger than a pinhead, from a cachou box; I pressed one against the door-jamb, the other on the door, down at the bottom. Then I tugged a hair out of my scalp and stretched it between the two blobs. We call this a witness; anyone opening the door has to tear the hair loose. I did the same thing on the garage door.

Days went by, but my witnesses remained intact. Then, one night around midnight, just as I was about to catch my bus home and say to hell with Quarteron and his whore, I saw a Citroën, lights all off, roll slowly up the street and stop in front of Lucienne's house.

A heavy-set man with his coat collar turned up got out of the car, went into the house and turned the lights on. From where I was hiding, behind the wall of a neighbouring house, I could see his shadow moving behind the closed blinds. Then the house went dark, the man came out and double-locked the door. What he did next really floored me: Quarteron—for it was he—bent down and, by the light of a flashlight, carefully replaced my witness!

When I told Fatso what had happened, he squinted thoughtfully at me. 'Stick to it, and take Hidoine with you,' he advised. 'These people have nasty suspicious minds, lad. And that's a good sign.'

Sitting behind Crocbois in the car, quaking with the cold, we continued our vigil at the corner of the rue du Maréchal-Foch and the rue de Fontenay. So as not to interrupt surveillance, we relieved our bladders into empty tin cans that Crocbois brought along. Despite our blankets and the thermos of coffee Marlyse had prepared for me, it took only two nights for us to catch our deaths. We were coughing and sniffling like clogged drains when, on the third night, Quarteron reappeared.

This time we were determined not to let him get away from us. As soon as he had left, Crocbois slipped the clutch in and took off after him, keeping about a hundred yards behind him to keep from being spotted.

We slid silently through Châtillon-sous-Bagneux and Montrouge; at the porte de Châtillon we turned off on to the outer boulevards. I had a hunch we were nearing our destination. When we turned into Boulogne-Billancourt, I asked Crocbois to close up a little on the Citroën.

He was about to speed up when a lorry crashed a red light at a crossroads and nearly flattened us. 'Son of a bitch!' Crocbois muttered. By the time he had swerved and straightened out again, Quarteron's car had vanished. We cruised around Billancourt, but found nothing. Eventually we gave up and went sulkily off to bed.

'God almighty, what lousy luck,' Hidoine fumed. 'What a damned stupid way to make a living!'

I told Fatso the next morning about our latest failure.

'That's too bad, Borniche,' he told me, 'because I've been finding out things. André Quarteron was a friend of Desgrandschamps, the guy Detective Superintendent Belin arrested after the Troyes hold-up. I am certain he is in touch with Buisson, but he's too cautious a man to risk hiding Émile in his own place. He must have farmed him out with a friend. You absolutely have to find him.'

Fatso was definitely getting on my nerves. He seemed to think that all he had to do was issue the order and it was done.

'I know that,' I said. 'But how?'

So the days went by.

I had tied up a fairly simple jewel theft case one evening and decided for a change to go for a drink at the Deux Marches. As I reached it, two men came out, bundled up in lumber jackets. I stood there, rooted to the spot. One of them was Quarteron, the other was a huge man I didn't recognize. I made way for them to pass by; they walked up the rue Gît-le Cœur, laughing like maniacs.

I entered the Deux Marches, took my coat off and hung it up and went to shake hands with Victor. 'Those friends of yours have lousy manners,' I said, 'They just pushed past me without even saying "hello".'

Victor's eyes opened wide in surprise. 'Which friends?'

'The two I passed coming in.'

Victor fell into the trap. 'Oh, Dédé and Antoine. Don't take it so personally. They were pretty tanked up and I'm sure they didn't recognize you. Want to roll dice for the first one?'

'Okay.'

I couldn't ask Victor for any information. He turns into a sphinx when he's questioned and, besides, he might warn his friends. In any case, luck had handed me the information that Victor and Quarteron knew each other. I would hang around the rue Gît-le-Cœur until I could pick up my customer and tail him.

I saw Antoine at the Deux Marches three evenings later. He was sitting crossways on the table, facing Victor. Both men looked upset. I walked over. 'What's the matter?' I asked. 'You look as though you were at a wake.'

'You couldn't have put it better, Roger,' Victor said, running a nervous hand through his hair. 'He's dead.'

Antoine crossed himself. 'Yeah,' he said. 'Dédé's dead.'

'What? How did it happen?' I asked, immediately supposing that André Quarteron's busy life had been cut short by an underworld bullet.

'He was making love with Lucienne,' Antoine told me. 'He had a very weak heart.'

Once more the thread had snapped in my hand.

20

One should never give up hope.

The next morning, skulking behind the tombstones in Ivry cemetery, I watched Quarteron's funeral from a distance. The cream of the underworld was there and I realized that the late Dédé must have carried a lot of weight to attract such a congress of villains. In the front rank of pallbearers was big Antoine, blubbering into a handkerchief the size of a towel.

The burial over, I huddled down in the back seat behind Crocbois and we prepared to tail Antoine as he drove away. From the cemetery, we trailed him along the avenue de Verdun to the porte de Choisy. From there we hit the exterior boulevards, crossed the Seine on the Auteuil viaduct and, still going fast, turned off at the porte de Saint-Cloud. As we shot into the rue de la Tourelle:

'Damn!' Crocbois exclaimed. 'This is where we were the other day.'

I took my eyes off the car ahead of us and looked around; we were in Boulogne, near the rue de Paris, and I too recognized the spot where we had lost Quarteron. I touched Crocbois on the shoulder. 'You're right,' I told him. 'Look!'

Antoine had slowed down before a block of flats and turned into its covered driveway. Crocbois and I saw him reappear and close the wooden doors to the street. It all took less than a minute.

That very afternoon, Hidoine and I began discreetly questioning the building's residents. We soon found out that Antoine lived there with his wife, a flower-seller nicknamed Liline, and their daughter Chantal.

'They've had a relative staying with them for some time,' the woman in the cleaner's shop next door told us.

'Oh?' asked Hidoine, innocently. 'Have you seen him?'

'Yes, once. He doesn't go out much and he doesn't seem like much of a talker. Their brother-in-law, I believe. A little guy, dark, well-dressed, with interesting black eyes.'

'We've got him,' brayed Fatso when I phoned him the news. 'But jump him in the street, by surprise, or it'll be a slaughter.'

It was late February and miserably cold. Hidoine and I worked in relays, either from the car or from the café next door, watching the building throughout the day, but there was no sign of Buisson. I began to worry; I wondered if he had found a new hideout, if the café waitress I had been carefully hustling had not, after all, tipped big Antoine off to our presence.

On 24 February, Fatso called us into his office. 'Listen,' he told us. 'I've been thinking. It's almost certain that Buisson was holed up with Antoine, who was a friend of Quarteron. So everything adds up. Whether he's still there remains to be seen. If we surround the building, we have to be sure there are no slip-ups. We're in the Prefecture's territory and if we mess it up they'll complain to the minister while they crow about our failure. I think we have to maintain surveillance. The moment Buisson sticks his nose out of the house, you jump on him. If you don't see him, that means he's moved to another hideout.'

'That can go on for quite a while, chief,' Hidoine remarked.

'That's your worry, not mine . . .'

'Obviously. And if we catch pneumonia?'

'You'll get a posthumous medal.'

That morning, almost at the same moment, Inspector Freddie Courchamp, his frozen hands in his pockets, looked up at a street number and walked into the tenement building on the rue de Paris. He knocked resolutely on the concierge's door.

'Chantal Borgeot?'

'Ground floor.'

Courchamp strolled casually towards the apartment door. He was investigating the death of a pretty young blond girl, Christiane Czerwonka, whose clothes were found neatly folded on a Paris quay and whose nude body was fished out of Marly lock. Suicide or murder? For the moment, no one knew. Among the facts Inspector Freddie Courchamp had learned was that, on the evening before her death, Christiane, nicknamed Cricri, had been seen at a dance in the company of a friend, Chantal Borgeot. Inspector Freddie Courchamp had come to question her.

He stopped at the door and listened. It was very quiet in the building and he thought he could hear panting noises coming from inside the flat. He knocked loudly at the door; the panting stopped at once. Courchamp knocked again. He heard footsteps shuffling across a tile floor. Then the door opened. A young woman appeared before him, her hair tousled, her eyes glowing with annoyance and her body obviously naked under her hastily crossed dressing gown. Inspector Freddie Courchamp now understood what the moaning had been about.

'Sorry to bother you,' he said graciously, shouldering his way into the flat. He glanced around the room. Through an open door, he saw a man sprawled in bed, hiding under a sheet. He marched officiously to the doorway. 'All right, on your feet!' he ordered. 'You can finish later. Get your clothes on and beat it. I need to have a private talk with your little girl friend, here.'

'Of course, sir.'

As Inspector Freddie Courchamp looked on mockingly, the small, dark man with black eyes jumped out of bed as though it were on fire. He threw on his clothes, not stopping to lace his shoes, grabbed his blue coat and trilby and fled to the door.

'Sure you haven't forgotten anything?' Inspector Freddie Courchamp snickered at the closing door.

Monsieur Émile had left one item behind: his Colt, hidden in a jar in the kitchen.

ROUND THREE

21

Time, luck and patience are a policeman's three chief weapons. There was nothing left for me to do but wait.

The arrest of a crack jewel thief named Paul the Sparkler involved me in a two-month-long series of operations in the diamond-cutting district around the rue Lafayette. Paul held out for two days, denying everything, until he was broken by the almost miraculous discovery of a five-carat stone in the head of a rag doll.

I learned from the newspapers and the Prefecture's reports that on 10 May 1948, two Social Security Administration employees in Draveil had been attacked by armed bandits who relieved them of the 70,000 francs they had just withdrawn from a postal savings account. A Colt was also taken. Among their assailants, inevitably, was the little man with black eyes. The job had Buisson written all over it.

On 27 May 1948, Fatso sent me scurrying out with Crocbois to the Villeneuve-Saint-Georges bureau of the SN to talk to two officers, Superintendent Prioux and Inspector Vigouroux, at whom somebody, we were told, had been taking potshots. I had known Prioux in the First Brigade, on the rue de Bassano—he had even been my section chief for a few months—and he gave me a warm welcome. We talked in the tiny room that functioned as his office. 'My friend,' he exclaimed, 'a hairsbreadth lower and I wouldn't be talking to you today—I'd have a split skull instead. They're pretty good shots, the bastards.'

He got up, walked over to the hat rack and took down a brown trilby, which he shoved under my nose; there were two neat holes, one on each side of it, just above the band. Prioux threw it on a chair and returned to his place at the desk, taking a pipe and tobacco pouch out of a drawer.

'If I had known who we were dealing with,' he said, tapping the bowl of his pipe against a corner of the desk, 'we would have gone about things differently, I can assure you, my dear Borniche. But we had no idea of what we were getting into.'

'How come, Superintendent?'

Prioux filled his pipe, meticulously gathering up the tobacco flakes scattered on his blotter. 'Hell, it started out as a routine operation, on a tip. Some fellow phoned the station to report that his wife had told him two gangsters were hiding in Charles Bouton's house at 125 rue des Prairies, in Vigneux. In fact, the guy turned out to be a cuckold whose wife had run off with Bouton—and Bouton is no great lover. We found all this out later. Anyway, the officer who took the call told us that the mugs in question were named Frisson and Bayaud.

'The names didn't mean anything to us, and they weren't on our wanted lists, but I decided to take Vigouroux with me and check, just in case. Off we went to the rue des Prairies, like lambs to the slaughter. The gate was closed. We rang, but there was no answer. Vigouroux didn't wait to be invited: he climbed over the fence and walked up to the house door. It wasn't locked. Vigouroux knocked. We waited, but nobody came. Then, as Vigouroux turned the knob and opened the door, a shot rang out. He jumped for cover just in time. I started to move, when a second shot rang out and the bullet went through my hat. Vigouroux and I took shelter behind a pillar and fired through the door. Then the shooting stopped from inside the house. We went in. All we found was a young woman, a looker; her teeth were chattering. The marksmen had escaped over some waste ground behind the house. And that, my friend, is how we were unfortunately foiled.'

Prioux came to the end of his recital and sat there puffing reflectively on his pipe until his head almost disappeared in the clouds of bluish smoke.

'What did the woman have to say?' I asked.

'Nothing. She didn't want to talk, but we found an identity card in the pocket of her coat. She's the wife of somebody named Caillaud.'

'Who did you say?'

'Caillaud. Francis Caillaud, an escapee from Fresnes. We identified him easily enough. And she finally admitted that her husband's companion was the famous Émile Buisson.'

Prioux tilted back in his chair, oblivious to the effect his

announcement had on me. So little Francis, hunted by every cop in
France since the Auberge d'Arbois hold-up, was finally identified.
Just because some woman happened to walk out on her husband.
Chance is truly the patron saint of policemen.

I asked Prioux to send for his prisoner. I was anxious to talk
to someone who, only hours before, had stood beside Monsieur
Émile.

Prioux was right; Caillaud's wife was very pretty. Looking at
her, so shy, so frightened, you would never suspect she shared the
life of a dangerous man. For she was very much a part of his life.
Caillaud took her with him wherever he hid out and, everywhere
they went she recreated a family setting for him, did the house-
work, prepared the meals for her husband and his friends. Without a trace of vulgarity, simply dressed, she was completely unlike
the gangsters' women I was used to meeting. I found it easy to be
courteous to her.

Prioux asked her to be seated on an unpainted wooden chair.
She did, her eyes watching me.

'Madame,' I said gently, 'you are undoubtedly going to be
charged with complicity in a serious offence. Your husband and
Buisson fired on officers of the law.'

Caillaud's wife nodded. 'I know, sir,' she breathed, dropping
her head.

'Now, I'm not going to pester you for long. I understand the
difficulty of your situation, but, unfortunately, your husband is in
the company of a killer who wastes no pity on anyone and must
be restrained from such attacks. Do you understand?'

She kept her eyes fixed on the tips of her shoes. I drew as close
to her as I dared and continued:

'It is in your interest, madame, and in your husband's, to help
us. I am sure that your honesty will earn the court's clemency.
Just tell me where you think they might be hiding.'

The woman raised her head; the look in the blue eyes she
trained on me was compounded of frankness and terror. 'I don't
know, sir,' she said. 'I don't know.'

She waited for the next question, her eyes still holding mine. I
confess to having felt a little sorry for her; she seemed so helpless.
And I believed she was telling the truth. I walked back to where
Prioux was sitting. 'Very well, madame,' I said, 'I have no more

questions. The superintendent has no choice but to turn you over
to the Corbeil magistrate. Oh—there is one more thing. How did
they get away?'

She swallowed hard, hesitated, torn between her impulse to tell
the truth and her fear of compromising her husband, of saying
anything that might put the police on his trail.

'On bicycles. They took two bikes they found leaning against
a fence.'

'Are they still armed?'

'Yes. They took the sub-machine guns with them.'

I could imagine the two fugitives, like giants of the road,
pedalling briskly through the suburban streets with their machine
guns across their handlebars

Yet despite all the road-blocks, not a single cop noticed them.

22

It was dark by the time I called the shop. The switchboard put me through to Fatso's office, but it was Paulette, his secretary, who answered.

'The boss there?'

'No.'

'Well, where is he?'

'I don't know. At the Deux Marches, perhaps.'

I hung up, said good-bye to Prioux and went out to the car.

'Where to?' Crocbois inquired.

'Victor's.'

I began to regret the decision long before we got there. I was all in, and if I began drinking in that condition I knew I was going to fall apart. When we got to Victor's, I went in just the same, determined to stay just long enough to knock back one *pastis*, report to Fatso on what I'd found out, then beat it home, where Marlyse was waiting for me.

The place was crowded. There were a number of Prefecture colleagues in attendance and, since they all had a head start on me, the air practically dripped soggy wit when I walked in. There were hordes of tourists, all in pairs, and a few criminal types. One big, laughing, chomping, drinking riot.

Fatso was draped over the table, playing dice with Victor and a short, silent, withdrawn young Corsican with long hair combed straight back.

'You know Jeannot?' Fatso asked me as he shook the dice in his palm.

'No.'

Jeannot stuck out his hand. I shook it.

'I'm Victor's second cousin,' he explained in a low, soft voice, 'Jean Orsetti.'

I glanced at him. 'Oh yes?' And I couldn't help adding, 'What do you do for a living?'

Fatso answered for him. 'A little pimping,' he said, turning towards him, 'eh, Jeannot?'

He laughed. Victor, who had just been eliminated from the game, left Jeannot and Fatso to fight it out. He served me a drink.

'He's a real man, that little guy,' he told me, ducking his chin at his relative. 'His word is gold. Listen, a few years ago, he got into trouble and wound up doing time in Riom. It happens. Well, one of the guards was a Corsican, like us. Naturally, he wasn't going to make any trouble for the kid, pester him, lean on him. They became friends after a while. They used to talk a lot, swap jokes and so on. You get the picture, eh?'

'Yes, I get it.'

'All right, so one day this screw says to Jeannot: "You are going to give me your word of honour, your word as a man that you won't do anything dumb, and I'll take you out with me from time to time in the evening to have a drink, lay a bird. But we must come back." Jeannot gave his word. Sacred. A Corsican never perjures himself. So they went out together, quite a few times. Jeannot had money, he could pay for his rounds. Chummy as two pigs in a trough, they were. One night, two crooks the kid had known in the old country came to Riom. They came into the *bistrot*, they saw the lad alone. The screw was playing billiards next door. "We've got a car outside," they told him. "Finish your drink and we'll take you out of here." Well, do you know what the boy did?'

'No. What?'

'He said no. That's right. He refused. He told them: "I gave my word. I stick to it." The two guys called him a stupid git and left. That's the sort of lad he is. He'll never double-cross anybody. A true Corsican!'

Fatso and Jeannot finished their game. I signalled to the boss that I wanted a word with him and he followed me into the street. I told him rapidly about the identification of Francis.

'Good,' he told me. 'Keep it up.'

We went back into the Deux Marches. Victor grabbed a bottle of *pastis* from under the table and served us, Jeannot Orsetti and himself.

'Business good, Chief Inspector?'

'Thriving, Victor.'

The four of us launched into a noisy, hard-fought dice game.

Two young English girls, not bad-looking and slightly sloshed, came up to us, laughing, leaving their husbands sitting at their table. To impress them, I dropped out of the game and did a string of card tricks that drew admiring little cries. A circle formed around me and I went from trick to trick while Victor poured out round after round.

Jeannot, who was close to me, looked discreetly at his watch. 'Shit!' he said. 'I'm out of cigarettes.'

I offered him one of mine, but he refused. 'American tobacco tears my lungs out,' he said. 'I'll run over to the shops and come back.'

'Hurry it up,' Victor told him dryly. 'Dolores is single-handed tonight for the cooking and serving. It would help if you could pitch in.'

Orsetti hurried along the rue Gît-le-Cœur, dived into the passage de l'Hirondelle and came out on the place Saint-Michel, where he entered a café-tobacconist's. He bought his cigarettes and walked out. Standing on the pavement, he slowly opened his pack of Gauloises, his eyes scanning the crowd, which was dense at that time of the evening. His dark, practiced gaze reassured him: no, he had not been followed. He moved off, skirting the square; when he reached the corner of the quai des Grands-Augustins, he ducked quickly into the Rôtisserie Périgourdine.

Ignoring the advancing headwaiter, Orsetti walked up to the second floor; his eyes swept over the occupied tables. Then he twisted slowly across the room to a table near the window where a little man in a dark suit sat alone enjoying a lobster in cream sauce. Orsetti sat down opposite him.

'Hi, Émile.'

'Hi, Jeannot. Have some dinner?'

'Impossible. There's a mob at Victor's tonight and I have to give him a hand.'

'Glass of champagne?'

'If you insist, Émile, but just a quick one.'

Buisson summoned the wine waiter to serve Orsetti. When they were alone again and Orsetti had put his glass down, Buisson asked:

'Well? You find one?'

'Yeh. I've found someone for you, a Wop.'

'Yaagh!' said Buisson. 'I don't go for them.'

'Nor me, but they make first-rate villains as a rule. And he's hard this one.'

'Who is he?'

'Désiré Polledri. To give you an idea of the kind of customer he is, he broke out of the Île-de-Ré over a year ago.'

'Okay,' Buisson said, setting his glass down. 'Bring him tomorrow, late morning. I'll introduce him to Francis.'

'I have to get back to Victor's.'

Orsetti rose and shook hands with Buisson. As he turned to leave, he glanced through the restaurant's panoramic windows at the dark, imposing bulk of the Prefecture building just across the Seine, on the quai des Orfèvres.

'Hey, Émile, do you like this view from here?'

'What do you think?' Buisson said with a delighted smile. 'They'll never think of looking for me two hundred yards from their own headquarters.'

'They might just happen to spot you though.'

'Not a chance. The photo they have of me is ten years old. Since then, they've never seen me close up.'

Orsetti left. Buisson finished his dinner, paid his check and then went quietly to the Sports Palace. There, in a comfortable ring-side seat, surrounded by famous people and puffing on an enormous cigar, he observed the Prefect of Police, seated only a few yards from him, out of the corner of his eye.

This was one of Monsieur Émile's traditions: every time he eluded the police, he treated himself to a bang-up feed and then went to a fight.

23

For nine months, I ignored Émile Buisson. Completely.

He had certainly formed still another gang, to judge by the regularity with which his description appeared in Prefectural reports on hold-ups. But I simply hadn't the time to worry about Buisson. At the end of June, I arrested seventy-seven members of the Crazy Pierre gang No. 2. This got me letters of commendation, but no promotion to chief inspector and no raise in pay. At one o'clock in the morning of a day in late July, on the roof of an apartment house on the rue Charlot, in Paris, I captured Crazy Pierre himself. I received the customary commendatory letters, but still no promotion, no money. In September, I invaded the lair of One-Eared Louis, Crazy Pierre's right-hand man. In March 1949, I apprehended four armed men who had held up and robbed some friends of the director of the Pasteur Institute. For this I received a full quota of smiles and handshakes. Nothing else.

I was lucky. My career was one long series of triumphs. People thought of me as the supercop, public servant No. 1. I was flattered, envied, spurred on with constant promises; a glorious future was predicted for me, my name would go down in history, I would have a pension to make a banker jealous. And I, at thirty a credulous, strutting fat-head, swallowed it all. Still spurning handcuffs, still unarmed, I made my arrests barehanded.

Fatso, staggering under the honours my prowess rained on him, sweet-talked me, called me 'a good lad', swore by me alone, devoured my reports voraciously, treated my pronouncements as oracular.

To Marlyse, I was the Tarzan of the police force, the terror of the underworld jungle. With my rare bonuses, I bought her a fashionable red coat and an electric kettle. Her admiration for me was so excessive that she was even considering marrying me so as to bear the name she so often saw spread over the newspapers. I had a good deal of difficulty in convincing her that I was unworthy of such devotion.

And then, abruptly, Monsieur Émile bounced back into my life.

One evening, patrolmen from the Vanves station on their rounds in Issy-les-Moulineaux spotted a car driving on the left side of the road, English style, with its headlights blazing away on high beam. The squad car had almost smacked into it. When the policemen blew their whistles, the car shot forward, zigzagging. The squad car set out after it, overtook it and forced it to the curb. The cops, feeling irritable, got out and walked towards the blocked car. They were only a yard or two from it when shots flamed from a window. Two of the policemen were hit; they rolled on the ground, howling in pain. The fusillade lasted only a few seconds. The man who had fired was overpowered. After a violent struggle, the driver, a giant with grey-flecked black hair, was also captured.

While the police battled with the furiously resisting pair, two other occupants of the car fled. Although the officers chased them through the dark, narrow streets of Issy, the fugitives finally gave them the slip.

The two prisoners spent an extremely trying night at the Vanves police station. Propped up on chairs, they were subjected to a methodical beating, an efficient, unrelenting pounding. In less than ten minutes their heads doubled in size and grew as lumpy as Jerusalem artichokes.

But nothing lasts forever. When the police, their tempers calmed, their nerves quieted, their fear avenged, proceeded to normal questioning procedure, they learned that the two citizens they were holding were named Francis Caillaud and Henri Bolec.

The spotlight in the eyes, the phone book thudding on his skull, the volleys of punches were wasted on Caillaud. He never said a word. Bolec was softer. It was he who informed the police, to their chagrin, that the two men who had slipped through their fingers were Émile Buisson and Désiré Polledri.

Unfortunately, it was too late to set up road-blocks.

I was assigned to a new case: a gang of hide thieves, operating on a nationwide basis, had already hit the big tanneries eighty-seven times. Questions were addressed in the Chamber of Deputies to the Minister of the Interior concerning the inefficiency of the police. Fatso ordered me to put the thieves out of business.

'Now that you've got reinforcements, Borniche,' he said, 'you ought to be able to take care of it in no time.'

The reinforcements had a name: Laurent Poiret. He was a young inspector, just appointed, a blond colossus with a face flattened by the thumping it had received in his former career as a wrestler. Poiret's strength was Herculean, but his stupidity was titanic.

He gave me conclusive proof of his density during an interrogation of Alfred Guémar, alias Frédo the Jeweller. Frédo denied he was Alfred Guémar. He denied it with such conviction that he even had me shaken. He insisted that his name was Albert Laugier; all his papers—identity card, passport, driver's licence, rent receipt, hunting licence—were all in that name. Some of these documents had been issued by the PP.

For six hours, Hidoine and I worked on him in relays. I put on the good-guy act, clowned around, did card tricks to break down his concentration, made coins disappear into my sleeves, told funny stories. Hidoine was the brute, banging on the table, threatening, glaring, then walking out, still roaring angrily, when I tipped him the wink. It was my turn. My eyes candid, my voice oily, I said:

'You're wrong to stonewall us like this, Frédo. My colleague isn't a bad guy, but if you keep it up, he is going to let himself go. Use your nut, Frédo. You tell me the truth, I write it down, you sign it and I put in a good word for you with the examining magistrate. Your sentence will be light as a feather.'

'My name is Albert Laugier, monsieur.'

'Son of a bitch,' I thought, 'son of a son of a flat-chested bitch.' Frédo hung on stubbornly, retiring into his false identity with truly lordly assurance. Not even Fatso, who appeared from time to time to read him the riot act, seemed to disturb him.

After seven hours of this, I thought of a slick trap.

Frédo was seated facing me. Hidoine, wearing his riding breeches, stood behind him. Poiret was leaning against the door. Slowly, smiling benignly, I opened my desk drawer and took out the ID card with the name Alfred Laugier on it. With surgical delicacy I peeled off the photograph, stopping from time to time to look at Frédo, who watched me, puzzled. Every time I stopped, I said in a honeyed voice:

'I have a surprise for you, Frédo, a lovely surprise. You'll see. Photos are always full of surprises.'

I finally got the picture off. I examined the back of it. Then I slammed my hand down on the desk. 'You see what I mean?' I exclaimed. 'You're a fraud, Frédo, your papers are fakes and I can prove it now.'

'How?' he asked in a weak voice.

'Simple, my lad. All photographers stamp the backs of their photos with the date and a reference number in case copies are wanted. Yours is dated 7 December 1948. But your identity card was issued 19 August 1948, four months earlier. Tell me how that could be. So you're not Laugier—it's that simple. You agree?'

'Yes,' he hissed.

It was at exactly that moment that the new recruit, Laurent Poiret, revealed his cunning. Bowled over by my demonstration, captivated by my intelligence, he sidled open-mouthed over to where I sat. He took the photograph in his thick, splayed fingers, examining it front and back, his eyes opening wider and wider. 'But Borniche,' he finally declared in his cavernous voice, 'where do you see a date? There's nothing on the back of this picture.'

Thanks to the acuteness of this intellectual of the public service, Frédo refused to sign the statement I wrote out. Since then, I have always felt some reservation about Poiret's support.

In any case, I plunged into the long, arduous investigation of the leather thefts. I had to question victims and witnesses, compare their stories with their written statements, examine the scenes of the crimes. At the end of a day, numb with fatigue, I would go home, change clothes and repaint my little flat; Marlyse wanted a pink bedroom.

One evening, however, I decided to forego the art work and have a drink at the Calanques, which I hadn't visited for ages. François Marcantoni was behind the bar, majestic in a new check suit and ultra-fashionable wristwatch, chatting with a young woman perched on a barstool.

I took my usual place at the end of the bar. François came towards me; he was smiling, but I had a feeling that there was a crack in his usually flawless poise.

'How's it going, Inspector? Shoot some dice for a round?'

'Not tonight, François. I'm just going to have one drink and then home. I'm all in.'

And so I was. I had talked that day to a dozen people involved in the hides thefts. I had to go out on searches, arrange confrontations, extract confessions; I earned my pay. So when François offered me a second glass of champagne, I refused, paid the tab, jumped off my stool and grabbed my coat. I was clumsy putting my arm into a sleeve and jostled somebody behind me. I turned. There was Orsetti, Victor's second cousin, looking a little pale, a little worried, staring at me. The man I had accidentally poked had been sitting at Orsetti's table, a little man with dark eyes and black hair. I looked at him and smiled. 'Sorry,' I said. 'I'm always throwing myself around.'

'Not at all,' he said. 'No harm done.'

A little embarrassed, I opened the door and stepped back to let them pass. The little man went out first, followed by Orsetti, to whom I whispered as he went by: 'Hey, you don't look too well this evening.'

'You're right, I don't feel on form at all,' he said in a tremulous voice. 'You look great, though.'

Outside in the street, I watched him and his friend disappear into the night. Then I walked up to the Étoile subway station, wondering what could be worrying François and little Jeannot.

Orsetti and his friend did not find a taxi until they reached the corner of the Champs-Élysées and the avenue George V. 'I was scared back there, Émile,' Orsetti said.

'Not me,' Buisson replied. 'I was all set to blow your chum's head off.'

ROUND FOUR

24

Beautiful! Really beautiful! I slouched at the table in my pyjamas, stirring my coffee and looking at Marlyse's breasts. She was bent over the sink washing, naked from the waist up. The washing mitten moved slowly over her skin and I saw her breasts sparkle as the light flashed on droplets of water.

The radio began spewing out the seven-thirty news without wrenching my mind from its fond contemplation. A feminine bosom is truly a sumptuous thing when it is well shaped: two breasts, geometric in form, balanced in weight, haughtily firm yet reasonably yielding—I was troubled and transported. Visions of savage rape beset me. Then the announcer's voice broke in:

'René Girier, the escape artist, has once again parted company with his guards. He escaped at five forty-five this morning from the Pont-l'Évêque prison, where he had been confined since January the twenty-seventh. An accomplice was waiting for him in a car. An intensive search has not yet located the two fugitives.'

The careful articulation stopped, to be followed by the warm, virile voice of singer Yves Montand. But I wasn't listening. Ideas were hooking up like chains of atoms in my head. It seemed logical that Girier had been reunited with Émile Buisson, his old jail-busting friend, as the nucleus of a new gang. Monsieur Émile must have been delighted with this unlooked-for reinforcement—his old mob had just been whittled down to almost nothing. I thought about Screwball, whose refusal to talk had led to a quashed indictment, while Dekker had been given twenty years hard labour. Jean-Baptiste was now back in his lair. I could see those cold nights of surveillance beginning again for Hidoine, Poiret and me at the rue du Faubourg-Saint-Martin, and as well as them our game of hide-and-seek with the men from the Prefecture. And I could almost hear Fatso sharpening up his tongue.

I sprang out of my chair and pushed Marlyse away from the sink. 'Let me in here, will you?' I barked.

'That's a pretty expression you're wearing,' she said stiffly. 'Is it the Girier escape that's eating you?'

I didn't even answer. I learned long ago that getting involved in a discussion with a woman is strictly a waste of time—either they don't listen to you or they don't give a damn.

I washed, shaved, gulped down my cold coffee, threw on my clothes and ran to the butcher's to order the day's meat. The *Parisien libéré* had gone to press too early to carry anything on the escape. Still going at high-hurdles speed, I raced down to the place Clichy to catch my bus, but this was turning out to be a bad day: the bus wafted by, jammed to the bumpers. It wasn't until the fourth bus that I succeeded in jumping on the rear platform, my fingers clutching the railing.

It was raining. And since, in my rush, I had left my raincoat at home, I arrived at the shop leaking water like a sponge. Christ, what a day! To top it all off, both lifts were out of order. It's crazy, the number of out-of-order lifts you can find in government buildings. I ran up the five flights of stairs. When, at eight thirty-five, I arrived, puffing, on the landing, I ran into Fatso on his way to the director's office with a file in his hand.

'Well, Borniche, at it bright and early this morning?' he asked. He opened the door to the corridor leading to the director's office, releasing a strong whiff of floor wax; before he disappeared, he tossed back: 'You know what you've got to do. Hidoine and Poiret are already here.'

I knew only too well what I had to do. I had to phone the prison at Pont-l'Évêque for information. Even that turned out to be impossible. Either I couldn't get through to the switchboard, or I couldn't get a dial tone, or it was engaged. Hidoine was changing clothes in the office while Poiret wolfed down a huge garlic-sausage sandwich. They both watched me work with the obvious relief of people who have narrowly escaped a disagreeable chore.

I still couldn't reach the prison, although I did finally manage to get the local police station. It was exactly ten forty-three a.m. The sergeant who had made the preliminary investigation told me that Girier had been extraordinarily docile from the moment he was locked up. His mildness, his willingness to help and his servility earned him assignment to the barbershop, where he energetically clipped the prisoners, the screws and the head screw. The job allowed him to wander unmolested through the prison; it took him no time at all to learn where everything was. More important, it gave him a chance to take impressions of the locks with the bit of soap he always carried in his pocket.

'Police.'

I tossed the word through the peephole at the two suspicious eyes examining me. With two turns of the lock, the gate to the Pont-l'Évêque prison swung open. I was surprised to find myself before a porter in a homespun prison uniform who looked me up and down.

'I want to see the head warder,' I said.

Without a word, the prisoner closed the gate, turned around and shuffled towards the office. I followed him, still surprised at being admitted by a prisoner and not a screw. The inmate opened the office door for me and indicated with a jerk of his chin that I was free to go in. I went in. My surprise was on its way to becoming shock: another prisoner, a huge fellow, sat nonchalantly with his elbows on the table.

'Monsieur?'

I looked around the room. No doubt about it: there were three other prisoners clerking in the office, but there was not a sign of a warder anywhere.

'Is the chief warder around or has he been locked in a cell?'

The mastodon showed no reaction. His tiny grey eyes stared unperturbed at me. 'Why do you want to see him?'

'I'm from the police,' I said impatiently.

'Oh! Okay. He's in the café across the street. But if I can help you . . . ?'

'It's the chief I want to see.'

Once more the first prisoner opened the gate. Still without opening his mouth, he pointed to the café À la Bolée facing the prison.

There were six of them there, folded over the bar: five screws and the chief, his hat with its two bands of silver braid shoved back on his head, sipping cider. I walked over and planted myself in front of the head man. 'Inspector Borniche, of the Sûreté,' I said in a voice streaked with irony. 'I have a question—nothing important, of course—but may I know who is guarding the prison just now?'

The chief gave me a conspiratorial wink and poked an elbow in my stomach. 'Delighted, Inspector,' he said in a thick voice. 'You're here about Girier, I hope?' He took off his starred hat and scratched his skull with his little finger. 'Okay, so that one was a special case—he fooled us. But the others—real lambs. Right, boys?'

He set the hat back on his head. As one man, the five warders agreed. 'You know,' the chief continued, 'nobody's going to steal the prison; it guards itself fine. So how about a jar of cider with us, Inspector? It's good stuff.'

His tongue clacked against his palate. I drank the glass of cider poured for me. That was a mistake. My stomach refused to join in the festivities. I thought it was time to end the party.

'Listen,' I said, 'I don't have much time. I need some information if I'm going to find Girier before he finds a safe hideout. What exactly can you tell me?'

The screw put down his glass. 'Me? Nothing. In fact, if there is one person who knows nothing it's me. And the same goes for all the others. Right boys?'

'Okay,' I said. 'Okay. So who does know something?'

The chief thought about that briefly. 'I can think of only one person,' he murmured. 'Georges Cudet, in the registration office. And even that's not certain. Come on, we'll go and see him.'

We recrossed the street. The prisoner-gatekeeper snapped a military salute. When we got to the office, the chief pointed to the giant who had been sitting at the desk before and who rose obsequiously when we walked in.

'This is Cudet, Pinky Cudet, my right-hand man,' the chief said by way of introduction. 'He's good at everything, provost, librarian—he even runs the place when I'm not here. Really makes them jump, too. Right, Georges?'

Pinky bowed. I questioned him for twenty minutes without getting a scrap of information from him. He didn't know anything either. He answered every question in a weepy voice. 'Girier, I didn't have much to do with him, my dear sir. We didn't like each other, him and me. I'm the last one he'd have told any secrets to. I swear on my mother's head, my dear sir.'

The chief plucked me by the sleeve, leading me to a corner of the room. Plastering his mouth to my ear, he whispered: 'You must believe him, Inspector. When he swears on his mother's head, he's telling the truth. I know human nature, you know.'

This comic-opera prison was giving me the willies. The connivance between the dim-witted guards and the bovine prisoners was obvious. I wasn't going to learn anything from this mafia. I decided to try the town police.

The inmate who had opened the gate for me earlier and who had been present when I questioned Cudet preceded me now, still mute, towards the exit. He fumbled his key into the lock and, out of the corner of his mouth, he muttered:

'Hey! Pinky's making a monkey out of you. He and Girier were thick as pigs. He let Girier phone Paris. Ask him for the phone chits, you'll see.'

'What?'

'Sure. Look at the chits, I tell you.'

'Why are you telling me this?'

'Because Pinky's got a big head—always making me clean out the shithouse.'

I don't like being taken for an idiot. It puts me in a mood to do very violent things. That bastard Pinky! And that sod of a screw! I went steaming back across the courtyard, where the prisoners were lolling around in the sun, smoking; I burst open the office door. The chief forgot his newspaper to fix me with a wide-eyed stare; I stalked across the room to where Cudet was sitting.

'Listen, you,' I said in a tone that brooked no argument, 'let me have a look at the telephone chits. I want them. And I want them quick! You're not automatic here, so there ought to be a record of all calls to Paris.'

Cudet went pale. He opened his mouth, shot a rabid look at the gatekeeper, who stood waiting with lowered eyes, and then did what I had told him. He pulled a cardboard box out of a file drawer; it was crammed with chits, about a hundred of them, rammed in every which way. I grabbed the box furiously and dumped the contents out on the table, pulled up a chair and went to it. It took me twenty minutes to sort them out. The Chancellery number appeared quite enough, and so did two Paris numbers, RIChelieu 93-- and MONtmartre 48--; in both cases, the last two digits had been scratched out. I whirled savagely on Cudet.

'What's this all about?' I demanded. 'Why were the last numbers defaced?'

Cudet gulped. 'How do I know?' he stammered. The lie shone in his eyes. This slop-pail had already made a fool of me once; he wasn't going to do it again. For once, I lost control of myself. I jumped for him, grabbed him by the scruff of the neck and shook him like a cat shaking a rat. That pried the chief loose from his chair. 'Calm yourself, Inspector,' he said in a panicky voice. 'Don't push him around. He's a nice fellow, Pinky is ...'

'No one is a nice fellow who makes a fool of me,' I fumed ... And if he doesn't spit out what he knows, he'll be spitting teeth instead, and damn soon.'

The chief was upset at seeing his protégé roughed up. 'Don't be a dope, Pinky,' he begged in a syrupy voice. 'Tell the inspector the truth. Tell him who fiddled those numbers. If you tell him what happened, he won't give you a bad time. If you don't, you'll be sent to another prison, and your wife, who lives right near here in Honfleur, won't be able to see you any more. You know I let her visit you in your cell when you want her to. She won't be able to do that anywhere else. Come on, Georges, tell.'

Cudet didn't need any more coaxing. He swallowed hard, then, with downcast eyes he admitted: 'It was Girier who told me to do that. He used to phone the hotel his wife was at in Paris.'

'Which hotel?'

'Chaptal, rue de La Rochefoucauld. Once, she even put on a friend of his, the Fishmonger, he called himself. I think that's the guy who came to get him. But for God's sake don't say it was me who squealed ...'

'What else?'

'That's all I know, honest.'

That wasn't quite all. I knew he could not have forgotten phone numbers he had noted down so often. A few more hints about what I was prepared to do to him stimulated his memory. I already knew one of the numbers was that of the Chaptal; now I had the other one, too: RIChelieu 93.67.

I left Pont-l'Évêque in a state of high excitement. Although he had never spilled a drop of blood, Girier was now with Émile Buisson, the most wanted man in the country. The jail-break team. Conclusion: by following Girier's trail, there was a good chance of its leading me to Monsieur Émile. What a double that would be!

25

The woman who managed the Hôtel Chaptal readily admitted that Girier and his wife Marinette lived there for two months in 1948. She also remembered that, in December, two short, stocky men, friends of Girier, had slept for several nights in room No. 15. She showed me the two names in the register: Maurice Yves, fishmonger, and Marc Giraldi, military pensioner.

'How come neither their addresses nor the numbers of their identity cards are mentioned?' I asked severely.

'You know, *monsieur l'inspecteur*, my night clerk didn't write everything down. I nagged him about it all the time, but he was hopeless. Poor man—he died two months ago.'

She was a wonderfully cool liar.

'Say, Borniche,' I was told the next morning by Poiret, whom I had sent to browse in the Prefecture's files, 'that's a very fishy fishmonger you've got.'

'What do you mean?'

'Well, he never goes near salt water. Except for a few birds he runs for pocket money, he specializes mainly in stick-ups. And you know who with?'

'How should I. . . ?'

'With Jacques the Niçois, Dédé the Italian and—hang on to your hat—with Émile Buisson. The PP is on it.'

'What?'

'Yeah. Homicide got a solid-gold tip: on 4 March, in Boulogne, they stuck up a couple of jewellers, Baudet and Guénot. They don't know if it was Buisson who fired, but, anyway, the result was two guys wounded and a cool million taken.'

'How did you learn all this?'

'Simple: Thuillat, of Homicide, is a friend of mine. He lives in my mother's hotel in Montmartre. So I went to see him and he told me all about it. You see? I'm not as dumb as you thought.'

Poiret's innocence amused me. 'Yes, indeed,' I said, 'for once you've outdone yourself. You must have taken a tonic. But while you were at it, you might have identified the Niçois and the Italian. That wouldn't have worn your brain out.'

'Well now, it may surprise you, but I thought of that.'

Poiret fumbled in his pockets, pulling out a miscellany of items, from which he extracted two police file photos. 'Look at these!' he said. 'The Niçois is Jacques Vérando, the Wop is Désiré Polledri. I swiped these from the PP file. I'm going to have them copied and then, when I get a chance, I'll slip them back where I got them.'

'Poiret,' I said, rising solemnly, 'I would like to buy you a drink. You have identified Buisson's new playmates. Well done! And Girier's friend Giraldi, who's he?'

'A Corsican from Sartène. Sentenced in absentia to twenty years with no remission and also to ten years exile. A model citizen. I'm going to get out the files.'

A few minutes later, I briefed Fatso on how the investigation was going. He was exultant. 'Borniche,' he intoned, 'if you want to make chief inspector, now is the time to make a splash, knock 'em dead. The PP snaffled Girier from under our noses in September 1947, so 1949 is our year for revenge. Besides, he's in our territory, since he escaped from a provincial prison. You get me, Borniche? Girier: I've got to have him.'

Too bad for Fatso. Despite all my informers, despite my nocturnal ramblings through the bars and nightclubs of Pigalle hoping to hear someone let something slip, despite the domestic scenes with Marlyse, who was feeling so neglected she threatened to go home to mother, despite Fatso's ranting and the hours of surveillance Hidoine, Poiret and I put in, we never caught so much as a glimpse of Girier and his friends.

There was a brief flare-up of hope when I found Marinette Girier's address in Montmartre. But she was leading her usual normal, peaceful life, trailing a platoon of Homicide and Flying Squad boys behind her every time she went out of doors.

One May morning, Poiret burst into the office; he was so excited he stuttered when he announced:

'Really bad news, Borniche: it seems Buisson is living with a pal in Le Plessis-Robinson. And the PP is on to it.'

He collapsed into a chair.

'Did Thuillat tell you that?' I asked him.

'Of course. He tells me everything, Thuillat. And let me tell you, the tip is good. We'd better do something.'

'Thuillat tells you everything? Why?'

Poiret assumed a knowing look. 'Blackmail, Borniche! I know how to play my cards, you know. Either he lets me in on what he knows, or my mother throws him out of the hotel. She gives him a special price, you see, and she even lets him take birds up to his room. I've got to get back and see what else there is.'

Poiret disappeared down the corridor. There was nothing I could do but pray to the god of cops to play favourites and keep my PP rivals from winning the victory I wanted so much for myself.

My prayer would be answered—through a man's death.

26

On the evening of 31 May 1949, Émile Buisson was seething with rage over an unfortunate accident. His followers, Jeannot Orsetti, Adrien Charmet, the ace car thief, and Désiré Polledri, who was responsible for his temper tantrum, remained prudently silent. They all knew Émile's rages could be deadly.

After the hold-ups in Saint-Ouen, which left one dead, and the attack on the Boulogne jewellers, Émile had planned a stick-up in Clamart—a construction foreman who was to transport twenty million francs in a bank bag.

On the appointed day, the gang waited outside the company office. Girier's friend Maurice Yves, known as the Fishmonger, was at the wheel of a car stolen by Charmet. They waited an hour —for nothing. The foreman never showed up. Disappointed and annoyed, Émile gave the order to retire. He went back to his hideout, Charmet's house in Le Plessis-Robinson. Yves, and Dédé Polledri went off to lose the hot car.

It was during this routine operation that disaster struck. Yves was driving. Polledri, sitting in the back, was trying to remove the clip from the machine gun. He was probably unfamiliar with the mechanism. In any case, the gun went off and, as luck would have it, the bullet smashed through Yves's head, spattering the windshield with a mixture of blood, brains and bone chips.

Although he was stunned by the detonation, Polledri managed to stop the car and clamber out. Luckily for him, Charmet, who was following them in his Peugeot to bring them back to the hide-out, was only about twenty yards behind. His face bloodless with shock, Polledri jumped in beside him. 'Get going,' he ordered.

Asking no questions, Charmet stepped on the gas, his nerves tight. As they drove, the Italian gave him an account of the Fishmonger's death. 'I'm scared, Adrien,' Polledri bleated. 'Christ, I'm scared. I'm sure Émile won't believe it was an accident. He's going to start imagining things . . .'

His eyes riveted on the traffic, Charmet agreed. 'He's not going to like it, that's for certain. I mean, for Christ's sake, Dédé, what a bloody daft thing to do!'

*

When Polledri, sweating, trembling, not daring to look at him, explained how stupidly he had killed Maurice Yves, Buisson did in fact explode with fury, as predicted. At one point, fearing Émile would kill him as he stood there, the Italian tried to excuse himself. 'The Fishmonger stamped on the brake when I wasn't expecting it,' he said. 'My finger was on the trigger and the gun went off.'

Buisson stared at him, so coldly that Polledri could feel ice forming in his spine. 'Adrien,' Buisson said, never shifting his gaze, 'is it true, what Dédé says? Did the Fishmonger really brake suddenly?'

'I don't know, Émile,' Charmet said quickly. 'I didn't see.'

'Think about it, Adrien. It's important.'

'I don't know, Émile.'

'Turd!' Buisson thought. 'Lying turd.'

Émile was a head shorter than Polledri, but that didn't stop him from grabbing the Italian by the throat. His fingers clamped viciously on Dédé's windpipe, he shoved the man back against the wall, banging his head against it savagely. Unprotesting, only half conscious, Polledri slid to the floor. This show of violence seemed to have eased the tension slightly. Buisson turned to Charmet.

'Where did it happen?' he asked.

'Boulevard de la Tour, in Le Plessis, Émile.'

'Is that far from here?'

'No, not really. Less than a kilometre.'

The veins stood out on Buisson's brow as he stood there, concentrating, casting furious glances at Polledri, who was too frightened to move, much less get up. Slowly, Buisson took out his wallet, removed some bank notes from it and tossed them on the table.

'Here, Adrien, that's for you.'

'What's this mean, Émile?'

'It means we're getting out of here. In an hour the neighbourhood will be crawling with cops. Believe me, between the Fishmonger's corpse and your gabby neighbours, it won't take them long to find their way here.'

'You can't guarantee that,' Charmet said. 'You see cops everywhere, Émile.'

'When a man is on the run, he does see cops everywhere, Adrien, and that's a fact. You're right. But it's by having second sight that he keeps from being picked up. It's when you think you're safe and clear that they jump you.'

Charmet, seeing Émile's rent payments evaporating, insisted: 'But, Émile, why should they think about me? I don't even have a record.'

Buisson shrugged. 'I've made up my mind, Adrien,' he said. 'I'm getting out. Pack my things.'

While Charmet did as he was told, Buisson turned to Orsetti, who was shocked by Maurice's death and Émile's violence with Polledri.

'Come on, Jeannot,' he said, forcing a smile. 'Don't look like that. You must have a little space for me in your dump.'

'Oh. Yes!' Orsetti gasped. 'We'll shove over for a few days.'

'How about me? What happens to me?'

It was Polledri. Still stretched out on the floor, propped on one elbow, the Italian spoke with a whimper. Fear distorted his handsome face. He was sweating, green. From the moment Charmet disappeared into the adjoining bedroom, where he could now be heard slamming drawers and grumbling as he stamped around the room, the conviction had grown in Polledri's mind that Buisson was going to kill him at any second. It wasn't as though Émile had never knocked anybody off before. The Italian knew that this was the second time within a few days that he had imprudently provoked the black-eyed little killer's suspicion and anger. This was playing with fire. Worse, it was inviting death. Buisson had still not digested the theft of 112 million francs in Moroccan bank notes in which Polledri had taken part with another gang in Puteaux on the night of 8–9 May. When he heard about it, Buisson had said very little. 'Well, Wop, so you're doing jobs on the side?' was his sole comment. But the tone had been knifelike. And Polledri had regretted with all his heart that he had not brought Émile in on the job.

And now he had Yves's death on his back. Swallowing hard, Polledri could not help reflecting that Russac had been liquidated for a lot less.

'What happens to me, Émile?' he repeated plaintively.

Buisson stared at him reflectively. There was no contempt in his eyes; his face was expressionless. He was calmly weighing his decision, deciding what fate he would mete out to this man, still cringing on the floor and sweating with terror, whom he no longer trusted.

'You've got a woman, is that right?'

'Yes,' Polledri said with an effort. 'Henriette Seguin. She has a hat shop in Albi. Why?'

'So that's where you go. When all this settles down, I'll call you if I need you.'

'Okay,' Polledri said humbly. Knowing he was going to live had made his heart pound, brought the blood to his face. He found it hard to focus his eyes.

'You'll leave tonight,' Buisson continued. 'Jeannot will go to the station with you. Maybe I'll go, too. I don't like to take chances with you.'

'It's not . . .' Polledri began, going white again.

'Not what?'

'Not . . . my last ride, Émile? Is it?'

'You're taking the train, Wop.'

Polledri left Paris. Émile moved into Jeannot's studio in the Square Rapp. When the Homicide men burst into the house in Le Plessis-Robinson the next day, they found only Charmet and his wife. Questioned at the quai des Orfèvres, the couple confessed everything.

Except the one detail they didn't know: Buisson's new hideout.

27

There were days when I suspected that the occupants of room 523 should be under lock and key. In a lunatic asylum, I mean.

23 May was one of those days. That morning, Hidoine was pirouetting slowly in front of me to show me the flower-printed cotton underpants he had bought half-price from an American black. A slit-eyed, grunting Poiret, was meanwhile, alternating shoulder exercises and shadow-boxing. 'I'm not as stupid as I look,' he repeated between punches. 'I was hot on the trail. I nearly had the bastards. And single-handed, too, damn it!'

It was a disheartening spectacle, but I didn't say anything. I was thinking about the PP report Fatso had given me to read; it told me all about Buisson's escape from our friends in Homicide, but no mention was made of Girier, who seemed simply to have disappeared into thin air.

It was at that moment that I realized how easy it is to make unforgivable blunders. Since Fatso assigned me to find Girier, I had done everything possible to lay my hands on him. Everything. Except for one detail: I had forgotten to find out whose telephone number it was that Georges Cudet had finally been persuaded to remember: RIChelieu 93.67. Caught up in the excitement of the hunt, annoyed by the dismal hours of surveillance, I had completely forgotten to check up on it.

Warning Hidoine and Poiret not to rat on me, I asked Information to give me the numerical list. Then I got the subscriber's name and address from a second operator. The number belonged to the Favart, a ritzy bar, just down the street from the Opéra-Comique. And the owner just happened to be a Corsican, by name Michel Varani.

'Get yourself dolled up,' I told Marlyse when I got home that evening. 'We're going out.'

'Oh, darling! How sweet!' she exclaimed. 'We haven't been to the pictures in such a long time!'

A little embarrassed, I kissed her before confessing that what I had in mind was not exactly a pleasure jaunt. 'Now listen, don't be upset, Marlyse,' I said. 'I wasn't thinking of the pictures. I had other plans.'

'What, then?' she asked, suddenly suspicious.

'Well . . . I have to keep an eye on a bar and if I went there alone I might be spotted. But if I went with you and we sat in a corner playing lovebirds . . .'

Marlyse went all thin-lipped. 'I thought it was funny,' she said. 'If you only knew how sick I am of your job and your Buisson and your Fatso and your shop. We never go out, never see anyone, never go dancing or go to the theatre. All I'm good for is to help you in your job.'

I put on my most persuasive manner: 'Help me out this time, Marlyse. It's the last time I'll ask you. It's important, you know.'

An hour later, we were sitting at a table against the wall at the Favart. It was a dark corner, and we played lovebirds and drank cocktails. Marlyse loves to play a part. Every time I nuzzled her, my eyes swept the bar and the room, but everything seemed normal, respectable, discreet, above board.

We did this for five nights in a row and it got me exactly nowhere. The owner, a big guy with greying hair and a lazy walk, got so used to us that he treated us like regulars.

I began to wonder if Pinky Cudet had been feeding me a line when he told me Girier had called that number so often.

One evening, a couple came in and sat down at the bar. The girl was blond, with a slender figure displayed to maximum advantage in a clinging dress; her beauty eclipsed even that of Marlyse, who was used to having men turn round to stare after her. It was the girl's companion who interested me, however. He was probably no more than thirty years old. There was something familiar about his blue eyes, his blond, wavy hair, his finely carved mouth and the muscular frame moving under his jacket. I knew I had seen him somewhere. I also knew from the way he looked furtively around him and his way of holding a cigarette cupped in his palm that this customer had been in prison.

The pair only stayed about ten minutes, just long enough for the blond man to talk quietly to the proprietor. Then they left. I restrained my impulse to follow him because I thought Varani might become suspicious. But Marlyse read my mind, and she thought faster than I did. 'I'm going to get some cigarettes,' she told me loudly. She flashed an angelic smile at Varani and disappeared. I just sat there playing with my cigarette lighter. It seemed to me she was gone an eternity. Moments later, she slipped back into her seat. 'It's 2409 RN 2,' she whispered, handing me a pack of Philip Morris.

I thanked her silently for her efficiency, embraced her tenderly and ordered a last cocktail. Then we got up to leave.

It was warm in Paris that evening, and Varani was taking the air in the doorway while appraising with a professional eye the few women who passed by along the rue Marivaux. Marlyse, slightly sozzled, hung tightly to my arm, making cow eyes at me and bubbling up in funny, stupid little giggles. Varani threw me a conspiratorial look as we passed him.

'See you tomorrow,' I said.

'See you tomorrow,' he agreed in his warm voice.

As soon as we were out of earshot, I asked Marlyse the question which had been burning my tongue: 'Well?'

'Well, it was very simple. A BMW was waiting for them in front of the Opéra-Comique. It was the guy who took the wheel. The number will tell you who he was. And one other thing. I don't know if it has any bearing on your inquiries but I've had this sentry-duty at the Favart up to the back teeth.'

The vehicle licensing gave me the name of the BMW's owner the next morning: Mathieu Robillard, a tailor, 26 rue Notre-Dame-de-Lorette, Paris 9th. That did it. Robillard, alias the Nantais, had been arrested with Girier by the Flying Squad some years earlier. The lead looked promising.

When I arrived at the rue Notre-Dame-de-Lorette, I learned that no one there had ever heard of the Nantais.

28

Suntanned and elegant in a tan gabardine suit nicely set off by a sky-blue shirt, Polledri returned from Albi on 8 June. His panic had left him. The few days he had spent with Henriette had restored him to his old, lovable self. His anxiety about Buisson's attitude had melted the day before, when, late in the morning, a phone call came from Paris. It was Émile.

'Everything all right, lad? Getting a good rest?'

Buisson's friendly manner tranquillized Polledri. He even ventured a jolly tone: 'Great! Nothing like a French bird to soothe your cares away.'

'Fine,' Buisson said. 'Don't burn up all your energy in bed. I need you. A nice set-up. You'll have to get back up here.'

'When?' asked Polledri, incredulous but delighted.

'Pretty soon. We'll get it going right away. If you like, have dinner with Jeannot and me the day after tomorrow at the Auberge Bressane. Eight o'clock okay? We'll settle things then. You know where it is?'

'Yes. I'll be there. *Ciao*.'

Polledri arrived at the gare d'Austerlitz at about seven p.m. The weather was perfect, the girls like flowers in their summer dresses, the beer he had drunk at the station had been ice cold. Unworried, glad to be alive, the Italian thought briefly of walking to his appointment to celebrate his return to the capital, but he finally decided against it; in that heat, he would arrive wilted, with his feet boiling in his brown and white moccasins. Since he had a little time to kill, he phoned a girlfriend who worked the streets around the Madeleine and invited her to end the evening with him. He'd come by and pick her up round about midnight. His evening now programmed, Polledri flagged down a cab and gave the driver the address of the restaurant in the avenue Bosquet where Monsieur Émile was waiting for him.

He was a good fifteen minutes early going into the Auberge Bressane, but Buisson was already there, at the bar, with Orsetti. As soon as they spotted him, both men put down their glasses, hopped off their stools and went to meet him. Orsetti was visibly happy to see his old pal again. With typical Corsican warmth, he threw his arms around him, embraced him, patted him affectionately on the back. When he released him, a smiling Buisson took his turn, pumping Polledri's hand heartily.

'Glad to see you back, Wop,' he said. 'You look great.'

Polledri felt a lump rise in his throat, and his eyes filled with tears. It was terrific to be with your old pals again. There was no anxiety now; his heart overflowed with friendship.

'Henriette okay?' Buisson asked, leading the way to the bar, where the bartender immediately poured out three glasses of champagne.

'Radiant, except that she cried when I left,' Polledri reported with joyous complacency, 'but, what the hell? I explained to her that work is work. How about you, Émile? How's your love life?'

'Oh, you know,' volunteered Buisson, who was usually close-mouthed about his emotional life, 'I got a little Breton girl right now. I'll introduce you to her one of these days.'

'A twenty-year-old beauty eating herself up with love for an old man,' joked Orsetti. The three men laughed, finished their drinks and ordered another round, sipped at it, passing the time in merry banter.

At their table, tucked inconspicuously in a corner, Buisson devoted considerable care to ordering their dinners, then broached the subject that had brought them together. He finished his *terrine* and, resuming his serious look, outlined his project.

'Look, this job is red-hot,' he said. 'If we pull it off, anybody who wants to retire after it's over will be able to live like a maharajah for the rest of his life.'

He stopped while the waitress cleared away the first-course dishes and served three plates of steamed chicken and rice. As soon as she had gone, he continued:

'I'm not alone on this job, but that's no worry. It will take a lot of people to bring it off. People with guts. I'm in touch with Girier, who busted out of Pont-l'Évêque with Jacques Vérando, the Niçois—you know him—and a solid crew.'

'Shit!' grunted Polledri. 'Are we hitting the Bank of France?'

'Almost,' Buisson replied placidly, 'almost; we're going to do a Crédit Lyonnais armoured car carrying a heavy load. Girier got the tip. He struck up an acquaintance in a café near the bank with two messengers who had just got their new trucks—they were bragging to the café owner about the security mechanisms.

Girier pretended he didn't believe them and they took him on a tour of one of the cars. There are still a few details missing. Girier ought to have them tonight or tomorrow from one of his pals, Mathieu the Nantais. As soon as we can set up the raid, we'll go into action. I expect it to be the day after tomorrow at the latest. That's why I asked you to get back in a hurry.'

'How about the cops?'

'What about the cops?' Orsetti asked. 'Don't worry. They don't know which way is up. Why, just last night I was at the Deux Marches and they were all there, as usual, packed in like anchovies lapping up on Victor's *pastis*. You know how it is, I always keep an ear out. Well, I can guarantee you that both the PP and the SN have lost Émile's track. As for Girier—they don't even know where to begin to look for him. So you see—there's nothing to get steamed up about.'

'I wasn't sweating,' Polledri retorted. 'It's just that, when you've been out of circulation, even for only a few days, you need to get back into the swing again.'

'You're right,' Buisson agreed, signalling the waitress to ask for the next course. There was silence again at the table while she served them.

'There is one thing we ought to settle now,' said Buisson gravely, looking Polledri straight in the eye. 'About the Fishmonger's wife. You're going to have to do something for her as soon as you get your cut.'

'Whatever you say, Émile!' Polledri said hurriedly, feeling fear well up in him at the very mention of the name.

'Okay, Wop,' Buisson said gently, pleased to see the other man tighten up. 'Then you agree that the poor girl deserves some compensation for your . . . clumsiness?'

'Naturally, Émile, naturally, I agree a hundred per cent, you bet. When you do something stupid like that you expect to pay for it; that's logical.'

'Good. Got any dough on you?'

Without answering, Polledri slipped his hand into his inside pocket and took out his wallet, opened it on the table and slid the bank notes out of it.

'How much?' Buisson asked.

'About two hundred thousand.'

'Fine. Slip me a hundred and ninety of them and I'll give it to the widow tomorrow. Keep ten thousand for the evening.'

'Thanks, Émile,' Polledri sighed, 'but if you want more—I mean, if she needs more, just ask, eh? Don't hold back.'

Buisson waved the notion away. 'No, that's good enough. Shit. Nearly two hundred thousand francs for a dumb bird, that's good money. That's a premium price per kilo of stupidity.'

They were at the cheese course. They had already emptied two bottles of light Bordeaux wine, which had brought the colour to their cheeks, when Polledri asked thoughtfully, 'How much will this job bring in?'

'If it's what we think, it should leave us about thirty million each. Most of it in old bills—you see the advantage there. There will be a cut for Mathieu the Nantais, too, but that won't be much.'

'Thirty million,' breathed Polledri ecstatically.

'Yes, or maybe even more.'

'Oh, you know, thirty million and I'm already a happy boy.'

'What'll you do with it?' Orsetti asked.

'I don't know,' Polledri said dreamily. 'I'd like to go somewhere a long way away with Henriette, buy a farm with a lot of land. Be a farmer—what the hell!'

'What an ambition!' Buisson sighed. 'And why not kids?'

'No, no—no kids. They smell.'

After two rounds of plum brandy, Émile paid the bill and rejoined his friends in the street.

'Where are we going?' asked Orsetti, hot to keep the party going.

Buisson shrugged indifferently, glanced at his watch. 'It's not even ten o'clock yet. At this time of night, the place is crawling with flatfeet. We can walk for a while—help us digest—and then, if you like, we can go have a drink on the Champs-Élysées.'

'Hold it!' Polledri said. 'I'm with you, but not for long. At midnight I have a date with a piece at the Madeleine.'

'She worth it?'

'Is she? A Grade A technician. She can tie me in knots when she wants to.'

'You mean you don't even have five minutes for a drink with us?' asked an indignant Orsetti, who not only had no date of his own but who was really a little jealous of Polledri's success with women.

'Okay, but no longer.'

The three men ambled along, crossing the rue Saint-Dominique.

When they reached the corner of the passage Landrieu, Buisson turned into it.

'Where are you going, Émile?' Orsetti asked, surprised.

'Down to the other end,' Buisson said. 'A pal of mine runs a place on the rue de l'Université. Lots of laughs.'

'In this bourgeois neighbourhood?'

'Why not? The bourgeois like their kicks too, they tank up and screw like everybody else, idiot. Since Polledri has hot pants and can't stay with us, we might as well go there. We can go on from there without him.'

Quietly, Buisson moved down the passage, his friends at his heels.

They had not gone a hundred yards before a car behind them blew its horn and flashed its lights to warn them out of the way. Orsetti stepped up on the pavement. Polledri felt Buisson's hand grasp his arm and draw him on to the narrow pavement on their left. The car, cruising slowly, was almost abreast of them.

Then, with lightning speed, Buisson moved Polledri in front of him. His hand plunged to his waist and came up holding a Colt. Polledri suspected nothing. He walked calmly along, not concerned about the car purring alongside him. He never saw the barrel of the Colt approach the back of his head. There was an explosion. Polledri's body clumped heavily to the pavement, thudding dully on the concrete. Standing over his victim, Buisson deliberately fired five more shots into him. There was still one cartridge left in the clip. Still taking his time, Buisson bent down and flipped the body over on its back with his left hand. The fingers flicked lightly over the hot, blood-spattered face, felt the lips, then pried the mouth open.

Without feeling the slightest disgust, Buisson gripped the Italian's tongue firmly and yanked it out. His other hand brought the barrel of the Colt up against the sticky flesh tugging against his fingers. A final shot echoed through the passage.

'Pile of shit!' Buisson said. 'Now you won't do any more jobs without me.'

He glared furiously at the end of tongue dangling from his fingers, then tossed it into the middle of the street. Finally he straightened up and climbed into the car Jacques Vérando had stopped alongside him. The car sped off as soon as he closed the door.

29

Buisson was amazed to learn from *Le Figaro* the morning after the shooting that Polledri, with six bullets in him, was still alive when the police ambulance delivered him to the Boucicaut Hospital. As a matter of fact, he had only two hours of life left in him—two hours that his suffering must have made to seem interminable. He regained consciousness just before he died, and the last faces he saw were those of the two policemen asking him who had shot him.

Polledri would gladly have told them. But he could no longer say anything. His tongue was in the passage Landrieu.

It took me no more than five minutes to identify the corpse. I knew that the official statement would have been written, as usual, by Mousset, the Homicide secretary. He is an even bigger fool than I am; he loves to see his name in the papers and he is the friend of every police reporter in town. Knowing this, I decided to use this publicity hound for my own purposes. I called him on the phone.

'Hello. Officer Mousset?' I asked.

'Yes.'

'This is Robiche, of *Ouest-France*.'

'Oh, yes. How are you, my friend?'

'Fine. Just fine. I'm calling you from Rennes because I'd like some details on the gang murder in the passage Landrieu.'

'Why, of course, of course. You'll mention me, won't you . . . ?'

'Naturally.'

'The victim's name is Polledri, Désiré Polledri, an Italian who had escaped from the Île-de-Ré and was wanted for armed robbery. Naturally, the papers we found on him were false, made out in the name of Lucien Souletis. But I soon identified him from his fingerprints.'

There was a pause. He was waiting for congratulations, and I didn't disappoint him. 'Bravo!' I said. 'And who bumped him off, officer?'

'Ah, now there you're asking me too much, my friend. My collaborator, Inspector Courchamp, has just begun his investigation. It was certainly a gang killing and cases like this can drag on for quite a while. Nevertheless, I can tell you, strictly confidentially, that the famous Émile Buisson is certainly involved. Charmet, whom I interrogated at length in connection with the Maurice Yves case, hinted to me that Buisson had been knocking Polledri around on the day of the murder. There! That's all I can tell you for the moment, but don't say anything about Buisson; it's no business of the boys at the Sûreté.'

'As a matter of fact,' I said hypocritically, 'I understand Inspector Borniche is on the Buisson case. That so?'

'Borniche! Borniche!' my informant snarled. 'He'll wind up like the rest of them. If he thinks Buisson is going to let himself be pinched by a twerp like that, he has another think coming.'

'Thank you, officer.'

I hung up. At least I had learned two facts: Polledri's identity, and Mousset's opinion of my intelligence. All I had to do now was to prove to the boys at the PP that I wasn't as big a fool as they thought.

The longer I looked at him, the more I thought him a dead ringer for the actor Pierre Dac. Same naked skull, same sparkling eye, same corpulence. Divisional Superintendent Paul Berliat held court on the sixth floor of the building housing the Surveillance du Territoire—the government's counter-espionage service—at 11 rue des Saussaies. He was certainly a crack technician, since the ST's director, Roger Wybot, had made him head of its radio-electrical communications service, otherwise known as the wire-tap section. At the moment, he was reading aloud the laconic note I had typed out at Fatso's instructions.

'Your habitual correspondent requests that you establish a connection with the subscriber to RIChelieu 93.67. It will be monitored by an employee of my unit. Signed: Biget, director, PJ.'

'Are you the one who's going to monitor this, Borniche?'

'Yes, sir. Me or Hidoine. Maybe Poiret . . .'

'Poiret?'

'He may not be very sharp, but even he is capable of trans-scribing what he hears.'

Berliat wrinkled his nose sceptically, then turned to indicate the wall on which the recorders were turning. 'He'll never make it if you monitor direct,' he said. 'As a favour to you, Borniche, I'm willing to interrupt a tap for the General Survey Section that's been dragging for a month now. That way, your calls will be recorded on cylinders. I'll lend you a dictaphone so that you can listen to them peacefully in your office. You can come and pick them up every morning. That do?'

'Thanks, Superintendent.'

Berliat handed me a key. It opened the hidden door to the corridor directly linking his unit to the Sûreté Nationale's PJ so that I would not have to go around through the rue des Saussaies courtyard with the recordings under my arm. Then he returned to his office.

I glanced around the laboratory. Electric wires hung down on all sides, forming complicated webs linked to recording devices stuck up on the walls like navigation instruments. It looked like a power station dating from Edison's first experiments.

An inspector in janitor's overalls, whom I had earlier mistaken for a repairman, offered me a welcoming cigarette and introduced himself.

'I'm Durand,' he said. 'You'd like to know how these gadgets work, would you?'

'Well . . .'

Durand explained that any phone line going through the central switchboard could be secretly siphoned off to the rue des Saussaies. The taps were installed at night; nobody bothered to tell any Post Office employees about them.

'Come back tomorrow,' he said. 'We'll do what's needed.'

The next day, I sat with earphones on and watched the wax cylinder turning beneath the dictaphone needle on my desk. Hidoine and, especially, Poiret, who was big-eyed with wonder, were straddling chairs and giving me moral support. (I needed it.) It was not until the fourth day that the recordings finally gave me something other than the dull chatter of the Favart's regulars:

'Mathieu? Hi. It's René. Did you call me?'

'Yes. I have to see you. What about tomorrow?'

Hidoine had just clapped an earphone to his ear. I grabbed his arm excitedly.

'What time?'

'How about seven o'clock? At the Terminus, porte de Vincennes. It's not far from your bus and it's quiet.'

'Okay.'

I turned to Poiret, who had been scratching his leg for the last quarter of an hour and trying to eavesdrop on the earphones.

'Listen, lump,' I said gently, 'you are going to do me a favour. Instead of stirring up your eczema, you are going to visit your chum Thuillat. You will check Mathieu Robillard in the PP's records; we know a fair amount about him, but there may be PP wanted circulars out on him that we haven't seen. You will do the same for Girier's mates, Vérando and Giraldi. Go through all that with a fine sieve, just in case they are Homicide informers.'

'Got it, Borniche.'

'Swell. We'll all meet tomorrow night at the Terminus, cours de Vincennes. Any objections?'

'At your service, "chief," ' said Hidoine, already on his way out in his seducer's uniform.

That evening at dinner, I outlined my programme for next day to Marlyse, telling her of the hopes I pinned on this new development.

'All right,' she sighed, casting her eyes up to heaven. 'Since duty calls, I'll go with you. I'd rather do that than spend an evening alone listening to the radio.'

30

It's nice to dream. Especially since it costs nothing. Nestled deep in Crocbois' car, crammed between Marlyse and Hidoine, I dreamed that I would soon have my revenge on Buisson, on Girier, on Clot and on Courchamp.

I had a good head start on my colleagues at the PP. While they were still looking for Girier, I was going to have him within arm's reach in just a few minutes.

The dreams went this way: scenario No. 1: if I wanted to, I could arrest him and that would be a sensational catch that would earn my promotion to chief inspector; scenario No. 2 was even more alluring, although it was riskier: if I let him run, if I found his hideout, if he led me to Buisson, I would be doubly successful and there was a chance of making superintendent.

The dreaming was too pleasant to stop. Suppose, just suppose, Girier were to go straight from his meeting at the Terminus to Buisson's place. Who could tell? Buisson might even come with him to the meeting.

The heat in the car was stifling. Fat streaks of sweat gleamed on Poiret's pink cheeks as he snored in the front seat. We were stationed on the boulevard Soult, on the far side of the cours de Vincennes, which gave us a long-range view of both Terminus exits, the one giving on the boulevard Davout and the other on the cours. It was six p.m. In sixty minutes I would know.

I am a mercurial individual, capable of going directly from blithering optimism to torturing doubt. Now my mood dipped again, and my happy daydreams turned to anxiety. There were a René and a Mathieu involved, well enough, but who knew for sure they were René Girier and Mathieu Robillard?

'Maybe it's not them, after all,' I muttered to myself.

Hidoine, who was silently admiring his brand-new riding boots, tore his gaze away and pinned it on me. 'Have you started talking to yourself, now?'

I told him what was worrying me, but it was Marlyse who added the philosophic note. 'You'll see when the time comes,' she said.

Silence once more settled over the car's occupants, shaken only by the regular snores of Poiret, whose chin was digging a hole in his chest. My moods left him indifferent. I should point out that, in order to pass unnoticed, he had outdone himself: he had got himself up in a house painter's jacket and pants. He had even brought along a prop, a can of red lead with two brushes soaking in it. In that rig, he could go into the Terminus for a glass of red wine without attracting attention. After that, I could make my decision. My main worry was not being recognized by Robillard, who had probably seen me with Marlyse at the Favart.

The minutes crept by. At six-forty, Hidoine's elbow dug into my ribs. 'Look!' he exclaimed. The sound made Poiret jump, muttering unintelligible noises before he came to. Crocbois, Marlyse and I stared at the Terminus.

'No,' Hidoine whispered, 'behind us, to the left. Don't all of you turn around at once.'

My curiosity was stronger than my caution. I screwed my head around and felt my blood flood back up to my heart; only ten yards away, with the light full on him, stood Girier, waiting calmly to cross the cours de Vincennes. How did he miss spotting us? A miracle! His profile was turned towards me and I reflected that, with his wavy blond hair and his round, thin-rimmed glasses, he looked exactly like the police photo I carried in my wallet. He was five feet eleven, all right, and there was obviously a powerful torso under his well-cut dark-blue suit.

'Nice-looking boy,' Marlyse conceded. 'Doesn't look anything like a gangster—more like a young intellectual.'

'Do we jump him?' asked Poiret, his hand already on the door handle.

I admit the temptation was strong. There was Girier, close to me, defenceless, his back turned, waiting for the light to change. He fished a cigarette out of his case and lighted it with the lack of concern of a man with an easy conscience.

'Do we jump him or what, damn it?' repeated Poiret.

'No. We'll wait and see what he does.'

'Aaagh!' he fumed. 'I'll never understand you. We sweat our guts out looking for these crooks and when we find them we let them skip. I'll tell you something. I'm not rich, but I'd gladly give a thousand francs right now to see the PP snatch him from under your nose.'

The traffic stopped for the red light. Girier strolled casually across the street along the pedestrian walk and disappeared into the Terminus café. Through the window, I caught sight of his tall silhouette passing the bar; then it vanished into the room at the right. I looked at my watch: still fifteen minutes to wait. Assuming nothing happened in the meantime.

The longer we waited, the tighter I could feel my nerves stretching and the more worried I got. I began to regret not having put Fatso in the picture. If we messed this up, there would have been two of us to look silly, which is the only way to get ahead in public service. Besides, I knew how Fatso's mind worked. He never put his money on outsiders; 'a bird in the hand is worth two in the bush', he always said. Now I had Girier and I didn't have Buisson; if René failed to contact Émile, if he was picked up by a PP detail, I would be marked as a fool for the rest of my life. I kept thinking of Fatso's dictum, 'Girier: I've got to have him.'

Since the handsome René's breakout, Fatso had forgotten all about Buisson. Girier was enough for him. By finessing like this, I was running the risk of seeing my promotion put off for a long, long time. All this was running through my mind when Marlyse announced quietly:

'Mathieu has just arrived, dear. He's parking his BMW under the railroad bridge and he's not alone.'

The traffic blocked my view of the car, but, moments later, I saw Robillard walk into the Terminus. Escorting him was a small, dark man wearing a brown hat pulled down over his eyes.

'Christ, who's that?'

I grabbed the binoculars from Hidoine's knees, but it was too late. By the time I had them focused the two men had disappeared into the café.

'By God, it's Buisson,' Poiret said. 'We'd better not blow it this time. I'll go into the *bistrot* through one door and you take the other. I'll get near Buisson—he won't suspect me in this rig—and dump the pot of paint on his head while you cover the other two. Okay?'

'Take it easy,' I said firmly. 'First we have to make sure it is Buisson, and then we have to check on whether there are really only the three of them in the place. Hidoine can go ahead and scout and let us know. Mathieu knows Marlyse and me by sight. You stick with us as back-up.'

'That's right,' Poiret complained, 'every time there's a hot pinch to make, it's made without me. Okay, have it your way. But if I'm not fucking well needed I might as well fuck off.'

Before I could stop him, he had opened the door and was off towards the place de la Nation with his pot of paint in his hand. I told Crocbois to bring him back without a fuss. Hidoine had already left the car and gone into the Terminus. Ten minutes later he was back.

'There are three of them sitting at a table in the back,' he said, 'but the little dark guy is not Buisson. He must be a Corsican, from his accent. I'd guess he's your Giraldi.'

'What makes you think so?'

'I went to take a leak and, as I passed their table, I heard Girier call him Marc. That's all I can tell you. What about Poiret?'

'Still not back. Stupid bugger. Hey, there's Crocbois.'

Our driver slid back under his wheel and turned to me to explain that he had searched the cours de Vincennes without seeing Poiret. He thought he must have ducked into a bar because he had lost sight of him all of a sudden. 'Let's hope he doesn't do anything stupid,' he concluded, combing his hair in the rear-view mirror.

It was almost eight o'clock when Girier, Robillard and Marc left the Terminus. They walked slowly, talking, to the BMW, then stood there talking some more. Mathieu finally opened the doors on the right-hand side and Girier took the front seat while Marc sank into the cushions in back. Mathieu took the wheel and the BMW took off.

'We're screwed,' Crocbois said. 'They're heading for the Throne monument; I'll never be able to catch up to them.'

He veered desperately left, cutting across the line of cars going towards Vincennes. Then, risking a smash-up, he cut broadside across the Paris-bound lane through a hail of curses and we reached the place de la Nation just as the light turned red.

'Crash it,' I yelled, but Crocbois was already through. The BMW was in front of us again. Two hundred yards farther on, it ploughed through a red light. When we got up to the signal, the cars speeding along the boulevards Soult and Davout blocked us. Crocbois tried to manoeuvre through them, but the shrill blast of a traffic cop's whistle and, even more, the fear of an accident stopped him. The policeman, his face twisted with rage, walked towards us. A traffic jam coagulated around us. We'd almost certainly lost them now.

Through the half-open window I waved my police card at him. 'We're on a tail,' Crocbois yelled. The policeman instantly stopped the cross traffic and we raced off, heading towards the Château de Vincennes. But we hit one red light after another. When we reached the castle, the BMW had disappeared and all our skittering around looking for it got us nowhere.

I was crushed. I should have listened to Poiret. Truth can sometimes come out of the mouths of imbeciles. The thing is to know exactly when that moment is.

'What do we do now?' Crocbois inquired.

I hadn't the slightest idea. When Fatso heard about our failure next morning, there was going to be hell to pay. Marlyse didn't say a word, just stroked my hand affectionately, trying to console me. Luckily, there was still the phone tap. Why not check it right now.

'To the shop,' I told Crocbois.

'At this time of night?'

'Why not?'

'Drop me off at the porte de Vincennes,' Hidoine said. 'It's not far from my place. I'll take the bus. I'm sick of your screw-ups.'

At the shop, more disappointment: nothing interesting had been recorded. I put the earphones back on my desk. Marlyse, who was reading a newspaper while she waited, raised her eyes.

'It's half past nine, Roger. We'll never find anywhere to eat.'

'That's all right with me. I'm not hungry.'

'But I am,' she insisted.

It was exactly at that moment that luck came back on our side. The phone rang.

'Good, it's you.'

I recognized Poiret's voice. 'Well, now, I'm in luck,' he said. 'I never thought you'd still be there. Get out here quick.'

'Out where?'

'Bry-sur-Marne. That's where they're eating.'

'What?'

'That's right. It's too long to explain. Get out here, I tell you. I'm on the quai Adrien-Mentienne, on the Marne. Bring some dough because I have to pay the taxi-driver and I don't have a sou on me. You'll see, I'm in a café at number 210, Pottier's. I'll wait for you.'

Feverishly, I called the garage to ask for a night-duty car because I assumed Crocbois had already left, but it was he who answered the phone.

'You're not gone yet?'

'I was just leaving.'

'Well, don't. We've had a break. I'll wait for you in front of number eleven.'

In the time it took to lock my office door, ring for the lift and steam out of the building with Marlyse at my heels, we were in Crocbois' car. He had gone around the block so as to be headed in the right direction. I gave him the address and the Citroën sped off through the Bois de Vincennes, Nogent, Le Perreux and arrived in Bry-sur-Marne. We got lost twice before we found the quai Adrien-Mentienne. Crocbois pulled up in front of the café. Poiret, his face flushed, his paint pot at his feet, was sitting at a table with a taxi-driver in a grey smock. He winked at me when I walked in and came to meet me.

'Seven hundred,' he said, 'not counting the drinks. A mere nothing. Don't say anything in front of him.'

I paid the driver, who drained his glass and left.

'When I left the car,' Poiret explained, 'I had to piss so bad my teeth were floating. You made me so mad, that was why. Then I said to myself: "I can't ditch them like this." So I came back. When I arrived, I saw the three of them walk out of the Terminus and climb into the BMW. A taxi happened to be passing, I jumped into it and gave the driver a song and dance about how the big blond was my wife's lover and I wanted to find out where he lived. The cabbie was a jealous type, so it went over big. He tagged them like a pro. Do I get a pat on the back?'

'You're wonderful. Then what?'

'Then, their car stopped in front of 224 quai Adrien-Mentienne, the Auberge des Oiseaux, where they are now tucking into their dinner.'

'And they're still there?'

'They were still there ten minutes ago. It's just next door.'

We walked out on the quay to the restaurant. Its lights illuminated the quay and the Marne. Through the window, I could see Girier and his two companions. The BMW was parked on the quay.

'Get back to the car and tell Marlyse to join me,' I whispered.

For an hour, Marlyse and I sat in the grass near the inn, necking, with our feet in the water. Finally, just before midnight, the three men came out of the restaurant. I could hear Girier taking leave of his two companions before ducking back into the inn.

The BMW made a U-turn and drove off towards Paris. Hidden in the shadows, I tried to see what floor Girier's room was on. Moments later, a light went on and, through the half-closed shutters, I saw a silhouette removing its coat and tie. Girier.

One up to me. Fatso was going to be pleased.

31

Well, no. Fatso wasn't pleased. Not in the slightest. When I began telling him about the previous evening's events, he seemed interested at first. Then he got up out of his chair and began pacing his office. As I got deeper into my story, making it as dramatic as I could, and arrived at the point where we reached Bry-sur-Marne, his face turned scarlet. And when I mentioned the name Giraldi, he blew up.

'Damn! Damn it to hell! Sonofabitchofagoddamwhore!' he yelled.

I looked at him, dumbfounded. I had never seen Fatso in such a state. He came, went, came, went, not listening any more. I coughed to remind him I was still there and he immediately planted himself in front of me. 'You don't understand,' he hollered. 'You can't understand.' Then he took off again, swivelled between two chairs, slammed shut the partly open door to his secretary's office, pulled his horn-rimmed glasses out of their case and slammed them on his desk. I tried to calm him.

'But this is good news, boss. Now we can bring Girier in whenever we want him, and maybe even Buisson.'

Fatso whirled suddenly around and stuck his face in mine again.

'I don't give a shit about Buisson,' he screamed, 'or Girier either. Do you hear me? I do not give a shit. It's that bastard Giraldi I want. He's going to pay for this, the little sod!'

He was off again, his hands in his pockets hiking up his jacket, his monumental buttocks straining against the cloth of his pants.

'I don't get it, chief.'

'You will, Borniche,' he said, coming to a halt again. He walked around behind his desk, collapsed into his chair, opened a drawer and hauled out a file with a green cover which told me the subject had been banished from the capital. As soon as I spotted the name written in capital letters on the cover, I realized that Poiret hadn't done his job completely; he had extracted the criminal and individual dossiers on Giraldi out of the files, but he had neglected to get the one on banishments now in Fatso's hands. Still, this oversight was not enough to explain my superior's rage or his livid complexion.

'Borniche,' Fatso said weakly, 'if you don't arrest Giraldi right away, I am done for. I've been covering him secretly for three months; he is walking around right now with an authorization I signed for him, in my own handwriting. If the guys from the PP collar him with Girier, I am all washed up. You can see that, can't you?'

I could see it all too clearly. Fatso had authorized Giraldi to circulate in Paris without consulting his individual file and, consequently, without realizing that Giraldi was under sentence of twenty years hard labour. This was imprudent. But it was also a very dirty trick the boss had pulled on me, and on Hidoine and Poiret.

This is why: every police service has its own informers and it fights its own battles by dealing an occasional low blow to its colleagues across the way. That's the way it is, it's absurd, it's illogical, but all right—let it go. But that Fatso should have his own private, personal informer and pull fast ones on us, his own men, the men who work for him—that is just Machiavellian.

It is true that if there were not so many different files and dossiers in so many different police sections, situations like this could never arise. It was Chief Inspector Roblin, the head of records, who explained it to me when I began my career. 'I'm going to tell you how it works,' he said, 'and works without anybody even suspecting anything. Suppose you were at the PP. Right? There is a Notices and Warrants Squad there which co-ordinates the hunt for wanted criminals. Right? A guy slips up in Paris, the prosecutor's office or the Seine Department judge issues a wanted notice, an arrest warrant or a custodial writ. Right? These arrive at the PP's offices and our colleagues, instead of relaying them to all police units right away, keep them under their elbows. That enables them, either on their own or through their informers, to lay hands on the citizen in question. If they succeed, they can collect additional expenses. If, on the other hand, their guy skips, then, and only then, do they pass on the wanted notice.'

'That's disgusting,' I'd commented.

'Disgusting or not, that's the way it is. It creates a healthy rivalry. And in the Sûreté, it's the same with the Paris and provincial offices. Superintendent Petit is the head of the group which receives the notices and warrants. When there is a guy to be pinched in Paris, it would be dumb to pass the tip on to the PP by circulating the wanted notice, right? Besides, there's a hell of a big advantage in this system.'

'Oh?'

'By God! When you pull in a gangster on the run, and the charge isn't too stiff, you don't absolutely have to lock him up. No, my friend. You make a deal with him. You tell him: "You slip us information and we'll look the other way a little". And you hide the wanted notice, which you only use in case the guy doesn't play straight with you. That's how every police service creates its informers. If we tossed everybody inside, we'd never know what was going on. That's obvious, my boy.'

It was so obvious that everybody in all the police units in the country got himself in a tangle over it. Every man for himself.

I was caught in a double bind. If I arrested Giraldi, his friend Girier was going to become suspicious and disappear. If I pulled them both in, the possibility of contact with Buisson was lost. And if the PP rounded them up, Fatso would be in trouble.

'Chief,' I asked politely, 'did your protégé give you any leads?'

'Not one,' Fatso groaned. 'He was introduced to me by an old Resistance friend and he swore he'd finger Girier for me. Says he's known him for years. Giraldi called me only yesterday, but it was all wind. He was careful not to tell me about his appointment at the Terminus with Mathieu and Girier.'

'Maybe he was waiting for the right moment to tip you off.'

'Are you kidding, Borniche? In any case, I can't let him wander around any more with my authorization in his pocket. I'm going to call him in and let him be sent up for twenty years. That'll teach him to mess around with me. Besides, there's no other way out.'

He mopped his brow. But he wasn't feeling any lower than I was. All that effort for nothing, just because Fatso outsmarted himself. With a scowl, he opened Giraldi's file and furiously tore up the copies of his letter of authorization. He clapped the bits into my hand. 'Flush this down the john for me,' he ordered.

I obeyed orders. After I'd pulled the chain, I went back to his office. He was on the phone when I walked in. 'It's him,' Fatso whispered. I listened as he spoke calmly to Giraldi, with the amiability of an old friend. He was really smooth, Fatso, when he wanted to con somebody. But his fury returned as soon as he hung up the phone.

'The bastard will be here in an hour. And is he going to have a rough time! Write me out the notification statement and his commitment slip and you'll see—I'll make hamburger out of him!'

I went back to my office, where Poiret, his mouth hanging open, was awaiting congratulations.

'The jailer pleased?' he asked me.

'Very. I told him about the way you tailed them and he was thrilled. He made me repeat my account of what you'd done and he even said that from now on he is going to use your method.'

Poiret's face turned purple with pleasure. He sort of hung himself on the wall and watched Hidoine concentrating on a cross-word puzzle. I added: 'He also made a few remarks about the stupidity of an idiot who takes a criminal's file out without thinking to check on whether the crook is actually under sentence, with a banishment decree against him. Like Giraldi, for instance.'

I showed him the green folder and Poiret's smile faded. It finally got through to him that I'd been putting him on. I took Giraldi's individual file out of the filing cabinet, slid a pair of statement forms into the typewriter and, under Poiret's astonished gaze, began to type out, in duplicate, the notification of sentence Fatso had asked for.

'You're putting Giraldi away?' Poiret asked over my shoulder.

'Yes.'

'I'll be damned!'

But I was suddenly not listening to Poiret. An idea struck me as I examined the court clerk's notice from Marseilles on Giraldi's sentence. I turned it and re-turned it in my fingers. Then I reached for the phone.

'Roblin?'

'Yes.'

'Borniche. I need some expert information, friend. When you get a notice of sentence, do you circulate it right away or do you pass it to Petit's group first?'

'Depends. Why?'

'Because I have a file here in which I don't see the distribution service's stamp, no number, no date . . .'

'What name?'

'Giraldi. Marc Giraldi.'

'Wait a second.'

Poiret came over and tried to listen on the supplementary earphone. I elbowed him away. Roblin came back on the line.

'No,' he confirmed, 'according to the file slip, the notice was not sent out. It must have arrived about the time Poiret took the file—I see it's marked out in his name. So it's been sitting here waiting for the file to come back.'

'I see. Thanks.'

I hung up and strode across the hall to Fatso's office. I explained to him that the PP officially knew nothing about Giraldi's sentences. 'Don't you see?' I said. 'We have nothing to worry about.'

Fatso brightened. 'All right,' he said. 'So we won't send on the bastard's notification, for the moment.'

He was satisfied. He didn't say anything, but I could tell from the way he shook my hand that Giraldi was not going to be arrested for a while yet. Now everybody was happy, for different reasons, but it had been a close shave.

I could go back to stalking Girier.

32

The Auberge des Oiseaux was a very quiet, very discreet place on the bank of the Marne. The dining room was huge. There was a bandstand at the far end of the room for the Sunday dances. The food was good, the rooms comfortable.

The owner was a likeable guy. He rushed to greet us when Marlyse and I arrived. I filled out my registration slip carefully, borrowing the name of a reporter I knew on the weekly magazine *Point de Vue-Images du Monde* and giving a phoney address. Marlyse didn't fill one out, and the owner gave me a conspiratorial wink.

A ravishingly beautiful waitress named Monique took our bags and led us to the second floor, room 13. Marlyse opened the shutters. The view over the Marne was superb, but Marlyse was not entirely satisfied.

'Are there any mosquitoes here, dear?'

I did not know and I did not give a damn. The only thing I was interested in was knowing what room Girier was in and if he was there, because I hadn't seen him when we arrived.

Marlyse sat on the edge of the bed, conscientiously writing the date in her diary: '12 July 1949—weather hot—No sign of René the Exile.' Her dishevelled hair, her provocative breasts, the way she sat with her beautifully tapering thighs not quite together made the stallion in me snort. Marlyse looked at me and understood. She laid aside the diary and let me press her back on the bed. I glued my mouth to hers, felt her tremble under me. I unhooked her bra. The country air was certainly a tonic.

The sound of a door slamming brought me to my feet. I ran to the window and saw Girier, a briefcase in his right hand, walking away from a Citroën parked carefully alongside the inn under the outside staircase. I made a mental note of the number, 8989 RQ 1, then I crossed the room and put my ear to the door. Girier's footsteps sounded on the stairs and stopped on the landing. I heard a key turning in a lock, a door closing. Stealthily, I opened my door and, barefoot, sneaked into the corridor. It seemed to me Girier had gone into No. 3, but I couldn't be sure. I went back to my room.

Marlyse had refastened her bra. She had also spread out on the table a dozen copies of the magazine I was supposed to work for. That would enlighten the chambermaid as to my occupation and the word would go down to the proprietor of the inn, who would accordingly consider me a bona fide newshound.

Six-thirty p.m. That was the time at which I had promised to call Fatso. The booth was near the bar, so I resigned myself to going into town to phone.

'Come on,' I said to Marlyse, 'let's go for a walk.'

Fatso was in the director's office when I called the shop, and Hidoine answered the phone. An impatient Hidoine, who gave top priority to his own irritation: 'Shit! Couldn't you have called earlier? I have a hot date at seven o'clock, as it happens. You have complicated my life.'

I could picture him in his riding habit, his crop under his arm, ready to charge up towards the place Saint-Augustin, his favourite rendezvous spot. I gave him the licence number of Girier's car. 'Get me a registration check right away,' I said. 'It's important.'

Hidoine didn't bother to answer. A sharp click told me he was already on to the internal exchange. A bare three minutes later he was back on the line: 'Car stolen 8 July from one André Graziani, manufacturer. That do you?'

'Yes,' I said. 'But for Christ's sake don't call me at the inn. It's dangerous. How's Poiret?'

'He's fine, just fine. See you.'

The bastard hung up. I rejoined Marlyse at the bar and we strolled back to the Auberge des Oiseaux arm in arm. Monique gave us a friendly wave as we went by, which caused my companion to stiffen with annoyance.

A record player was whinnying a popular waltz tune when we entered the dining room. We sat down at the table reserved for us, in front of an open window. Life was good at the Auberge des Oiseaux.

Monique had just brought us the cheese board. I glanced out through the window—and almost fell out of my chair. Before me, walking primly along the quay with a pretty woman on his arm, was Fatso. He pretended not to see me but, when he had moved a little farther off, he beckoned discreetly. The timing was lousy; Girier appeared at that moment, still holding his briefcase, and sat down near me. With a detached air, he unfolded a *France-*

Soir and began reading while waiting for the menu. I waited a few minutes, then got up. So did Marlyse. Girier's eyes followed us as we smooched our way out to the quay. When we had moved beyond his radar range, Fatso heaved himself up out of the grass in which he had been lying with his young woman.

'I have news,' he said, pumping my hand. 'And you?'

'Girier is here, but he's alone. I think he is in room number three, next to mine.'

'Good,' Fatso grunted. 'I've had a tap put on the inn's phone. Hidoine and Poiret are monitoring.'

'Fine. How about the Favart?'

'That's just why I've come to see you. We picked up an interesting call: Mathieu phoned. He's on to a sensational job to replace the Crédit Lyonnais stick-up, which is considered too dangerous. It's an attack on two messengers from the French Cartridge Works, rue Bertin-Poirée. He's expecting a haul of fifty million. The job is set for 19 July. According to Mathieu, Girier is in on it. But Buisson has been keeping his neck tucked in since Polledri's body was found and he hasn't yet given his answer. The job was set up by Giraldi's brother-in-law, who is the cashier in the joint. Mathieu will drive the car; Girier has agreed to provide the gunmen.'

I was ruined. We obviously couldn't let the hold-up take place, which meant I would have to arrest Girier before he could lead me to Buisson. Once more, I had followed a track that, at the last moment, brought me back where I started. I stalled for time.

'Listen, chief,' I pleaded, 'since the hold-up is not scheduled to happen for days yet, maybe we needn't collar Girier right away. Suppose he has a meeting with Buisson within the next couple of days or even the next few hours. Why throw away a chance at Émile just by rushing things? What do you say?'

My argument shook Fatso's resolution. Basically, he was as anxious as I was to lay hands on Buisson.

'All right,' he said. 'I may be making a mistake, but I'll give you a few more days. But I warn you, Borniche: if it misfires you'll take the entire responsibility, all the blame goes to you. Understood?'

'Understood, chief.'

Fatso went away happy. With a scapegoat arranged in advance he was covered every which way.

*

I went back to the Auberge des Oiseaux and sat on the terrace to smoke a cigarette. Girier came out and sat down next to me. I smiled a greeting and offered him a cigarette.

'No, thanks,' he said. 'I only smoke French.'

The ice was broken, as the saying goes. The more I studied him, the more likeable he seemed. It was hard to believe that this courteous young man could be a criminal. Marlyse's newspaper slipped to the ground. Girier bent lithely, picked it up and replaced it on her knees.

'You like it here?' he asked me.

'Oh,' I said, 'we just arrived today. It's nice to get out where there's some grass for a few days, especially now, when it's so sultry in Paris.'

Monique went by. Her short skirt was packed tight, and I caught Girier's eager glance.

'Good-looking, eh?'

'Yes,' Girier agreed. 'Nice machinery.'

He puffed on his cigarette a couple of times, knocked the ash off into the saucer. 'So you're a reporter?' he asked me nonchalantly.

The grapevine had worked fast. I had filled in my registration slip only four hours ago, and he already knew what was on it.

'Yes. It has its fascinating moments, but you'll never get rich at it,' I said. 'We work like Americans, follow orders like Germans and get paid like Frenchmen. See what I mean?'

He laughed. That began a friendly conversation that went on for over an hour. He told me he was in a business which sometimes obliged him to be away for days at a time.

'How did you know I was a reporter?' I asked him at one point. 'I don't know anybody here, unless you went to my rag once and saw me there.'

He laughed again, showing his teeth; I noticed two of them on the right side were missing.

'Simple,' he replied suavely. 'I often carry large sums of money in my briefcase. So I ask the owner to fill me in on his customers. Just a simple precaution, you see.'

Did I see! I paid for my round and we returned to our respective rooms. I was going to have to watch myself with a wise guy like Girier around. There was only one thing more important: not losing him.

The next morning I phoned Fatso from Ma Pottier's café.

'The job is set for the nineteenth,' he told me excitedly. 'Everything's lined up. They're to stage a rehearsal on the eighteenth at four o'clock. Robillard talked too much on the telephone. Girier and a hard guy named Marius Poulenard will be the guns. Buisson refused to join in. He's been replaced by the brothers Louis and André Biraut. They are very special specialists, the Birauts—they dress up as gendarmes, stop bank vans on the road on pretext of checking their papers and relieve the guards of their cargo. They are nasty customers—there is a fistful of warrants out for them already. An all-round crew, this one. We're going to nail them.'

'But, chief,' I groaned, 'that blows all my plans sky-high.'

'Borniche,' Fatso said forcefully, 'I cannot run the risk of letting Girier stage his stick-up just so that you can collar Buisson. If there is shooting, I will be the one held responsible, especially if there are bystanders killed or wounded.'

'What do you plan to do, then?' I asked dismally.

'I am going to take all these playful fellows out of circulation. They're to meet today at the Favart bar. We'll pick them up one by one. I'll expect you at the office at two o'clock. Be on time for once.'

'And Girier?'

'From what I've been told, he will not be at the meeting today. That's the way stars are: they don't come on until the last minute. So let him be in his hidey-hole. There's still an outside chance he'll contact Buisson before then.'

At two p.m. on the dot I was at the rue des Saussaies. I left Marlyse in Bry-sur-Marne to sun herself on the beach alongside the disturbingly muscular torso of René Girier. Fatso had set his operation up efficiently. He had asked for reinforcements from other units at the shop and we had Superintendent Boury and Inspectors Bouteiller and Gard to lend us a hand.

Two Citroëns headed towards the rue Marivaux. At four p.m. I passed in front of the bar, scouting, and saw that the place was stuffed with villains. At five o'clock, a tall, svelte Marius Poulenard came out with his mistress on his arm, turned into the boulevard towards a cinema. He was quickly overpowered, handcuffed and shoved into one of our cars. The Biraut brothers' turn was next, and they were followed into the cars by the famous Marc Giraldi, at whom I was getting my first look. He immediately denied he was an outlaw, protested at being disturbed, showed me Fatso's authorization to stay in Paris, which he kept carefully folded in his wallet. I put it with equal care in my pocket and signalled to Fatso that the mission was complete.

There was, unfortunately, one man missing from the roll-call: Mathieu Robillard. Our reinforcements had failed to spot him when he left.

When I went back to Bry-sur-Marne that evening, leaving it to my colleagues to grill the prisoners and search their homes, Girier was completely relaxed. He had spent a splendid day with Marlyse and Monique, of whom he was in open pursuit. He dined at our table that evening and bought us a bottle of champagne. 'I am on to a fantastic deal on the stock market,' he told me. 'If everything goes right, by the day after tomorrow I'll have doubled or tripled my capital.'

I almost choked on my champagne and wondered if I ought to send for Fatso in a hurry; as soon as Girier heard about the arrest of his accomplices, he would up anchor. But I could not phone from the hotel. And it was so late now that the café next door was closed.

When I entered the dining room the next morning, the owner told me that our friend's business had obliged him to depart suddenly and that he would not be back for ten days. The Citroën was gone. Three days later, I learned from a phone message that the car had been found abandoned in the 20th arrondissement. Girier had vanished. There was one consolation: Fatso had recovered the compromising letter he had given Giraldi. But the road leading to Buisson had once more come to a dead end.

33

The newspapers were tipped off to the story of how the French Cartridge Works caper was foiled. They ate it up. Examining Magistrate Daniault was assigned to prepare the case against our prisoners on charges of consorting with known criminals.

Superintendent Clot pointedly informed his lackeys what he thought of them for letting themselves be diddled in the middle of Paris, on their own patch, by their colleagues from the Sûreté. He summoned his deputy, Morin, stared at him sternly for a long moment to give ample time for his displeasure to sink in. He finally found his voice again. 'Morin,' he then said, 'the Sûreté is not going to make an idiot out of me for long. Girier is in Paris. We have got to find him. And Girier means Buisson. How many men do you have available now?'

This was the vacation period, which meant that Chief Inspector Morin needed very little time to make the count. 'Eighteen, sir,' he replied.

'That's three times as many as you need,' Clot declared. 'Each of your boys must have at least five informers in every racket. So I expect to see Girier here before the new court term starts. And Buisson too. Buck up.'

Morin left his chief's office looking as though he had just been cut out of his rich aunt's will. The brass, he reflected, has a different conception of the police from the man on the beat's. So he summoned Inspector Bouygues. 'Old man,' he inquired, 'how many men do you have available?'

Bouygues, a fat little guy who wore a floppy beret all the year round, waddled right into the trap. 'Six,' he said.

Morin calculated rapidly. 'That's lucky, my friend,' he said. 'Since each of your boys must have fifteen informers to feed him tips, you should be able to pick up Girier and Buisson for me before the new court session.'

Bouygues' eyes popped. 'What do you mean, fifteen, informers? If you think they can be collected that easy, and us without a centime to pay out to them . . .'

'I don't give a gold-plated damn, friend. Buck up.'

Inspector Bouygues went into action.

*

I was running hard after Girier, too. One evening, the tap on the Favart's telephone produced the information that he had a date with Robillard at six p.m. at the bar of the Hotel Terrasse, rue Caulaincourt, in Montmartre. I rubbed my hands. Fatso rubbed his hands. To hell with Buisson; we were going to nab Girier. Who could say? Maybe he would even tell us where the killer was hiding.

Fatso and I left Crocbois nearby and walked to the Terrasse, our eyes swivelling like the flashing light on a squad car. It was five-thirty and we wanted to case the place. We were no more than fifty yards from the entrance when we saw Girier and Robillard rush out of the hotel and, talking heatedly, get into a car.

The car took off and we stupidly began sprinting after it. Naturally, Fatso pulled up after fifty yards, his chest on fire, suffocating. I kept going for another twenty yards, hoping the car would slow down at the corner of the rue Lepic, but I finally gave out too, the blood pounding in my temples. Fatso caught up with me. I looked at him. He looked at me. We were white as communion wafers. But we had not yet drained the cup of humiliation.

The next day we felt even sillier. The *Parisien libéré* informed us that Inspector Morin of the PP had arrested René Girier and Mathieu Robillard in a hideout in Montfermeil.

It was really too dumb! Because of a change of timetable that had not been recorded on our tap, we had been made to look grotesque on two counts. First, the PP had nabbed Girier on our territory. Second, it was as well informed as we were, and it had succeeded where we had failed.

When I arrived at the office, Fatso was apoplectic. 'This time we have been royally screwed,' he thundered. 'Morin grabbed Girier in a zone we are supposed to be covering. Nice work, Borniche! Hell, I should never have listened to you in Bry-sur-Marne. But I'm too good to you, I give you too much rope. Now, thanks to you, I can't show my face.'

He shut up long enough to straighten his tie. Then the volcano erupted again: 'How did they do it? Do you have any idea?'

I stuck my neck out: 'No. Possibly they tailed Girier's wife.'

Fatso sat down and, without looking at me, opened his desk drawer. 'Makes no difference in any case,' he said. 'If the PP knows I was on the case, I'm going to look like a damn fool. Thanks, Borniche. I'll remember this.'

I understood that the interview was over and, head bowed, I sloped off. I was in a fog. All I knew was that I had wanted to score a double with Girier and Buisson. And I had. I had lost them both.

When I showed up at Superintendent Clot's office two days later to take delivery of his prize, Girier was still on the grill. His arm cuffed to a tomato-coloured velvet chair, face drawn, he was parrying the rapid-fire questions Officer Lemoine shot at him from behind his typewriter.

My visit, although justified by our investigation of the French Cartridge Works case, did not seem to go down well with my PP friends. And, in fact, it was just a pretext. My real and exclusive interest was still Buisson. And this was not the time to let Girier ripen too long on the vine at the quai des Orfèvres. You never know when a moment of weakness will come.

When I walked into the office, Girier turned away from me indifferently. Then he did a double take and I could read the amazement on his face as he recognized me. 'The bastards!' he exclaimed. 'Have they arrested you too?'

I reassured him on that count. While I cuffed him to Poiret's wrist and led him to Crocbois' car, I heard him chuckle: 'Now that's a good one, that is, a real good one. I should hire you as a reporter.'

'And I'd hire you, René,' I retorted. 'You'd pass anywhere for a financier.'

But Girier was no more talkative with me than he was with my rivals across the river. He professed total amnesia concerning his connection with Buisson. 'What I don't understand,' he said as I left him, 'is how they managed to find my hideout. Some son of a bitch must have turned me in.'

The 'son of a bitch' had led the PP to Girier. It was up to me to find someone else who would lead me to Buisson. But who? Monsieur Émile only works with men he is sure of. And, at the slightest doubt, he reaches for his gun . . .

ROUND FIVE

34

Modern psychologists would classify Simon Loubier as a person with a slightly above-average IQ. He is a louse, of course, but he has a brain and he uses it.

Of average height, muscular, quick to react, with a puffy face and frizzy hair, Loubier is not, so to speak, a man crushed by the weight of his scruples. He can't stand being crossed. The moment his affairs begin to wander a little off course, Simon blows up, and finds relief only in violence. It was for having revised his superior's profile with his fists that he lost his accounting job with a firm in which he had been thought a promising young man. Because he killed a storekeeper who objected to Simon's trying to burglarize his premises, he was picked up by the police, although he was released for lack of evidence. And it was because he had seriously damaged an accomplice he suspected of ratting on him that he enjoyed an alarming and flattering reputation in gangland.

Simon was always ready to welcome opportunity. But when he ran into Hughes Grosjean, a small-time pimp he had known in the Army in North Africa, in a café on the rue de Vaugirard, he was feeling curmudgeonly. Some days before he had bungled a stick-up of two railway workers who were transporting railway funds. His failure was the more regrettable for the fact that he was almost broke.

'Maybe I have a deal for you,' suggested Grosjean, who had listened patiently to his friend's song of woe.

'If it's some grocer's cash register, you can stuff it you know where,' Simon replied discourteously, glaring at Grosjean's simian features.

'Okay, Simon. Since serious jobs don't seem to appeal to you, I know someone else who's sure to jump at it. I have this feeling your nerves are a little ragged just now. You'd do better to go and calm down with the whores then come back when you're ready to be less of a pain in the arse.'

'All right,' Loubier growled. 'Unwrap it and let's look at it.'

Grosjean shrugged, paused, lowering his voice and glancing behind him to make sure the barman was at the other end of the counter.

'In Saint-Maur,' he explained, 'I have this neighbour, Georges Dezalleux, a carpenter, who let me in on a terrific gimmick. He's a nice chap, this carpenter, and absolutely straight: everything he told me was just in passing, in a *bistrot* over a *pastis*.'

'All right, all right. Let's have it, for God's sake!'

'What's the big hurry?' Grosjean complained, glaring at his friend. 'I need to explain it from the beginning. So anyway, my carpenter told me he is working in the basement of a bank that's being built. It's not finished yet, but the safes are already in and that's where the dough is stored every night. There's a bundle of it. Every morning, two guys come and cart the money to the old bank building, which will be abandoned when the new one is finished. You understand?'

'When's the work supposed to be finished?' Loubier asked.

'In a week at the most. That's why we need to get a move on if you're interested.'

Loubier thought it over briefly, weighing the possibilities of success. 'You know the route the two guys take?'

'Do I! I watched them two days in a row. It's simple—they only have one street to cross. But it's millions they carry in their satchel.'

A light went on in Loubier's eyes, but he remained lost in thought for some minutes more before he decided.

'I'll buy it,' he said. 'Slip me the name of the bank, the address and the times.'

Grosjean flashed a mocking smile. 'Easy does it, chum. First, I want to know what my cut will be.'

'How much are you expecting out of it?'

'Me?'

'Yes, you.'

'Well, at least as much as the guys who pull it off.'

Loubier did some fast mental arithmetic. 'You're on,' he said with an indifferent shrug. 'Word of honour.'

'Good. It's the Banque régionale d'Escompte et de Dépôt in Champigny. The new building, where the dough is left to cool, is at number eighty-seven avenue Jean-Jaurès. That's where the two messengers leave from every morning at eight-thirty. They have a short trip, no more than fifty yards—the old bank is across the street at number eighty-eight. Which means there's not much time to operate—a minute, tops.'

'Don't give yourself a headache,' said Loubier, untroubled by such details. 'I'll see you tomorrow at your place. So long.'

'So long.'

There was one man, Loubier reflected as he walked up the rue de Vaugirard, who could negotiate this deal perfectly. And that was Émile Buisson. For some time now, the little killer's reputation had been rising steadily in the underworld. Everybody in every dive in France more or less knew that most of the armed robberies being carried off in Paris and its suburbs were his work.

The payroll snatch at the municipal garage in Boulogne-Billancourt: 1,880,273 francs. The stick-up of the Salavin Corp. cashier in Paris: a round million. One hundred thousand francs taken from a Social Security cashier at Neuilly-Plaisance; 300,000 in cash plus 250,000 in stamps from a tobacconist on the boulevard de Courcelles in Paris; 996,000, his watch, his identity papers and his pistol from Monsieur Battarel, a Family Allowances Fund payments agent, on the road to Étampes.

All the stick-ups were signed by the hand of the master, Buisson. His success gave Monsieur Émile a monopoly on the stick-up market; every criminal fresh out of stir, the small-fry as well as the veterans, pined to be tapped to join the Buisson gang. But it was not easy to reach Monsieur Émile. He was said to patronize certain bars, chiefly La Ribote on the rue de Liège, or the Favart at the Opéra-Comique, but his visits to them were rare, rapid and unpredictable.

Everything in life is a question of contacts. Whether it is to bring off a political manoeuvre, triumph in a military career, make good as a businessman, the intermediaries have to be there. The same is true in the underworld. The prisons and penitentiaries are the post-graduate schools, the thieves' Polytechnic, their Oxbridge, their Fine Arts School. It is there that they cement their friendships, forge their alliances. It was inside that Loubier had got to know Orsetti. It's another country.

So it was of Orsetti that Loubier first thought when he got the idea about Buisson. Orsetti had not shown his face at the Deux Marches since Polledri's murder. He was lying low in his apartment on the avenue Rapp and the only place he would consider going for a quick one was the Rotonde in Montparnasse, because it had two entrances and a vast expanse of window across its front that allowed him to see what was going on in the street.

Loubier knew this, so it was there that the taxi dropped him around six p.m. It was early January 1950, and cold. The heat inside the huge café took his breath away. It was a fetid kind of heat, weighted with cigarette smoke and the insidious, sickly-sweet smells of the aperitifs people were drinking.

Loubier's eye ran down the line of men propped up at the bar. No Orsetti. He pushed through the room, jostling clusters of secretaries and sales girls whose jaws were swollen by mouthfuls of sandwich, and a group of noisy regulars flagellating a pinball machine. He reached a smaller room with round tables which functioned as a bunker for lovebirds with nowhere else to go.

Orsetti was sitting at a table well away from the couples grappling with each other between bites. He was talking excitedly to Henri Bolec, Francis Caillaud's Breton pal, who had just been released from prison.

'I'm in luck,' Loubier thought as he headed towards the two men. They stopped talking when they saw him, waiting until he pulled up a chair.

'How's tricks?' he asked.

'Lousy,' Orsetti said, his face frozen.

Loubier lighted a crippled Gauloise, tossed his pack on the table, called the waiter, ordered a round of *pastis* and leaned towards the other men.

'What's biting you, Jeannot?'

'Émile,' Orsetti said in a low, vibrant voice. 'He sent Henri to bring me to work for him.'

'So? That's good, isn't it?'

Orsetti took a long pull at his drink, set the glass down. 'You think so, do you?' he asked. 'Listen, I've had enough of working with madmen. Quite enough. What he did to my friend Polledri was disgusting. Émile's nuts, and I don't like it.'

'Oh, come on, Jeannot,' Bolec ventured, 'you must admit the Wop was a messy operator. Sooner or later he'd have pulled one that would have put us all inside. There are times when you've got to be merciless, think of your own safety.'

Orsetti shook his head. 'You poor sap,' he said in a pitying tone, 'you're so stupid it hurts. Not one of us—you understand? —is safe from Émile's fits. Get it into your head that the day he thinks he's in danger he won't hesitate to knock us all off one after the other. He's sick, Émile, he's in love with murder. He's an insatiable necrophage.'

'A what?' asked Bolec, alarmed.

'Necrophage, you Breton bonehead. A guy who lives on corpses, who feeds on rotting bodies.'

'Necrophage or not,' Loubier said, throwing his cigarette butt on the floor, 'at the moment there isn't a better heist man around. And, as it happens, I have a job to propose to him that's worth the trip.'

'Well, you tell Henri all about it, because I'm off,' Orsetti said as he rose.

Bolec tried to hold the little Corsican back. 'At least stay and hear what it's about,' he growled.

'No,' Orsetti said curtly, 'I don't work with killers. *Ciao.*'

They watched him go, their eyes following the diminutive figure until, seconds later, it was swallowed up in the darkness. The waiter who served them moved off.

'Well?' Bolec asked.

'Listen, you've got to take me to Buisson,' he began. 'I've got this fantastic job, right up his alley. Only I can't do it alone and I don't want to mess around with slobs. With Émile it's different, see?'

Bolec ran his hand through his greying hair. 'You're right there,' he said. 'But Émile's not that hard up for work. Everybody wants to team up with him. But he's a suspicious guy, you know, and he wants the best—no softies.'

Loubier's head snapped back. 'Listen, Henri, I'm not soft and Émile knows it. I can blast a guy without fainting or losing any sleep over it.'

'I'll talk to him about it, Simon,' Bolec promised. 'Maybe he'll go for it. He's no ball of fire for the moment. He was working with Jacques Vérando and his lot, but they didn't get along—the Niçois wants to give the orders. Just between you and me, I can tell you: Émile wants to put together a new squad with the best men on the street.'

'Has he already taken some on?' Loubier asked, his throat suddenly dry.

'There's me, of course, and Happy has been in for a couple of months. Screwball, his brother, who is just out of stir, would love to re-enlist, but Émile doesn't want him. He thinks there's too close a watch on Screwball and that he would be risky for us. He wanted me to ask Orsetti to come back in, but you saw his reaction. Corsicans are soft-hearted; Émile gunned his pal the Wop so Jeannot goes around with a long face. You must know something about this—you're Corsican too, aren't you?'

'Me? I can live without old wives' tales. All that interests me is meeting Émile and putting together my operation with him. Will you set it up for me?'

The Breton got up, leaving the check for Loubier. 'It's a deal,' he said. 'Come to La Ribote at noon tomorrow. I'll warn Émile. If he wants to see you, he'll be there.'

Buisson arrived half an hour early for the appointment, minutely inspecting the area around La Ribote before entering. He approved highly of Loubier's caution in walking by the bar without stopping, continuing as far as the next corner before turning around. From where he stood, Buisson could see the Corsican put his right hand in his coat pocket, reverse direction and retrace his steps. If he had been followed, he would have found himself nose to nose with his surprised shadow and the tag would have been blown.

Buisson liked that kind of prudence. Pleased with his new recruit, he waited a few minutes longer, then walked slowly on, every sense alert, entering La Ribote just slightly late, as became a boss.

Over glasses of champagne, the two men quickly reached an agreement. Buisson, who knew Loubier's reputation as a gunman, recognized in him the new lieutenant he had so sorely lacked since Caillaud's capture and the revelation of Orsetti's soft heart.

He was enthusiastic about the Champigny hold-up; it was just the kind of job he loved, one that required precise timing, speed and decision. A Buisson special.

'Great,' he said, draining his glass. 'Today is Saturday. This is what I propose: tomorrow we'll go and give the place a good look over, fix the date for the job and then go and treat ourselves to a slap-up meal.'

'Sounds terrific, Émile. Have you heard about Bolec?'

'No,' said Buisson, suddenly suspicious.

'The stupid bastard has got a sore throat. I'm afraid he won't be back in shape for a week.'

'That's all right,' said the leader, relieved. 'Happy will do just as well at the wheel as the Breton.'

'Okay, Émile. And you don't think we'll need a fourth for a job like this? You never know how it can go.'

'You have somebody in mind?'

'Yes. A good friend. A solid boy: Pierre Labori. Ten years breaking rocks and never a peep out of him.'

'If he's a friend of yours, he's all right by me,' Buisson conceded. 'Bring him along for the reconnaissance tomorrow; I'll show Happy the spot later. That way the citizens won't see us all together.'

On Sunday, 8 January, Happy gulped down his glass of port, set it on the table, wiped his mouth, slapped his girlfriend Christiane on the bottom and got up out of his chair.

'Shall we be off?'

Buisson rose and pecked his Yvette on the lips. 'We won't be long, sweetie,' he promised.

The two men buttoned their coats, turned up their collars and walked out of the café near the station. It was six p.m. Night had already fallen and it was bitter cold. Walking fast, they soon reached the avenue Jean-Jaurès. Another hundred yards, walking shoulder to shoulder, and Buisson slowed down. 'The stuff's in there,' he said.

Through narrowed eyes, Happy gazed at the still incomplete façade of the new bank while Buisson took out his package of Gauloises and offered him one. A match crackled and while Happy leaned over the flame, Buisson whispered: 'You see, the old branch is just across the street. Just look a little to the left and you'll see it.'

Happy drew on his cigarette, pivoting to take in the old building on the opposite pavement.

'Got it?' asked Buisson. 'Let's go.'

They crossed the avenue slowly, passing in front of the condemned bank building, which also had a side entrance on the rue Pierre-Renaudel. They walked on a little way, then Buisson stopped before the door to a courtyard bordering the rear of the building and pretended to relight his cigarette. 'Take a good look,' he murmured. 'This courtyard is where the two messengers bring the loot every morning; they go in by the little staff entrance on the right.'

'Right,' said Happy. 'So I'll have the car waiting at the end of the street, on the corner of the rue Joséphine, and we'll scram by the rue de Verdun. Now we can get back to the ladies.'

About an hour later, Happy dropped Émile and Yvette at the Hôtel Gallien, 120 avenue Foch, in Saint-Maur. Happy knew Fernand, who ran the hotel, but he had omitted to tell him the true identity of the new guest who had registered under the name of Jean Lucien.

Buisson and Yvette shared a comfortable room on the second floor. He choose it because the window gave on the garden some four yards below, which gave him an escape route in case he needed one.

It was a quiet life they led. Because of his well-groomed appearance, his dark suits, the conservative daily *Figaro* that was always tucked under his arm, and his courteous manners, everyone, from the owner to the barflies, took him for a mild little notary public indulging himself in a few weeks of good times with his mistress. Émile's reputation was so good that he spent many an evening shooting long games of pool with the local gendarmes.

Buisson was happy with Yvette. He was crazy about her. The two girls who made up the rooms, and to whom he peeled off huge tips, took special care of him. When the bed they made up around noon bore traces of the notary's amorousness, they envied Yvette her luck in digging up a guy in his forties who was rich, generous and still virile.

And, in fact, Buisson lavished attentions and kindnesses on Yvette in a way that would have astonished the underworld. To his own surprise, she stirred in him yearnings for a normal life, a desire to escape the life of a hunted man, the only life he had really ever known.

At night, with Yvette sleeping beside him while he vetted the hotel noises for indications of danger, he would sometimes think of the Odette he used to love. The two girls were much alike, physically. Both were small and slender, both dark-haired and blue-eyed; they had the same lithe movements, the same smile, the same soft lips, the same way of sighing when they surrendered themselves, the same modesty in lovemaking.

He had met Odette in 1940, a few months before he stupidly let himself be arrested by the Germans on the train. She remained faithful to him despite the separation. So faithful that, on 29 October 1941, in Troyes prison, they were married, standing between two detectives armed with machine guns and a squad of nervous prison guards.

Odette was pregnant; the baby was due the following March. It was because of Odette and their unborn son that his conduct had been so exemplary in prison. He had made up his mind, then: as soon as he was released he would take his wife and child far from France, to South America, maybe, or Australia, to begin a new life.

In the darkness of his hotel room, Émile recalled totally the savage feeling that had swept through him when Odette told him of their daughter's birth. The resignation into which he had let himself slide, his passive acceptance of imprisonment—all that was suddenly effaced. Buisson ached for his freedom because he ached to see his daughter. Right away! This was why, entirely forgetting his fine resolutions, he had tried to murder the warder Louis Vincent.

After the attempt failed, he was thrown into solitary for ninety days. Tragic news awaited him on his return to his cell: a letter from Odette told him their daughter had died of meningitis. 'When you read this letter,' she wrote in her small, tight hand, 'I will probably no longer be here. I am doomed, and in the eyes of the doctors and nurses I see clearly that there is no longer anything they can do to cure my tuberculosis. Then, too, I feel my strength going every day and my cough tears me apart. So I am going to die, darling Émile, and I confess that I am glad. I can't go on living now that our little one is gone. Nor can I go on living after the frightful murder you tried to commit and which would prevent my loving you from now on. Be kind and ask your family to go and put some flowers on our child's grave. Maybe it's a good thing she never knew her parents. I see now that God has been good to her.'

The letter was some weeks old when he saw it. Odette, too, was dead by that time. He did not weep. He would never weep again.

Since then, Émile had never loved any woman. Every female he encountered in his path was viewed merely as an instrument for the maintenance of his glandular equilibrium. He thought of women as nuisances, fickle. As a way to spend an evening, he usually rated their company below a good dinner or a boxing match.

He had clung to that practical point of view until the evening he met Yvette at the bar of the Calanques. She had just turned twenty. She knew who he was, how he lived, yet she loved and admired him. He knew, on the other hand, that she was the last woman he would love, that after her there would be no one. He was forty-eight years old. If everything went smoothly, he would end his life with her. If not . . .

Yvette had asked him once why they didn't run away from France. Obtaining a false passport and crossing the border would have been child's play for him. But he refused. Stupidly—as he repeatedly assured himself—Émile had bound himself to his deaf sister Jeanne. Whenever he had a little money, he gave her part of it so that she could consult the best ear specialists in the country.

Besides, you had to be young to emigrate. At his age, Émile no longer felt curious about new horizons. He was at home in Paris, he had his habits, his friends, his hideouts. The underworld respected him, even if it did not always approve of what he did. The Corsicans, particularly, reproached him for making too many waves. Every time Émile went into action, he stung the police to a frenzy which meant they would invade all the underworld villages, pull in the pimps, round up the girls, demand action from their informers. A lot of commotion just over one man. Buisson knew that some of them would willingly hand him over to the police for the sake of peace. That was why he trusted almost no one. Fewer still knew his hiding-places.

Only Happy knew he was living in Saint-Maur, on the south-eastern rim of Paris. But there was always a chance Happy might be followed. So, on the evening of 9 January, he summoned him to the Café des Cascades at the Porte-Dorée. They sat in a corner of the room, facing each other over glasses of *pastis*. 'I've been chewing over our job,' Buisson said, 'and I know how we're going to operate.'

'How's that, Émile?'

'You'll know when the time comes. I wanted to see you to let you know that the stick-up is set for Wednesday, the eleventh. You be here, with the car and the other two boys, at seven o'clock in the morning. Sharp.'

'Christ!' sighed Happy, 'it's practically that now.'

35

Stepping out of the doorway of the building at No. 2, Buisson crossed the broad pavement of the place Édouard-Renard towards the black Peugeot which had just stopped in front of the Café des Cascades. He got into the back of the car.

'The others?'

'They're coming,' said Happy. 'They're guzzling coffee in the *bistrot*.'

Émile said nothing. Hidden in the car's shadows, he took out his Colt for a last check. Loubier and Labori finally arrived. Simon took his place next to Happy; his inscrutable friend sat with Buisson and didn't open his mouth.

The sun had not yet risen, and it was cold. Happy stepped on the gas, heading for Champigny.

At the same time, Roger Goumont, manager of the Banque régionale d'Escompte et de Dépôt, was eating his breakfast bread and butter and wondering whether to take his MAB 7.65 pistol with him; his head cashier, Félix Sentou, had failed to hear his alarm clock go off and now he jumped out of bed and ran for the shower.

Eight-ten a.m. It was still dark. The Peugeot nosed in to the curb near the entrance to the old bank building; three men got out and strolled along the avenue Jean-Jaurès. The car moved off again, turned into the rue Pierre-Renaudel and took up its station in front of the staff door, its motor purring.

As usual, Buisson was entirely calm. He was dimly aware that his heart was beating a little faster, but it was not from fear or nerves; every time he went into action he felt a kind of exultation, exactly as though he were about to mount a woman for the first time.

He stood motionless at the curb, like someone looking for a taxi or waiting for a friend to stop and pick him up. He even turned his back to the new bank building. But he was on the alert for any sound, any footstep coming from the building site. Seconds before, he had checked to make sure his henchmen were obeying their orders. Loubier was standing in front of the old building like an impatient customer waiting for the doors to open. Labori was stationed in the rue Pierre-Renaudel, a few steps from the entrance to the passageway the two bank employees would come through.

A yellowish light began to seep through the darkness, Buisson hoped the bank men would come out before it was full day. The darkness was a godsend. Not only would it make it impossible for any witnesses to identify them, but it would help them to get away faster if anything went wrong.

He barely repressed a start when, suddenly, he heard voices behind him saying something he couldn't catch. Hurried footsteps rang on the pavement, moving towards the street. Émile whirled around. Everything about him at that moment bespoke the lurking animal bunching itself to spring.

Silent on his rubber soles, he strode towards the two shadowy figures crossing the avenue. The first, the smaller of the two, was the cashier, according to Loubier's description; a satchel was dangling from his hand. The second was the manager, walking with his right hand in his overcoat pocket. Émile could imagine the fingers clutching the gun butt. 'Poor cunt,' he couldn't help thinking. And what, indeed, could the 'poor cunt' do against competition like this? Émile knew that by the time the manager got his pistol out, his guts would be a lead mine.

As he drew near the two men walking peacefully along, unmindful of the danger stalking them, Buisson reflected with a tight little smile that the manager wasn't the type to fire through his coat—his wife would give him hell for making a hole in it.

The two bank men were now alongside the old building; the doors were still locked, but there were lights on inside. Goumont didn't even glance at Loubier, who was irritably rattling the doorknob. Buisson, now only four yards behind them, heaved a sigh of relief. His one worry had now left him. Until then, he had been afraid the men might use the main entrance, in which case neither he nor his accomplices would have had time enough to act.

He had been following his victims for only a few seconds. It was growing rapidly lighter despite the cloudy sky. He quickened his pace, turning into the narrow passageway almost on the heels of the bank men, who were still unaware of his presence. The cashier stopped before the small staff door. The manager was just behind him. He was about to enter the courtyard when Émile's voice, terrible, like a knife in his ribs, stopped him.

'Don't move. Hands up.'

Goumont turned around. He cast an astounded look at the little black-eyed man with a gun in his hand. He had no idea what kind of man he was facing. With the stupidity of innocence, he moved his arm, trying to draw his gun. All he had time to do was to begin his move—just a hint of a movement, no more than a twitch. An explosion sent violent sound waves through the passageway. Goumont felt a powerful, nerve-stunning, burning sensation in his stomach. His eyes opened wide, as if to express surprise—'Heavens! No worse than that?' If that was what he really thought, the second bullet destroyed the illusion. There was an awful searing feeling, like red-hot pincers tearing at his stomach. Then, suffocated by the pain, unable to make a sound, Goumont sank down on the paving-stones, his body twisted up as though the foetal position could somehow compress the pain.

At the sound of the two shots, Labori raced into the passage to back Buisson up, but there was nothing for him to do. He had just entered it when he saw Émile fire at Sentou. With numbing speed, Émile grasped the satchel, ripping it from the cashier's hand even before the poor man could fall down. Still careful and methodical, Buisson peered at his victims to make sure they were incapacitated. Then he raced for the car. As he emerged from the passageway, he saw Labori. 'Get to the car,' he ordered. 'We're getting out.'

Loubier was already beside Happy, gun in hand, ready to open fire. Labori dived headlong into the back of the Peugeot, followed by Émile. Happy had the car leaping forward even before the door was closed.

The few passers-by who had happened to witness the hold-up had taken shelter in nearby driveways, throwing themselves flat on their faces. They saw the Peugeot spear through the rue Pierre-Renaudel and career into the rue Joséphine.

It was eight thirty-one a.m. In the car speeding towards Saint-Maur, Buisson opened the satchel and inspected the loot, gauging the amount. 'There's at least four million here,' he said in a satisfied voice. 'I'd have thought there'd be more, from the size of the bag.'

His estimate was remarkably accurate: the satchel contained 4,200,000 francs in cash, plus 100,000 in cheques.

36

Propped comfortably on two pillows, with Yvette's head on his shoulder, Émile reviewed the pile of newspapers the maid had brought him. A tray with the remains of their breakfast on it was on the bedside table.

While Yvette's fingers snaked under his striped pyjama top and professionally stroked his chest, sending little shivers of pleasure through him, he read the morning dailies' irritatingly inaccurate accounts of the robbery, the absurd testimony of the few available witnesses and the vague, cautious statements of Superintendent Friedrich and his aide, Inspector Nouzeilles, of the PP's 11th territorial squad.

'No problems?' asked Yvette, gluing herself even closer against him and slipping one leg between his.

'No problems,' Buisson said. 'Just in case, though, I am going to ask a friend to find us a new flop. And I'm staying away from the others for a while.'

'What a shame, Émile. We're so comfortable here . . .'

As he did every morning around ten o'clock, Buisson drew her to him. And, as always, she gave him his way. Her love for Émile had grown stronger since he told her the story of his childhood. They had been lying in bed, relaxed after making love. Impelled by the need for a deeper knowledge of this man who knew so well how to stir her, she had asked him in her naïve little voice:

'Darling, how come you don't have an honest, quiet life like other people?'

Émile had looked at her without answering. He lit a cigarette, still silent. He moved a few inches away from her and then, staring at the ceiling, he told her his story.

'My father, Auguste, was a lush, like most of the fathers in our neighbourhood in Digoin,' he recalled. 'He built bakers' ovens but he chucked all his earnings away in the *bistrots*. When he came home, pissed to the eyes, plastered like a farmhouse wall, he would eat without saying a word, then, suddenly, he would get up and start whacking at my mother, either to get the blood going in his arms or to crawl up on her.

'My mother, Reine, took the knocks without trying to defend herself. She just screamed like an animal and yelled for help. But nobody in the neighbourhood stuck his nose in—anyway, the same thing was going on in their houses. The only people who did step in were my older brother, Jean-Baptiste—we call him Screwball—and me. I was six years old. I would ram into my father's legs as hard as I could. He was so full of wine that I sometimes managed to knock him over. As soon as he hit the ground, Screwball would tap him on the nut, just a short-arm smack, with a big, heavy ladle, and knock him silly. We'd leave him lying there on the tile floor and we would all go to bed.

'We didn't win all the time, obviously. Sometimes my pa would lash out with a couple of slaps that sent us flying to the other end of the kitchen. Then he'd drag my mother off with him. That explains why she was pregnant ten times. Five of my brothers and sisters died at birth.

'I ought to point out that my mother gave birth all alone in the kitchen. When the pains came, she stretched herself out on the floor, pulled up her skirt, spread her legs and pushed, bellowing like a cow.

'Me and Screwball, we stayed there near her, waiting for the baby to come. We put water on to boil, cooled it and as soon as the brat came out, after Ma herself cut the cord, we washed it. We didn't give a damn whether it lived or not.

'Screwball was all for going and burying it in a certain field we already knew quite well, because it was there we'd buried the foetusses my mother used to dig out of herself with knitting needles, moaning a little as she did it. Screwball wasn't entirely wrong. There were already seven of us to feed—my parents and the five of us kids who had escaped the field.

'Since my old man never brought home a franc, Screwball and me took charge of that problem. As my older brother, he taught me to steal chickens and swipe things out of shops. As soon as we entered a shop, I took advantage of my smallness and slipped behind the counter while Screwball distracted the shopkeeper somehow or other—he never bought anything, naturally. When he left, the woman would return to the back of the shop. I would empty the cash drawer without making any noise. I was always very good with my hands. Then I beat it too.

'We had to steal to eat. My pig of a father insisted on it. I remember like it was yesterday when my mother prepared a present for my seventh birthday, a potato baked in the ashes. I adored them. She handed me the potato at the table. I reached out my hand. My pa knocked my wrist with his knife handle and said, 'When we're hungry, Mimile, we go out and look for our bread and butter.' And he ate my potato. I realized that night that I would have to make it all on my own.

'The old lady had already died, mad as a hatter, by the time Screwball was back from the war before everybody else—he deserted in 1917. I was delighted to see him and we decided that, from then on, him and me would always stick together to the death.'

It was not long after he moved out of the Hôtel Gallien that Buisson received news which, while it did not panic him, nevertheless upset him. He had just taken a room at the Auberge de la Grenouille in Saint-Vrain, run by Bolec's friend, old Georges, when he heard that Dezalleux, the carpenter who had unwittingly given Grosjean the idea for the Champigny hold-up, had been found hanging from a beam in his house. Like all the workmen employed in the construction of the new bank building and all the bank staff as well, Dezalleux had been questioned repeatedly by the police. His nerve had cracked. He was not long in realizing that it was his gabbing that had given Grosjean the idea for the crime. Remorse for his carelessness, fear of prison, shame at his dishonour and a surfeit of aperitifs led him to suicide.

Buisson didn't kid himself. He knew the police would now question everybody who knew Dezalleux and that, sooner or later, they would get to Grosjean. It was just a matter of time, but the danger was there, growing, inevitable.

If he could have afforded it, Émile would have left with Yvette for the South of France. From there they could have slipped into Italy, a country rich in cruise ports; from there you could sail for anywhere. But Émile's means no longer allowed him to wander around playing the tourist. Of the round million the Champigny caper had netted him, there was 200,000 left at most. He blamed the enormous hole in his reserves on a moment of tenderness for which he had been kicking himself, with appropriate oaths, ever since.

'How could I have been such an arsehole?' he raged, pacing his room. 'Jesus I was an arsehole!'

'Calm down, darling,' said Yvette, frightened by his fury. 'A good deed is always rewarded.'

But it was true that Buisson had good cause to repent his

generosity. It all happened a few days after the Champigny
hold-up. Émile and Yvette were returning from an outing in the
country when they heard shouts, racking sobs and the sound of
pleading coming from a house near the inn. Curious, they stopped
before the wooden fence of the tiny garden fronting the house.
They saw two women come out of the house, cross the garden
and walk towards them. One, elderly and built like a farm horse,
was scowling; the other, a young woman whose face was wet
with tears, sniffled hopelessly, blotting her nose and eyes with her
handkerchief. 'Please . . .' she kept saying, 'I beg you . . . please . . .'

'What's going on?' Émile asked, stepping towards them.

The older woman told him in a scornful, vinegary voice.
'What's happening,' she shrilled, 'is that when you bring children
into the world and you give them out to nurse, you have to pay
for their keep. When you open your thighs for fun, you have to
open your purse later on and feed the fruit of your sin. Madame'
—she pointed her finger at the young woman—'gave me her son
to bring up. But she hasn't paid me for five months. So I say I'm
fed up and I'm throwing her and her brat out.'

What happened then was simply ludicrous. Yvette had been
upset by the young mother's distress; she tightened her grasp on
Émile's arm and he could see tears in her eyes. So, moved by the
drama before him, shaken by that gust of generosity which he
had been regretting ever since, he put his hand in his pocket and
pulled out a roll of bills—his share of the loot, which he always
carried with him. Drunk with kindness, he gave the nurse 500,000
francs, which covered the arrears and two more years of care.
Before the mother could thank him, he turned on his heel and
walked away.

Buisson had been broke since that day. What with the money
he bestowed on the wet nurse, the cash he gave to his sister and
his own bed and board, which came to 100,000 francs a month,
he was on the brink of ruin.

'What I need,' he told Yvette as she gazed confidently at him,
'is another caper.'

That baby's bottles were to cost a man's life. The new job
Buisson needed was proposed to him by Henri Bolec. Through
the Hunchback, he arranged a meeting with Buisson at the Café
des Cascades.

'It's an easy job, Émile,' he said. 'A pal of mine told me that the daily receipts of the Versailles tram system are all collected by a cashier who then takes them to the company's office at thirteen rue Colbert every evening.'

'Great! You sure of that?'

'Positive, Émile. I did some nosing around; the carrier, whose name is Bourven, arrives at the office every evening around seven-thirty. I even asked a buddy to lend us a hand—little Grigot. He'll go along with us; he needs to square some of his track debts.'

On 17 February 1950, having inspected the set-up several times, Buisson set off for Versailles. Bolec was at the wheel of a stolen Simca. Buisson and Grigot, both armed, waited a few yards from the entrance to the tram company's head office.

The carrier's car arrived at seven-thirty. Unsuspecting, Bourven got out, carrying his satchel, and walked towards an office clerk advancing to meet him. They were no more than a few yards apart when Grigot, eager to impress Buisson, leaped forward ahead of his boss. Waving his 7.65 automatic, he grabbed the bag away from Bourven, shouting, 'That's mine,' and sent a bullet ripping into the man's right side.

Despite his wound and the thick ooze of blood from it, the cashier tried to run after Grigot, but, staggering and in pain, he collapsed in the street as the bandits' car pulled away.

Émile was annoyed to find that the satchel contained only 154,900 francs. Two days later, the trolley company's cashier, his liver burst by the bullet, died in Versailles Hospital.

37

The Brasserie du Sentier, on the boulevard Bonne-Nouvelle, is a large café for small bourgeois and big textile merchants. Its owner is a massive woman with a thick, crimson nose who surveys the peaceful activity of her establishment through eyes as narrow as buttonholes. She is occasionally roused from her lethargy; at such moments you can hear her cavernous voice harassing her two waiters, a little fat man and a tall thin one, neither of whom takes any notice of her.

The wall at the far end of the room has an odd, curved recess in it. This is the favourite niche of lovers, who, removed from the public stare, find compensation for their housing problems in a variety of clandestine manoeuvres.

This was the corner Buisson chose for his meeting with the Hunchback. His unofficial brother-in-law had phoned Saint-Vrain that morning, an action justifiable only by extremely grave happenings, to tell him he had to see him as soon as possible. 'All hell's broken loose,' he'd observed before hanging up.

They had selected this particular café because it was close to the Hunchback's lair and because it was always crowded.

'Things are real bad, Émile.'

'What things?'

'The cops are on the warpath. They've taken in Happy and Pinel and only a while ago grabbed Bolec. They keep taking Grosjean in for questioning, but he's keeping his mouth shut for the moment.'

'I don't give a damn about Pinel—I don't know him,' Buisson murmured, 'but Happy and Bolec, that's rough. Do you know how the cops got to them?'

'More or less. I heard about it from Grosjean. As usual, it all boils down to stupidity. Some wild man, I don't know who, tipped the police that there were stolen cars tucked away in Happy's sheds in Saint-Mandé. The flatties had no proof, so they watched the place.

'Pinel brought in a hot car one day. The cops took the number and checked; the wagon belonged to a medic who had complained about it when it was pinched. When Pinel went back the next day they jumped him and hauled him away. The moron admitted that

Happy owned the sheds and that he supplied hot cars for stick-ups. So they kept on watching. When Happy showed up, they put the arm on him too.'

'Did he talk?'

'Like a dictaphone. He admitted being in on the Champigny job; the son of a bitch squealed on you as well as Bolec.'

'Are you sure?'

'I'm telling you. He even told them that you'd got matey with him after the bank heist and bragged about having knocked off the two carriers.'

Buisson scratched his ear. 'How about the others?'

'Labori has left the *bistrot* in the passage Saint-Martin and is hiding out with a skirt in Montmartre. Loubier skipped to Auvergne, where his wife's family lives. He came back a few days ago and Orsetti found him a flop with some mate of his in the suburbs. As you can see, it's leaking all over. What do you think you'll do, Émile?'

Buisson, worried, thought about it for a long moment before replying. Then he drained his glass and rose. 'I'm going to call Yvette,' he said. 'I want her to pack our stuff and meet me in Paris. The Saint-Vrain hideout isn't safe any more. Hunchback, old pal, with all these so-called hard men shooting their mouths off the minute the police frown at them, the underworld these days is just a collection of clowns.'

Buisson moved to the cash desk at his usual unflurried pace, asked for a telephone token and shut himself into the phone booth. He was back two minutes later. But his pallor and the furious light in his eyes told the Hunchback that something else had gone wrong. Buisson sat down beside him, ordered two cognacs and waited to speak until they were served.

'There's no answer at the inn,' he muttered, taking a gulp of brandy. 'It went faster than I thought.' He gulped down the rest of his drink. He was still unflustered and lucid; he could feel the police vice closing on him, but he was not going to let it crush him without a fight.

'Tomorrow, here, same time,' he ordered. 'Bring me a gun and a grenade. See you, Hunchback.'

'Where are you going, Émile?'

'Never mind. See you tomorrow.'

38

On 3 August 1949, near Cannes, four bandits relieved the Begum Aga Khan of 200 million francs worth of jewellery, including the famous Marquise, a diamond as big as a robin's egg, and every police unit in France was shaken with violent convulsions.

The Marseilles police just couldn't cope; Lloyds had offered a huge reward, bringing informers swarming out of the woodwork, and setting police against police. The Sûreté's Director-General, who was breeding ulcers because of what he considered his men's incompetence, took retaliatory measures. Albert Biget was brought down from the North to replace the Southerner, Valantin, at the head of the PJ; Chief Superintendent Spotti, a friend of the big boss, was detached from the Bordeaux office and placed over Fatso, who until then had functioned as chief of section. My group was also swept up in the tide. It was dismantled, reorganized and rebaptized the GRB, which in plain language means: 'Group for the Repression of Banditry.' I stayed on the squad with Fatso, of course, but I was henceforth teamed with a lusty, good-natured cluck of a super named Charles Gillard, plus an emaciated fellow, Maurice Hours, who came from Nîmes and was exasperated by the Parisien accent. Hidoine and Poiret were shunted off to other duties.

Fatso had become invisible. He brooded in his office, waiting for Spotti to decide to send for him for a briefing on pending cases. Communication in this cold war was by memos only. The old fifth-floor auction gallery had been transformed into a cathedral where shadowy civil servants flitted silently from office to office. Everybody kept watch on everybody else. The only disturbing sound was the bullfrog plaint of Poiret making his resentment at his transfer echo down the line of sullenly closed doors. 'This place gives me the creeps,' he boomed. 'If this keeps up, I'm chucking it in and joining the traffic cops.'

Luckily, there was still Victor's. When we met at the Deux Marches, Fatso and I could compare notes without worrying about being overheard by some big-eared chatterbox. One evening in January, Fatso let his hair down. 'What's going to become of us, Borniche?' he sighed, clutching his glass of *pastis*. 'My super's stripe is out of sight as long as Spotti is there. Isn't there anything we could try . . . ?'

'Like what, chief?'

'How do I know? Don't you have any cases kicking around, something that would make a big noise?'

'Buisson?'

'Ugh! Buisson,' he said, a weary shrug making visible the disillusionment in his voice. 'I've given up on him. We're just too unlucky, my boy. We muffed our chance at Bry-sur-Marne. As for the new crew, Gillard is great at drawing up reports, but he doesn't like to ferret; Hours is a first-rate police officer, but he's fresh from the South and doesn't know a soul in Paris. Me? I'm nailed to my desk; all I have to do is leave it for one minute and I'll either find I've been saddled with some foul-up or that Spotti has horned in on a juicy case. This isn't the time for me to go gallivanting around.'

'How about Mathieu, chief?'

'Mathieu who?'

'Mathieu the Nantais. Robillard, if you prefer. Suppose we plugged him into the circuit.'

The *pastis* bottle in his hand, a smiling Victor Marchetti came up to us. 'My round, kiddies,' he announced cheerfully. 'Everything okay?'

He poured for both of us, his left hand sliding a jug of water towards us.

'Just fine,' I said, pouring water drop by drop into Fatso's glass —he didn't like his *pastis* too wet. 'We were just talking about Orsetti. What's become of him? We never see him around any more. He's not ill, is he?'

Victor cleared his throat and wagged his head rapidly, which made his forelock bounce. 'I don't think so,' he said. 'It's been quite a while since the boy phoned me. I don't know why not. Excuse me, I have to go and finish my game.'

He smiled again, but I thought the smile seemed forced this time. He walked slowly back to a table where two reporters were rolling dice. Fatso had also noticed the Corsican's discomfiture.

'You see that?' he said. 'He doesn't seem to like being asked about Jeannot. I wonder what goes there . . . So, you want to hook Robillard into the circuit?'

'Yes, but with us, not against us.'

'How?'

I unfolded the plan I had been mulling over for the past few days.

The idea had come to me just like that, out of the blue, while I was standing in my kitchen with an apron around my middle drying the dishes Marlyse handed me. As I dabbed absently at them with my teacloth, I thought about Buisson, whose cronies had a way of disappearing over the years; they either died violently, faded under intense heat from the police or were retired from circulation by a judge.

Among his old henchmen, only one, Francis Caillaud, seemed to me to be worthy of interest. Since Émile's escape, Caillaud had been his most faithful lieutenant. He had joined in his boss's robberies, shared his hideouts. He was with Buisson at the Auberge d'Arbois, at the botanical gardens, in Vigneux, in Boulogne. He had fought the police savagely to give Émile a chance to escape. Overpowered, beaten, he had refused to talk. He had truly acted the faithful aide, and Émile must have appreciated his loyalty. For a while, Dekker had occupied my thoughts. But his confession during the Russac investigation could only work against him. The more I thought about it, the more convinced I became that Caillaud was the cornerstone of this operation. I was sure he was still pally with Buisson. Some quiet nosing around at the Santé prison had disclosed that he regularly received lavish food packages from an anonymous donor.

'What are you thinking about, dear?' Marlyse had asked me.

'About Caillaud. You know, if I could have myself put inside and share a cell with Caillaud for a month or two, long enough to win his confidence, I'm sure I could make him talk, so that sooner or later he would give me Buisson's hideout.'

Marlyse raised her eyes to heaven. 'Don't talk nonsense, Roger,' she advised very calmly, as though she were humouring a madman. 'Can you honestly see yourself fooling Caillaud in his cell? What you need is a criminal, a veteran criminal who knows the gang well and who agrees to work for you.'

Marlyse often comes to my rescue at difficult moments. I put down the plate I was manhandling and looked into her eyes. 'You're right,' I exclaimed in a tone of wonder. 'And I know just the guy I need. Robillard. What do you think?'

'I think you'd need a pretty good hold on him.'

'Robillard is Girier's friend. I can have him sent up for

associating with undesirable persons in the French Cartridge
Works case. The Begum's jewels made me forget all about him.
He just came out of stir. Maybe he wouldn't like the idea of
going right back in.'

'Is that all you have on him?'

'No. Poiret told me—he surprises me a little more every day,
that boy—that he is wanted by the Rouen police for a heist while
masquerading as a cop in Étretat. Poiret was on night duty when
he got the message and he passed it on to me. So I've got all I
need for a pretty good hold on Mathieu, as you put it. And I can
do even better than that. The directors of the Banque régionale
d'Escompte et de Dépôt have just announced publicly that they
are offering a reward of one million francs to anyone providing
information leading to the arrest of the Champigny hold-up men.
Since there are nine chances out of ten that the little man with
dark eyes who fired at the carriers was Buisson, Robillard might
be tempted. How does that sound to you?'

When I explained my idea to Fatso at the Deux Marches, he
listened thoughtfully, analysing my plan as I laid it out.

'Your idea isn't bad, Borniche,' he said. 'And if the Maison
threw in another 500,000 francs in reward money, that might be
enough to make up his mind. We'll talk some more about it
tomorrow.'

Once more, we left the Deux Marches feeling confident of the
future, exactly as we had two years earlier when I had hoped to
catch Buisson in his rue Bichat hideout.

The next day, I arrived at the office to learn that Spotti, Fatso
and Gillard were in Marseilles, where our people had finally
arrested three of the men who had burgled the Begum. I was
disappointed; I would have liked to go along. But the joyrides
were for the brass, not for humble slaves like me. Two days later,
Spotti in person called me from the Bishop's palace in Marseilles.

'Borniche,' he said, 'we still don't have the fourth man. He's
in Paris and we want him—now!'

Orders are orders; I arrested the fourth man and Hours took
him down to Marseilles. He had hardly arrived before Spotti
called me again, from police headquarters this time. 'Borniche,'
he said, 'we don't have the informer on the job. We want him—
now!'

So I went looking for the new mystery man, in company with

Berilley, an inspector from another group. We learned from the informer's wife that he was in Alsace. The Strasbourg police picked him up and shipped him off to Marseilles.

Two days later, while the newspapers celebrated the prowess of the police, Fatso's voice vibrated through the telephone receiver. 'Borniche,' he humphed, 'you haven't forgotten Mathieu, I trust?'

No, I hadn't forgotten him. In fact, I thought about very little else. I had found his hideout in Joinville-le-Pont, and had learned that his wife was seriously ill. Lying in wait near the apartment building they lived in, I waylaid the doctor treating her:

'Police, Doctor. Is it serious?'

'Leukaemia.'

The medic had violated professional secrecy, but that was all right with me. He had put another ace in my hand.

Unfortunately, the business of the Begum's baubles popped up again. The Marseilles police had made an almost miraculous discovery: a packet of jewels, laid by an unknown hand at the foot of a tree in the very courtyard of the bishop's palace. It did not, however, contain the Marquise, which was worth over sixty million all by itself. The insurance people were fretting. So Fatso turned to me.

'The Marquise is still missing, Borniche,' he cooed.

'What do you want me to do about it?'

'Find it!' Fatso, when he's feeling peremptory, can be hard on the hearing.

So I found the Marquise, on 7 March. The press was called in to the rue des Saussaies and Fatso was beside himself; this was his revenge on Spotti.

'And now for Buisson,' he ordered.

I had Mathieu Robillard in my office the very next day.

39

With his armour of affability and his nice manners, the Nantais could have moved easily in any circle. He is—I have to admit it—a charmer, and I felt a twinge of jealousy in his presence in spite of myself.

Prison had not affected his lordly air. He looked just as I had seen him eight months before at the Favart, blond, blue-eyed, heavily muscled.

He was on the defensive when he walked into my office. He searched my face carefully, probably wondering where he had seen me before. He waited calmly, but my first question threw him off guard.

'Well, Mathieu, tell me: the BMW—is it a good car?'

Robillard stared at me in surprise. Two surly police officers had picked him up that morning, ransacked his rooms, hustled him to the rue des Saussaies and tossed him into a cell for three hours after removing his belt, tie and shoelaces. And here I was, talking not about capers, but about cars. Something must have gone haywire in my thinkbox, that was for sure.

I stood up, walked round to the other side of the table and sat straddling a chair near him.

'However you can be sure that I didn't bring you down here just to chat about cars, Mathieu,' I said, 'although I must say yours was running like a dream when it picked up your friend Girier at Pont-l'Évêque.' He was breathing faster now. 'Nor do I wish to think of the ticket you ought to have picked up getting away from the Favart, the Terminus at the porte de Vincennes or the Auberge des Oiseaux in Bry-sur-Marne. You're a hot pilot; I know, I was there. Not to mention your skill at the wheel in the police impersonation deal in Étretat; my colleagues in Rouen, who are in charge of the case, have already told me enough about the way you take curves on two wheels. No, I'm not interested in demonstrating to you that the police are not as stupid as they seem to be. What I want to do is arrest Émile Buisson. And I think that between us, if we come to a proper understanding, we can do it.'

Robillard listened to all this without showing a flicker of

reaction. Only the jumping of his Adam's apple told me that my needling had hit home.

'I don't see what you're getting at,' he said finally. 'I don't know Buisson. I've never heard of him, so I really don't see . . .'

I took a cigarette out of my pocket and lit it, drawing easily on it at first and puffing out bluish clouds which rose in spirals towards the ceiling. 'You're being stupid, Mathieu!' I told him.

'Word of honour, Inspector,' he said, still off balance.

'Don't make me laugh with your word of honour. A man's word means what it says, you know, and if you are going to drag yours through every mud puddle you come across, why, I'm going to end up not believing you. So! You were saying that you don't know Buisson?'

Robillard nodded his head. 'So naturally,' I went on, 'you didn't work with him planning the stick-up of the Crédit Lyonnais truck.' He looked at me in amazement and I hid my satisfaction at having scored another point. 'Stop playing games with me, Mathieu. I've got enough on you to get you a nice, long lease on a cell. Everything I've told you is solid, all wrapped up, with no leaks. I haven't used it against you yet because I've had more important things to worry about. Now I've got to have Buisson. That's flat. Take it or leave it.'

I stood up and picked Robillard's file up off the table. I pretended to look through it for a while. Then I looked up.

'So?'

'So nothing. I don't know Buisson, I don't know where he's holed up and even if I did know, I wouldn't turn him in. I'm not an informer.'

'Just now,' I said, 'I listed in passing the charges hanging over you. What's more, I have an arrest warrant for the Étretat job. So I can put you inside as of now.'

'If that's the way you want it, Inspector,' replied Robillard, who had regained his self-control. 'Your threats don't impress me. It may not be all that jolly inside, but I know my way around. A good lawyer can always get you out. And in any case I would rather go back there than become a turd. I'll swallow a lot in life, I'll forgive a lot of faults but not a big mouth. I'm a thief, Monsieur Borniche, not a killer. But if somebody ratted on me, I think I'd strangle him with my bare hands with ferocious pleasure.'

I heard Robillard through. And I knew his profession of faith was sincere. Nevertheless, he had to work for me. Whatever the cost. Even at the cost of making me hate myself.

'All right,' I said quietly, 'I won't insist, Mathieu. I know about the famous law of silence, although I must say that in the circles you travel in there is a lot of blabbing and not much respect for that law any more than any other.'

As I played with a coin, making it disappear and reappear in my fingers, I added, softly and without looking at him:

'Mathieu, you're wrong to hold out this way. Because you're forgetting something.'

'Oh? What's that?'

'Something important, Mathieu, something very important to you.'

His grin was mocking. 'Really, Inspector? I don't see what it could be.'

This was the moment, and I knew it, when I had to behave like a son of a bitch. This was the moment to sock him hard in the emotions, to wipe that complacent smile off his face, to act like a shit, using the safety of society as my alibi.

'Your wife, Mathieu.'

'What about my wife?' he asked, frowning.

'Your wife. If I put you in stir, you'll never see her again. I know she's ill, very ill. You stand to get six years, with no remission. Do you think she'll still be there, alive, when you get out? Waiting for you?'

I raised my head. My eyes held his. And the hatred, the contempt I saw for me in his face made me squirm in my skin.

'It's disgusting, what you're doing.'

Robillard's voice was harsh. His fists were clenched. I could feel the tension in him; he was ready to spring at me. But he hung on to himself. He knew I'd told him the truth. He was torn between his revulsion at having to work for the police and his love for the woman whose days were numbered unless a miracle saved her. I don't rate any credit for following the way his mind worked. I had had enough practice in criminal psychology. He and I belonged to two worlds which had been facing each other down through the ages, fighting an unceasing war—two worlds separated by their laws, their morality, their ruses and their perils.

I looked at Robillard. His face was twisted with rage and anguish. I fired the *coup de grâce*:

'Remember that, when you're in stir, she'll be alone, at a time when your presence will be more important to her than ever before. Remember that she won't be able to help you, or visit you. Remember . . .'

'That's enough!'

Robillard's voice was strident. Once more, our eyes met, and this time I knew I had won. His struggle to maintain his honour was over.

'What do you want?' he asked me.

'I told you: Buisson. For you, it will mean freedom, to begin with, and absolution for your sins; the warrant issued by the magistrate in Étretat will be locked in my drawer until we can intercede with him. Then there's the money. The Champigny bank is offering a reward of one million for the arrest of the robbers. The money will go into your pocket. In addition, the Maison will give you five hundred thousand for your co-operation. A million and a half altogether—that will pay for a lot of first-rate doctoring for your wife. That's worth the effort, no?'

He dropped his eyes, said nothing.

'Well,' I asked in my most honeyed tones, 'is it yes or no?'

'It's yes,' he sighed.

I put on my understanding voice: 'You see? I knew we'd wind up understanding each other, you and I.'

'Listen,' he said, looking me straight in the eye, 'spare me your comments and get to what I have to do.'

'Simple. You're going inside.'

'What?' he shouted, appalled.

'Don't get excited and let me explain: I'm going to have you locked up in the Santé, where you will arrange to become chummy with a guy named Francis Caillaud. You know him?'

'Absolutely not.'

'Well, you'll meet him. You'll become his pal, his confidant. I know that Caillaud, even though he's in stir, knows how to reach Buisson. You have to find out how. As soon as you have what we need, I'll spring you. Okay?'

The Nantais, his shoulders drooping, got up and walked out of my office without answering. I have never felt so disgusted with myself.

Everything was ready. The next day, his bundle of spare clothes in his hand, Mathieu Robillard entered the Santé, charged with harbouring fugitives from the law in the French Cartridge Works hold-up.

I had let the governor in on the scheme, after getting the approval of the examining magistrate and the prosecutor's office. It was worth bending a few rules to lay hands on Buisson. I left Mathieu at the registration office. He walked through the gate without turning around, and I watched him and his guard disappear into the strict-surveillance section. Now there was nothing for me to do but hope the Nantais knew how to act his part.

40

Caillaud immediately spotted the newcomer during the exercise period. Robillard was at the tail-end of the squad, walking in circles some ten yards behind him. When they came abreast of each other (each in his own circle), Caillaud whistled softly at him. The guard pretended not to hear him. Mathieu heard him though. He snatched the cigarette Caillaud threw him out of the air, thanked him with a slight nod and slipped the Gauloise into his jacket pocket. Then he went back to walking his circle.

It wasn't until he got back to his cell that Mathieu shook the tobacco out of the cigarette and read the message inside: 'I been told about you. Get behind me tomorrow.'

The next day, Mathieu took advantage of a brief mix-up of the prisoners to slip deftly into line behind Caillaud. As soon as they began walking, Francis whispered, 'Any news of the little guy?'

The 'little guy' was Buisson. Robillard played dumb.

'I don't know any little guys.'

Caillaud was so surprised he almost missed his step.

'Émile,' he hissed.

'Don't know any Émile,' Robillard insisted stubbornly.

'Shit! You know Buisson, don't you?'

'I don't know Buisson,' Robillard declared firmly. 'Just what the hell do you want?'

Francis kept walking. He secretly approved of Mathieu's attitude, but he kept probing. 'It's just that—I would have liked word of him. I hear some friends of his, Bolec, Happy, got pulled in . . .'

'So ask them and get off my back,' Mathieu told him sharply.

He was satisfied with his performance. His behaviour had been totally natural. Francis dropped the subject for the moment. The Nantais was not talkative and the way he looked at you discouraged any notion of crossing him. Even in stir.

When the exercise period ended, Mathieu went back to his cell. He had been in prison for two weeks now, and he was getting impatient. He had left only once, for a hearing at which his indictment was read out to him. Since then, nothing. His anxiety over his wife, about whether she could hold out, was growing daily. Then a key turned in the lock. 'Visitor,' the guard told him.

Mathieu's head snapped up in surprise. He wasn't expecting any visitors. Shuffling behind the warden, he went across the central hall and into the lawyers' room. Two men in raincoats, one of them a big man with a head like a doll's, the other with a deeply lined face under a crown of grey hair, were waiting for him. They had come about the Étretat caper. Mathieu angrily walked into the room ahead of them, while the guard began pacing the corridor outside.

Mathieu didn't understand. What about the promises they'd made him? If he claimed the Sûreté's protection, the coppers would certainly go easy on him; the Étretat business would be closed. But he would be branded as an informer. If he kept his mouth shut, he would be prosecuted and transferred to Normandy. What the hell was he to do?

'I'm not saying anything without my lawyer here,' he growled, playing for time.

'What did you say?' asked the big cop, frowning.

'I said I want my lawyer here before I say anything.'

'Look, mate, are you ill or something?'

'There's nothing wrong with me. I've just got nothing to say to you. Full stop.'

'I'll give you full stop, right in the mouth, you little turd,' thundered the big man, his hand already raised to strike.

Robillard leaped back. 'What did you say?'

'You heard me, turd,' the giant repeated, advancing on him, 'I'm going to flush you down where you belong if you don't start talking.'

The insult hit Mathieu in the pit of his stomach. He went white. Furious, he overturned the table on which the detectives had placed their typewriter. Grabbing a chair and waving it like a club, he defied his tormentors.

'Just try it, you great pig, and see what happens . . .'

The warder had been watching. He hastily unlocked the door while Mathieu, foaming at the mouth, continued to scream insults. 'Turd yourself. You cunt . . .' And, still foaming with rage, he was led back to his cell.

He wasn't the only one who was foaming. Poiret was just as livid when he recounted the episode to me the next day. I couldn't help laughing. 'So he called you a cunt, did he? And you an ex-wrestling champion!'

'Yes, me!' he said, rolling his enormous eyes and shaking his macelike fists. 'If I hadn't been on duty, I can tell you I'd have smashed your Mathieu's head in for him! I cracked the glass on my watch picking up the papers he knocked over. He was lucky they took him away in time.'

That afternoon, a guard on either side of him, the Nantais appeared before the governor.

'Playing the hard man, eh, Robillard?' he muttered without looking up. 'Two weeks in solitary.'

As he walked down to his solitary cell, his blanket under his arm, Robillard reflected that the punishment was heavy for what he'd done. Word of his rebellion had flashed around the strict-surveillance unit, winning the inmates' unanimous approval.

When he had served his two weeks, Mathieu left his hole to learn that, at the governor's order, he had been moved to another cell. The new one, with a sign reading 'Dangerous' on the door, was next to Caillaud's.

The two men communicated via the heating pipe. It was not an ideal channel, but it was good enough to enable them to get to know each other better and, finally, to become friends. They spoke about their wives, but never about Émile. Mathieu prudently waited for Francis to open up; he knew he had won his confidence.

Twenty days went by. The assistant governor kept me informed of Robillard's conduct: he was becoming more and more defiant of the guards, he terrorized the prisoners, even threatened to go on a hunger strike if the judge didn't hurry up and decide his case. Only his next-door neighbour, Caillaud, seemed to have any influence on him. So the assistant governor had sent for Francis.

'Caillaud,' he said, 'from what I've been told, you seem to get on pretty well with Robillard.'

'Me, sir?' Caillaud said, turning his cap in his hands.

'Yes, you. I'm not blaming you, understand. What I want to know is: do you think Robillard would be less belligerent if I put him in your cell?'

'I don't know, sir.'

'Well, we'll give it a try, Caillaud, and if it doesn't work out, you let me know.'

'Yes, sir.'

The very next day, Robillard was installed in Caillaud's cell. It was more than he had hoped for.

41

A new trail suddenly appeared.

While I was interviewing the examining magistrate, who also filled me in on Robillard's activities, there was a knock at the door. It was my brother officer Sol, of the First Mobile Brigade, my first service unit. He had come to ask permission to remove Bolec from prison for questioning. We were both pleased to see each other again, and we went down to the Brasserie du Palais to celebrate the reunion. It was there that I learned that Bolec, the Breton, had already been gone over several times and was on the point of giving Sol's boss, Superintendent Denis, some valuable information on Buisson's possible hideouts.

'He's got hot nuts for his woman, the Breton has,' Sol told me, grinning. 'So we let him see her. It's touching. We promised him that if he helps us nab Buisson we'll let him climb her.'

I knew Superintendent Denis well—I had worked with him in the First Brigade—and I was acquainted with his professional ability, his courtesy and his humanity. He was dangerous competition. We worked for the same firm, but I was going to have to put a spoke in his wheel, too. I would have preferred doing it to some other cop.

Fatso was alarmed when I told him what I'd learned. Here we were, close to the end again, and once again, a new team had come along and dynamited our plans.

'As though we didn't have trouble enough with the PP,' he grumbled. 'Listen, Borniche, you have got to get Bolec out of there and arrange for him to go to bed with his wife. And right away!'

I gaped at him, stunned, but Fatso was serious.

'Where do you want him to do it, chief? In the office?'

'If that's the way you want it, Borniche. Or anywhere else you choose. I don't give a damn.'

Sure, he didn't give a damn. His neck wasn't on the block. I gave it some thought. Not the office—impossible. Not a hotel, either—Bolec might escape. So where? At his place in Clamart, in the conjugal bedroom, where else? I could see to security.

There isn't anything you don't get to do in this racket. Even pimping.

When I showed up at the Palace of Justice the next day to request my permit, the magistrate's eyes twinkled behind his gold-rimmed glasses.

'He must be a gold-mine, this Bolec. You're all eager to get at him.'

I left him with his illusions. Backed up by Maurice Hours and Poiret, whom I had requested as reinforcement, we all trooped out to Clamart.

The Bolecs lived in a three-storey house on the allée des Matrets. His wife, Mireille, a tall, twenty-eight-year-old Breton woman with blond hair and green eyes, welcomed us awkwardly and broke into tears when she saw her husband handcuffed to Poiret.

To give them a chance to relax with each other, we pretended to search the house. This didn't take us long—the PP had been there before us. I checked the place carefully. The bedroom on the second floor wouldn't do as a love nest; the window was too close to the tin roof of a garage. The one above it, on the other hand, had only a small aperture which could easily be watched from the landing window. It seemed a dandy place to me, even if there wasn't any bed in it. Bolec was in front of me, his one good eye devouring his wife.

'Uncuff him,' I told Poiret.

The great bear clawed about in his pocket for the key. Not there. He sighed and kept searching, finally locating it on his key ring. He fumbled with the lock and the bracelets popped open.

'Kiss her,' I told Bolec, 'I'll give you ten minutes. And no tricks. We're watching the window.'

I pushed Bolec and his wife into the room, shut the door and took up my station with Poiret on the landing. Two hours later I took Bolec back to the prison. I hadn't asked him anything, but, in the registration office, he took me aside.

'Thanks, Inspector,' he said. 'You're all right. I'll give you a tip: Buisson is at Mme Rousseau's, 168 quai Louis-Blériot in Paris. I took him there myself on 30 March. Be careful—he's got a grenade so he can blow himself up along with the cop who traps him.'

Late that afternoon, Fatso and I were on the quai Louis-Blériot, a stone's throw from the Auteuil viaduct.

'I should have put on overalls,' I told Fatso. 'They'd have made me practically invisible round here.'

Fatso didn't say anything. I knew he was nervous, probably impatient to get up close to Buisson. We split up and walked past the front of the building in opposite directions, exchanging eye signals as we went by. We met under the viaduct to compare notes. I expected him to say he hadn't seen any more than I had, which was nothing at all. But he had other things on his mind.

'You see, Borniche, I'm really worried about bungling this Buisson thing. I've known since yesterday that I'm on the promotion list.'

'Congratulations, chief. That must be good news.'

'If you like. I'm number eight. There are only seven openings.'

'Oh.'

'The Director-General did it deliberately, of course. He gave priority to the ones who helped him with his clean-up operation.'

'You think so, chief?'

'I know so. I'd have done better to go into politics. It's scandalous.'

I nodded agreement. But I was really thinking that I was not on the promotion list and probably never would be unless I made a sensational catch. Fatso had never hidden that from me; for the past three years, he had been dangling two carrots before me: 'If you arrest Buisson . . .'; 'If you arrest Girier . . .' True, up to that point, Buisson had eluded me. But my promotion list wasn't to be posted until June, and by that time . . .

The concierge interviewed me through her peephole. She took me for a salesman, and salesmen and pedlars were banned from the building. It said so in the entrance, on a sign just above the Police Emergency number, probably placed there to impress on the obstinate that the sign meant business. Fatso waited for me on the pavement. I showed her my badge. Yes, the concierge knew Mme Rousseau well, she also knew her nice boarder, a small man with big black eyes, who dressed well, wore a trilby and often carried a black briefcase. 'He's a notary,' she whispered. 'He sometimes has to go out of town on business. He left here the day before yesterday. He must have had an accident, because the police came not long afterwards.'

The police!

As I went up in the lift, I was thinking that Bolec must have given the same information to the competition. He must have been screwing like a jackrabbit.

Mme Rousseau was alone when I rang her doorbell. Tiny, weasel-faced and white-haired, she told me Monsieur Lucien had lodged with her for two weeks. He had come to her through an ad she'd placed in the paper because her flat was too big for a lone woman. She had known nothing of the little man's history until some policemen from the First Brigade came to see her and found a hand grenade in his wardrobe closet. There had been no word since then. But he had been honourable, Monsieur Lucien —he had left the rent money in an envelope before he left.

I left the building both disappointed and pleased. Disappointed that Buisson had disappeared again, pleased because Bolec's tip was no help to our rivals either. The only possible trail left was the one that led through Robillard.

And no one else knew about that but me.

42

'God almighty, what the hell is he doing?'

We were packed into a staff Citroën behind Montuire, the group's new driver. And Fatso could no longer contain his impatience. It was nine p.m. We had already been waiting for two hours at the corner of the rue de la Santé and the rue Jean-Dolent. The judge had told us Robillard would be getting out this evening. A number of prisoners had already come out, one at a time. Some were met by parents or friends; others headed straight for the café across the street, À la Bonne Santé. Robillard was supposed to have been sprung at seven o'clock, but there was still no sign of him.

'I hope to God they haven't stuck him with another confinement order,' Fatso moaned. 'That's all we need.'

I wasn't any more confident than he was. Only Montuire remained phlegmatic, immune to our anxiety. Another half-hour went by. I was burning up cigarettes as though they were SOS flares.

Fatso's exclamation made even Montuire jump. There was Robillard on the prison doorstep, his bundle in his hand, lost in his big rumpled suit and hesitating about which way to walk. Finally he ambled towards our car. As he approached, I lowered the window.

'Psst!'

Robillard slowed down. He recognized me, turned round, looked carefully in every direction, then slipped into the front seat. Montuire had the car moving by the time the door closed.

'Well?'

The question came from Fatso, even before he had shaken hands with Robillard. I introduced them. The car purred along the boulevard Arago, circled the place Denfert-Rochereau and turned up the avenue du Maine. His left elbow resting on the back of the seat, Mathieu turned to me.

'Francis doesn't know where Émile is holed up,' he said, 'but his brother-in-law, the Hunchback, is in permanent contact with him. I've got a letter of recommendation to him.'

'No kidding?'

'Honest.'

'Let's see it,' I said, unable to restrain my impatience.

'I can't. It's sewn into the shoulder of my jacket. I'm supposed to take it to the Hunchback tomorrow. I think it'll go all right.'

'It should work,' I said. 'The toughest part is over. Now we have to see if Buisson will show himself.'

Montuire dropped us off at the rue des Saussaies. The main door was closed. When we unlocked it and went in, the men in the guard post stared at us in amazement. They weren't used to people working overtime.

We went up to my office. We had the shoulder of Mathieu's jacket unsewn in a matter of seconds. In it was a carefully folded bit of square-ruled paper. Caillaud had an odd handwriting, back-slanting. The message was peppered with misspellings. In the clearly legible signature, the double 'l' was rigidly parallel, like a pair of gateposts.

'My dear Émile,' it said. 'The friend I am recomending you is sure, duble-sure, even. I have juged him, you can trust him compleetly. Be careful with Ribot the breton, he has been intergated a number of times by the cops. Hugs and kisses. francis Caillaud.'

That was all. But, under the signature, Caillaud had drawn a double circle with a dot in its centre, like a target. Mathieu smiled when he saw my bafflement. 'It's their recognition sign,' he explained. 'It tells Émile the note was really written by Francis.'

We had to photograph the letter, but no one answered the laboratory phone. Even more important, it had to be put back in the jacket shoulder and sewn in again.

So, at eleven p.m., in the harsh light of my office, Mathieu Robillard dangled a leg off the corner of my desk and sewed up his sleeve with the thread he had saved when we'd opened it; he had stowed it with his needle on the underside of his lapel. The thread was a little short, but Mathieu promised he wouldn't make any sudden movements.

'Why don't we get some dinner?' Fatso suggested.

Understandably, Mathieu preferred to go home. So we grabbed a quick bite at the Saint-Lazare Station and ferried him out to Joinville-le-Pont in the Citroën. We got through the Bois de Vincennes in record time.

'I have a date at noon tomorrow with the Hunchback at the Petit-Saint-Denis café,' he said as we neared his home. 'We can get together later, at two o'clock. Good enough?'

'Fine, but where?'

'I don't know. How about the Thermomètre, at the République?'

I had a hard time getting to sleep *that* night, too.

In his carefully pressed dark blue business suit, with his hair trimmed and his cheeks freshly shaved, Mathieu was almost unrecognizable when, at noon on the dot, he walked into the Petit-Saint-Denis. He had left his BMW at the porte Saint-Denis.

I watched him go in from a hiding-place in the driveway of a run-down block of flats. I couldn't resist the temptation. The Hunchback was already there, at a table in the back, his hair plastered back and impeccably parted, a glass of red wine in front of him. The sun's rays glinting on the café windows prevented me from seeing clearly what went on, but at twelve-thirty I saw the two men come out, walk to the BMW and drive off in it. All I could do now was wait for my meeting with Robillard. I wasn't hungry. I just wandered aimlessly around the neighbourhood.

Mathieu didn't show up at the Thermomètre until after three. I had already phoned the shop several times to find out if Fatso had heard from him. All I had succeeded in doing was making a nervous wreck of him. 'You'll see,' he predicted. 'We are going to look very sick. Your precious Mathieu is going to take off into the brush and we are going to look ridiculous.'

I thought it prudent not to say anything and to go on waiting. When Mathieu did show up, his face had the flushed look of a man who has just had a very luscious lunch.

'It's repulsive, what I'm doing,' he said as he dropped into a chair. 'The Hunchback invited me to chow at his place. There's a framed photo of Émile on the sideboard, with a dried-up flower in the corner of it.'

'Skip the sentiment,' I said. 'He does. So what happened?'

'We opened up the shoulder and the Hunchback read the letter. He said he'd let me know, that I should leave him my phone number, and then we changed the subject. They're really just a bunch of poor bastards.'

'We'll remember that,' I said. 'What phone number did you give him?'

'The *bistrot* next door to my place. I told the Hunchback to be careful. That reminds me, I need a helping hand. It's my wife's illness . . . money, you see.'

I promised I'd speak to Fatso about it. Despite my desire to be nice to him, especially at that point, I didn't have a sou to give him. This was late May and my bankroll was as thin as a loan shark's smile.

'Call me tomorrow,' I said. 'I'll have it straightened out by then.'

I watched Robillard leave. I was ashamed for him of the way he lived, but I was just as ashamed of what I was forcing him to do. I never dreamed when I joined the police that I would end up fostering lies and deceit and betrayal so openly. I had been brought up to believe in fundamental principles of right and wrong by a father who slapped my face whenever, as a child, I told tales about my older sister. No matter how I tried to rationalize what I was doing, telling myself that it was for the good of society, to protect innocent people from a killer's bullets, my conscience still gnawed at me. I was determined to get out of the Grande Maison as soon as I could.

'Get out of my hair with your scruples,' Fatso cut in when I tried to tell him how I felt. 'You don't make a police force out of moralists. When you get to be my age . . .'

43

29 May 1950. A Monday morning. I would mark it with a cross: Mathieu made contact with Buisson. Just as I had begun to despair of hearing from him, he called me. I was to meet him at once, at the Café de la Paix, on the place de l'Opéra. It was noon; it would be twelve-fifteen before I could get there. Mathieu's no fool; he always calls at lunchtime. I knew what that meant, but this time he was pushing it a little hard. The Café de la Paix, on the kind of money I had . . .

With a little sigh, Fatso advanced me 20,000 francs, which immediately vanished into my pocket. Ten minutes later I joined a beaming Mathieu looking regal in a brand-new check suit. I confess I don't understand how he does it; he never has any money, but he is always superbly turned out.

'We're in,' he said as I sat down. 'The Hunchback phoned me. I'm picking him up tomorrow at ten o'clock and we're going to see Émile. Buisson's in Boulogne. I don't have the address, but I know he's short of dough. I promised to bring him twenty thousand.'

I couldn't believe it—Mathieu must have been reading my mind. Twenty thousand was exactly the amount I had on me, except for a hundred-franc bill of my own. I handed him the money, regretfully, promising to dig up some more for him the next day.

'That's not all,' Mathieu added. 'I need a gun.'

'A gun?'

'For Émile. And cartridges, at least fifty of them. He feels a need for some artillery in these troubled times.'

'Look, are you out of your mind? I'm not giving you any gun so that Buisson can embroider on us with it when we go for him.'

'That's your worry, Inspector. No boom-boom, no Buisson,' Robillard said, stretching his legs comfortably. I could feel the pleasure radiating from him at my confusion. We had suddenly changed roles; he was running the show now. 'If I don't take him the gun,' he went on persuasively, 'Buisson won't trust me.'

'All right, all right, I see that,' I said. 'But it's a decision I can't take on my own. I'll have to talk to my boss. If you like, we can meet at four o'clock at the Terminus near Saint-Lazare.'

Fatso came very near to having a fit when I told him about my conversation with Robillard. He understood the absurdity of our position as well as I did. But, after mulling it over for a while, he came up with an idea for offsetting the danger involved in giving Buisson a gun. On the platform of the bus in which we travelled to the Saint-Lazare Station—he insisted on coming along—he explained it to me.

'Don't worry about this, Borniche,' he explained. 'I've got a plan. We'll shadow Robillard out to Boulogne-Billancourt. And we'll surround the house Buisson's hiding in, and too bad if anybody gets hurt.'

We didn't even have time to order a drink at the Terminus. Mathieu was waiting for us and the first thing he did was to demolish Fatso's scheme. 'You give me your word you won't tail my car, all right?' he said. 'I don't want the Hunchback spotting something; if he does, we're finished. Besides, I don't want Émile making a sieve out of me.'

Fatso gave his word, but I could see the string attached to it. I looked at him and he blinked back. So, feeling more than a little queasy, I hauled a neatly tied little package out of my pocket containing the gun and ammunition for Monsieur Émile.

The gun was a nine-millimetre Mauser. It was mine, not the government's. I had come across it one day while searching an apartment, back when I was just starting out in the service. The Mauser had been appropriated, sealed and forgotten, like a lot of weapons in that weird post-war period. I had carefully cleaned and oiled it; I even tried it out once in open country, firing at a tin can nailed to a tree. It was an amazingly accurate weapon—I hit the can nine times out of nine. It had sat in my drawer ever since; every once in a while I would take it out and look at it.

It hurt me to turn it over, thinking that Buisson might some day use me for a target.

As we had agreed, we met again the next afternoon at four, in the same café. 'Mission accomplished,' Robillard told me. 'I saw Buisson, spent two hours with him, in fact. He was delighted when I gave him the gun. He's a likeable guy. You know where he is?'

'Hardly. Or why would we be oiling your palm so generously?'

'Staying with a poor slob named Jean the Painter on the rue de Billancourt. Émile met him some years back, through Bolec. When the Breton was arrested, Émile holed up there. He pays a thousand francs a day for his food, which is ruinous. I have to find him another hideout, a safer one.'

'Where does he want to go?'

'Haven't a clue,' Mathieu replied. 'He's left it up to me. I'm to pick him up Thursday morning, the day after tomorrow, with the Hunchback. Between now and then I have to look for something. Do you know a quiet place?'

This was getting richer and richer. Not only did I have to supply Monsieur Émile with money, a gun and ammunition, now I had to find him a hideaway. What next? But my annoyance quickly subsided; the situation had its promising side. Arresting Buisson would be risky. Somebody was certainly going to get hurt, as Fatso put it. Whereas the bloodshed could perhaps be kept to a minimum if I could take Buisson in a quiet, out-of-the-way place. 'Okay,' I said, 'be at the shop at nine tomorrow morning.'

Robillard didn't show up at nine however. He had burned out a bearing in his BMW and was still in Joinville-le-Pont when he let me know about it. I was furious. We had only one day to find somewhere for Émile; there was no time to lose. 'I'll wait for you at the Château de Vincennes, outside the Métro entrance, in half an hour. And don't dawdle.'

Fatso poked his head in through my office door. His face took on a sick look when he saw me alone. I explained what had happened and he walked off muttering to himself. Not a very auspicious beginning.

At nine-thirty, I picked Robillard up at the meeting-place. He was annoyed over the car breakdown. 'It's going to cost me another twenty thou,' he said. I didn't pick up the hint. It occurred to me that his life seemed to be divided up like a bar of chocolate—at 20,000 francs a square. We shared the back seat of the Citroën. Montuire was driving.

'Where are we going?' I asked him.

The car moved slowly off, made a U-turn at the bus terminal and headed towards Paris. 'Follow the exterior boulevards to the left.' Robillard ordered. 'We'll pick up the autoroute.'

Montuire nodded; we were soon at the porte de Saint-Cloud.

'It wouldn't be a hot idea for Émile to see me with you in a police car,' Mathieu muttered, slouching deep in his seat.

We zipped through the boulevard de la Reine to the autoroute tunnel. It was ten a.m.

'I thought of seeing a mate of mine in Fécamp,' Robillard said, 'an ex-lawbreaker who runs a rooming house, but that's a long way out, 125 miles at least.'

I calculated rapidly. 'We can be there by one o'clock without busting ourselves,' I said. 'In time for lunch. An outing in the country.'

Montuire stepped on the gas. It wasn't long before we ran out of dual carriageway and were on National Highway 12 heading towards Évreux. On the Bonnières rise, Robillard turned to me. 'I also have a buddy in Rouen, but he's a pimp and I don't think Émile would approve of that,' he mused.

'I doubt it,' I said. 'Pimps have a reputation as double-crossers.' I could have bitten my tongue off as soon as I said it, but Mathieu didn't say anything. We went through Pacy-sur-Eure, then Évreux. Ten kilometres beyond the town we noticed a sign on the left-hand side of the road indicating Auberge de la Mère Odue.

'Hey!' Mathieu exclaimed, 'a friend of mine runs that place. Jesus! I forgot all about it. No point in going any farther. Pull up two hundred yards from here and let me get to work.'

'What are you going to do?'

'I'm going to drop into his place for a meal as though I had just come from Deauville. You wait for me in the field and I'll pick me up in two or three hours. Lend me the car.'

'And how about us? Where are we supposed to eat?'

'Oh, sorry. All right then, let's push on to the next town; we can come back here later.'

The pork-butcher in Saint-Martin-la-Campagne made us some enormous sandwiches of ham and pâté and we drove back to the Four Corners, near the inn in the township of Claville. Montuire turned the wheel over to Robillard. He and I stretched out in the grass and chewed at our sandwiches, our eyes glued to the black Citroën now parked in front of la Mère Odue's restaurant.

Two hours later, I saw Mathieu emerge from the inn with a young man in a chef's white uniform. Robillard was looking pleased with himself when he rejoined us. Grignard, the hotel owner, had agreed to house his friend, who needed peace, good food and fresh air. Nobody had talked about money—that was secondary.

We drove back to Paris, both relieved and jumpy. Tomorrow at this time, if all went according to plan, Buisson would be safely within my reach, but out of range of my enterprising rivals. Tomorrow would be 1 June. 10 June was a Saturday, which meant we could question him undisturbed all day Sunday without having to announce the arrest.

'We're home,' Montuire announced. I looked up and saw that we were well and truly at the rue des Saussaies. Now I had to tell Fatso about the latest snag: Robillard no longer had a car in which to chauffeur Buisson to Claville. And we couldn't put off his leaving for the new hideout.

'First the dough, then the gun, the bullets, a cosy little hideout, and now I've got to find the right car for Monsieur Émile,' I fumed. 'We're becoming the Salvation Army.'

'Just a temporary hitch, Borniche,' Fatso clucked. 'I know where to find just what we need. Rendezvous tomorrow morning, the three of us, in front of my place.'

The man's resourcefulness amazed me.

44

The chief's idea was a disaster.

H-hour was eight-thirty a.m., in front of the Cluny café (in the Latin Quarter). Fatso, Robillard and I were waiting on the street corner for a *Paris-Presse* reporter who had agreed to lend us a car in exchange for exclusive rights to the story. He was on time, but I almost had a stroke when I saw the car he pulled up in— a bright red Simca with white stripes and the name of his rag printed in huge black letters on its flanks.

The reporter squealed to a halt and waved cheerfully at us.

'Like it?' he asked.

'Marvellous,' Fatso growled. 'Just the thing for following the Tour de France. Unfortunately it's a little conspicuous for our purposes.'

He dickered with the reporter briefly. Then the man drove off, vexed and disappointed. We were in the soup. We had a bare two hours in which to find a car for Robillard. 'Now what do we do?' Fatso groaned, mopping his forehead. 'We're screwed. If Mathieu isn't on time or if he shows up without a car, Émile will smell a rat.'

I didn't know what to do. The first problem was to warn the Hunchback about the mishap, then find the kind of car Buisson liked—a black Peugeot, for example. It was at that point that, miraculously, an idea came to me.

I remembered that a young inspector in the Petit group used to dazzle his girl friend by renting a car in Montmartre, at a place on the rue Duhesme, near his home.*

'You get over to the Hunchback's,' I told Mathieu. 'We'll meet here in an hour. Tell him you've had a breakdown and that you're waiting for a replacement.'

Twenty minutes later, Fatso and I got out of a taxi in front of the rental agency. We chose a black Peugeot. The agreement was quickly drawn up. Signature, comprehensive insurance, deposit. Deposit? I didn't have a franc on me. Fatso unflinchingly took out his cheque book and wrote a cheque for the 50,000-franc deposit. Then he showed his ID card. When the clerk read his

---

* Private cars were rare in France in 1950 and car rental agencies virtually unknown.

profession, 'Police Chief Inspector', he was reassured. I took the wheel, we zoomed through Paris and parked in front of the Cluny, where Mathieu Robillard was pacing up and down the street.

'I was right not to go and see the Hunchback,' he said. 'You're here already. And the Peugeot is perfect.'

I gave him the car keys and papers. 'Be careful, Mathieu,' I warned him. 'Keep those papers well hidden if you don't want to add your name to the list of Émile's corpses. They're in a cop's name. And a chief inspector, to boot.'

At ten forty-five, Fatso and I were downing our sixth coffee. At eleven, we were, in our thoughts, with the Hunchback and Mathieu in Boulogne. At eleven-five we mentally watched them leave there with Buisson.

At eleven-ten, a uniformed policeman with a Sten gun stationed himself at the intersection of the boulevard Saint-Michel and the boulevard Saint-Germain, while carloads of police began manning every intersection in sight. I was curious—that's my job, after all—and I went to find out what was happening.

'There's been a number three alarm,' the policeman told me when he'd seen my badge. 'A robbery. They got away in a black Peugeot and we're stopping every car of that description. If they don't stop, we fire.'

I ran back to the Cluny and told Fatso what was going on. He nearly fainted. 'We're fucked,' he moaned, closing his eyes. 'Either Mathieu will stop for the block or he'll try to crash it. Either way, Buisson will start shooting. That's certain. He'll defend his hide. And we'll be accessories to murder because we supplied the car, the gun, the dough and everything. Not to mention failure to apprehend a criminal we were ordered to arrest, not to send for a drive in the country. It will mean total disgrace.'

He swabbed his brow again. If Buisson fired, it would be with the gun I supplied, firing my own bullets. And Mathieu would spill his guts. No judge, still less our superiors, would ever believe we were only trying to make a splash. Not on your life! Our rivals would take us joyously to pieces. Of all the half-wit ways to operate, they'd gurgle; we'll take them fruit on visiting days. How were we to explain that we were just trying to protect our informer and win promotion at the same time?

We just about stopped living until noon. We phoned the Grande Maison regularly to ask if there were any news. And at

six o'clock on the nose, while I was in Fatso's office, a message
reached us from the country: 'Parcel arrived safely.' It was
Mathieu.

Fatso and I fell into each other's arms.

Émile liked the Auberge de la Mère Odue. He was immediately
accepted by the owner and before the Hunchback and Mathieu
left he insisted on a round of champagne.

The room he occupied on the ground floor of the main building
was large and bright and looked out over the fields. From his window, Émile could watch herds of cattle grazing only yards away
in a pasture of an intense shade of green. He was awoken by birds
twittering in a nearby copse, and Grignard lent him an air rifle.
The food was excellent. Émile sucked in huge lungfuls of fresh
air, forgetting the noxious atmosphere of the capital, forgetting
about police traps, even forgetting about his old friends at the
Santé. Mathieu Robillard had rescued him in the nick of time.

Robillard and the Hunchback promised to bring his sister
Jeanne to see him on 7 June. He was waiting for them. No kidding, Émile reflected, Mathieu was a valuable man to have
around, just as Francis had said he was. He'd try to set up a
worthwhile job with him, to reimburse him for his expenses. Then,
equipped with new identity papers, he would go travelling abroad.
To South America. Monsieur Émile dreamed happily on.

'Mathieu's a real asset,' declared the Hunchback, slightly
pissed, when lunch was over. 'He drives like a pro. If we'd been
tailed, the guy behind us would really have had some pedalling
to do.'

Buisson didn't appreciate the Hunchback's assurance; it set his
suspicions twitching. But his 'brother-in-law', cocky as a knife-
fighter in a schoolyard, calmed him down. 'Don't worry, Émile.
I was careful. And the cop who can kid me is still in his old man's
balls.'

45

10 June 1950. I hadn't slept a wink. I was scared. This was the big day. The Buisson case had become my case, the case of my life. I couldn't, I mustn't spoil it. Marlyse had slept peacefully beside me, her naked body occasionally touching mine. I could smell her warmth, the perfume of her skin, could hear her regular breathing and, in spite of all this, I felt lonely. Panic, insidious panic, crept gradually over me, knotting my throat, twisting my stomach into a Chinese puzzle.

Around three a.m. I had got up and, groped my way to the kitchen through the darkness for a drink of water. A few minutes later my mouth was dry again. I went back to bed, tossing and turning, unable to rid myself of the mental picture of Buisson that haunted me. I was gripped by an unintelligible terror. It ground me down, that feeling; I had never known anything like it until that night.

I made love to Marlyse in the hope that it would put me to sleep—a natural therapy I sometimes employ against insomnia. It usually works. My hand moved softly over Marlyse's body and she smiled in her sleep—whether consciously or unconsciously, I couldn't tell—and sighed softly, surrendering herself without waking.

But when it was all over, there I lay with my eyes wide open, feeling unsatisfied and worried, watching the day steal through the blinds. I finally dropped off to sleep at six a.m. At seven-thirty the alarm clock went off.

'Roger,' Marlyse mumbled, 'couldn't you make the coffee this morning, darling?'

My eyes swollen, I struggled to my feet feeling like the inside of a boxer's glove after a title fight. The room spun around me for a moment, but it finally settled down. I was putting on my dressing gown when Marlyse, her eyes still shut, piped up.

'Roger?' she said.

'Yes.'

'Roger, do you think it's normal, at my age?'

'Do I think what's normal?'

'Having sexy dreams.'

'You ought to see a doctor. I've always thought you were a sex fiend.'

'Oh dear, you are in a nasty mood this morning.'

I didn't say anything. There are times when I wonder if Marlyse isn't as stupid as her mother.

It was eleven a.m. when the powerful Delahaye lent me by a lawyer friend, Paul Villard, rolled up on to the shoulder of the Western Autoroute behind the black Sûreté Citroën. Standing alongside it, smoking, were Fatso, Gillard and Hours.

'You don't look in particularly good shape this morning,' Fatso said with a worried frown.

'I got to sleep late, chief,' I said, 'but don't worry. It'll be all right.'

'Good,' he replied. 'Well, let's not waste time. You understand, Borniche, that at the slightest alert, the smallest hitch, you will signal to us in any way you can.'

'Yes, chief.'

'Right. As we agreed, Hours and I will wait in the clump of trees at the far edge of the highway. We'll be able to get to you in a minute at the most.'

'Yes, chief.'

'Good. Come to think of it, are you armed?'

'No, chief.'

'That is stupid, Borniche, very stupid. Well, it's your skin. Do you at least have handcuffs?'

'They're in Marlyse's handbag. She'll pass them to me when I need them.'

'All right. Well, good luck, my boy. Take Gillard with you and we'll see you later. With Buisson.'

'See you later, chief.'

Fatso shook me by the hand, hanging on to it, looking me straight in the eye. A little theatrical perhaps, but it was comforting.

I got back behind the wheel of the Delahaye, where Marlyse was waiting for me, filing her nails. Gillard got in the back. With a deep-throated growl, the car started off.

For fifteen miles or so I forgot about Buisson, about Fatso, about my promotion, about the whole circus. Barring a miracle, I would never have the money to buy a machine like this one and I wanted to enjoy it while I could. I played with the accelerator and the gears, passing other cars as though they were nailed to the road, making the tyres complain as I skidded round bends. Well behind me, the Citroën laboured like a mule trying to follow a racehorse. It caught up to us from time to time. I could imagine Fatso grinding his teeth back there; he would certainly be taking a dim view of my playfulness and cursing every time I pulled away from them.

From time to time I glanced at Gillard's reflection in the rear-view mirror. He was curled up well back against the cushions, his face tense, carefully not looking at the landscape leaping towards us. He was a relic of the days when people got excited about hitting sixty miles an hours; the needle on my speedometer was hovering around a hundred and he was obviously beginning.

We drove as far as Évreux that way. There we stopped again. More handshaking. Since there was a chance that I would be dead in the very near future, Fatso spared me his comments on my driving. I couldn't do anything wrong this morning—I could pull his ears, cut off his necktie, step on his toes, rumple his hair, make faces at him and he wouldn't protest. He had that indulgent attitude towards me we display to those who salute you as they are about to die.

The Delahaye was alone on the road when we got moving again; Fatso had agreed to give me a lead, then take a side road to his station in the trees.

When I drove Mathieu to Claville, I had noticed the two petrol pumps, one economy and one premium, outside the Auberge de la Mère Odue. I stopped the car alongside the premium pump. A Delahaye is fun but it is voracious. It drank up more than eight gallons of petrol doing the seventy-five miles from Paris to Claville. This gave me a good excuse for stopping to fill the tank.

Giving a short, imperious blast on the horn, I swung open my door, pivoted on my tail on the leather upholstery and got out, standing in my shirt sleeves in the sun, relaxed and confident, the very image of the prosperous young executive. I stretched lazily, flashing a fatuous, great-lover smile at Marlyse. Then, hands on my hips and legs wide apart, I watched the owner's wife trot towards me. She hauled up before me, pink with perspiration, her lips moist, her blouse stretched tight across a prettily rounded bosom which was heaving like a schooner in a storm.

'Fill it up, please, madame.'

We grinned at each other while she filled the tank. She was a real sweetie.

'While you're at it,' I said when she had cut off the flow of fuel, 'would you mind checking the oil?'

'Certainly, sir,' she said. 'That's what I'm here for.'

I raised the hood of the sleek car, glancing around for the rod that should have been there to prop it up. But the rod was gone. I had to hold the thing up myself.

The woman was wiping the dipstick with a rag when, suddenly, a small, dark-haired man with black eyes appeared in the inn door. He stared at me. Then he contemplated the car.

I had the shakes. For the first time, after three years of searching, of failure, of humiliation, I was looking at Buisson. He was here, only two yards from me, standing with his hands on his hips, looking interested. If I hadn't had to hold up that damned bonnet I might have been tempted to jump him right there. But if I let go, I might decapitate the poor creature who was stabbing at the motor with the dipstick. And I risked wasting that precious fraction of a second Buisson needed to draw his gun and shoot me down at point-blank range. At that distance, he couldn't miss. Of course, Gillard, who was almost invisible in the back seat, would have time to draw and gun him down in turn. That's called a conditional in the grammar books. But by that time I would be strictly past tense, a corpse without a future.

In those few moments, feeling Buisson's suspicious stare scrutinizing me like an X-ray machine, it wasn't fear which kept me from acting—my panic had fled the moment the little man in shirt sleeves appeared. I rejected the risk for a very simple reason: I wanted Buisson.

He turned on his heel and disappeared inside the inn. I cursed the missing bonnet prop. If I hadn't had one hand immobilized, I could have found an excuse to get nearer to Buisson. It would have been all over by that time. I'd have had him.

My only consolation was the knowledge that Buisson was still there. It was up to me to see to it that he didn't get away from us as he had from the PP's men.

I peeked at my watch; it was twenty minutes past noon.

'Can we lunch here, madame?'

'Of course, sir. We serve meals.'

'Splendid! If you don't mind, I'll park the car in the courtyard, in the shade under the plane tree.'

'Of course, sir.'

'Set a table for us, would you? And get out a bottle of wine—the best.'

I ran the car into the courtyard behind the inn and we all got out. While Marlyse brushed the creases out of her dress and I locked the doors, Buisson showed up again, five yards away, among the strawberries in the vegetable garden. He was watching us. I felt his flinty, merciless stare pierce me. He was slight and furtive-looking, but there was something imposing about him.

That was the moment that Gillard, whose back was turned to him, chose to announce: 'Hey, Borniche! I've left my gun in the car.'

'For Christ's sake shut up!' I hissed, terrified that Buisson might have heard him. I grabbed Marlyse by the arm and led her towards the dining-room door, inquiring as we went whether the little 6.35-millimetre gun I had given her was still in her purse. She nodded. I confess that up to then Marlyse amazed me. Did she realize the danger we were in? I wasn't sure. All I knew was that she was astoundingly calm, as though this whole operation were just a day in the country.

We went into the inn. The room we entered was the bar. On our left, a typical dining room, with red and white checkered table-cloths and curtains, whitewashed walls, exposed beams. The kitchen was to the right through a swinging mini-door which allowed the owner to keep an eye out for arriving clients and to pass plates through to the waitress.

'Would you rather lunch inside or on the terrace,' the proprietress asked as she handed us menus. I pretended to consult my friends, but I answered almost at once. 'Inside,' I said. 'It's cooler and we'll hear less traffic noise. You can give us three *pastis* while we wait.'

While she busied herself behind the zinc-topped bar, we chose our lunch: potted pork, mixed salad, stuffed rabbit and a bottle of Saint-Émilion. Time passed, but there was still no sign of Buisson. We had to play for time.

'Another round,' I ordered, 'and a drink for the cook.' I peered back into the kitchen, where the owner nodded his thanks. I could hardly sit still. I glanced around the dining room again. No Buisson. There was a piano in a corner; I sat down at it and began playing a blues tune. Marlyse leaned on my shoulder, humming. Gillard just looked worried.

The minutes passed. Now it was twelve-thirty; remembering my promise to Fatso to make my move as soon as possible wasn't making me any calmer. I had to find some way to warn him, or he might come bumbling in there and do something stupid. Then I saw an old bugle hanging on the wall. I got up and took it down. Gillard was right behind me.

'Now you'll hear something,' I said.

I moistened my lips and screwed the horn into them. The sound was tremendous, a fine, martial mess call that must have shattered every eardrum in the region. I only hoped Fatso, hiding in the woods across the way, had heard and understood.

'Here we are, here we are,' said the owner, bustling in with an armload of dishes. 'No use getting impatient. Sit yourselves down.'

I chose the table near the window, in the centre of the outside wall. Gillard and I sat with our backs to the kitchen, opposite Marlyse. That way, I hoped to avoid rousing the black-eyed killer's hyperactive suspicions.

'Do you see him?' I asked Marlyse.

'No. There's nobody at the table there but the owner, for the moment.'

We dug into the first course. I had already gulped down the pâté and salad when Marlyse kicked me. 'He's just crossed the kitchen,' she murmured, 'but he's gone out again, through the back door into the courtyard.'

I felt my stomach turn to cement. I didn't think I would ever be hungry again. I poured myself a glass of wine, then Marlyse kicked me again. 'He's back . . . He's carrying a dish of strawberries . . . He's disappeared . . . Now he's here again . . . He's sitting at the owner's table and he's beginning his lunch. He's facing us.'

The last item bothered me. I wondered how I was going to get near him. I had thought he'd be sitting near us in the dining room; in any case, I never dreamed he'd take his meals in the kitchen with the proprietor. He could keep an eye on everything from there.

There were seven or eight yards of potentially fatal space between the two tables, and I had to have a convincing reason to get near Émile without his doing any fancy needlework on me with the Mauser.

46

I nibbled thoughtfully at my rabbit, unable to come up with a pretext for approaching Buisson. He was chewing stolidly, never taking his eyes off us.

'What do we do?' Gillard asked.

'I don't know. You worried?'

'Worried? You're kidding. My teeth are chattering like I had palsy. How about you?'

'I'm okay. But I've got to get over there . . .'

I put my napkin on the table, pushed back my chair, got up and, trying to look natural, walked towards the kitchen. I still hadn't the faintest idea what I was going to do or say when I got there. I walked through the bar to the swinging door, but at this point Buisson, who had watched me all the way across the room, gave me a look that froze me. I was sure it was suicide to go any farther. His right hand put down the knife it was holding and slid stealthily towards his pocket. For a moment, I felt drained. It was a weird sensation—as though I were just a large envelope with no skeleton inside. The blood left my cheeks, my heart beat like a steam pump and my legs felt as though they were melting into the floor. Call it fear or call it acute awareness of danger, the effect is the same: I was petrified.

I got to within a few steps of Buisson, who was still staring at me, ready to move. We were separated by the owner, who had his back to me and who was continuing to stuff his face, and by the table with its burden of greasy dishes. I finally found my tongue again. 'I would like to phone Deauville, madame,' I said in a surprisingly firm voice that probably didn't cost me any more than ten years of my life to control. 'Can I do that from here?'

Luckily, I had spotted a wall telephone in an angle of the kitchen, between a dish cabinet and the window giving on the street. It was my only hope.

'Certainly, sir. What number do you want?'

'432.'

I could just as well have said 73 or 852. What difference did it make what number I dreamed up?

To restore Buisson's confidence, I went back to my table. From where I sat, I could hear the owner's wife crank the handle, ask for the number and hang up again. She came out to tell me, 'They'll call back, sir.'

'Is this going to work?' Gillard whispered.

'I hope so. If not, you'll be finishing your lunch without me.'

At that moment, the phone rang. I felt the blood rush to my head; a hot wave washed across my cheeks. I got to my feet, my muscles stiffened and my body tense, and hit the trail back to the kitchen. Calvary is the word for it. Twice my eyes met Buisson's and a kind of panic swept over me. Discouraged, I told myself I would never manage alone to get under this killer's guard and overpower him. His reflexes had been honed by years of flight; Monsieur Émile mounted a fierce and permanent guard over himself.

Once more, Buisson's look stopped me at the kitchen door. And that look took on a scowling, terrifying, murderous iciness when the woman, who was standing behind him with the receiver in her hand, informed me in a surprised voice: 'They say there is no such number.'

It cost me a tremendous effort not to swallow hard—the bouncing of my Adam's apple wouldn't have escaped Buisson; he'd have known what it meant. And I had to control my voice, which wanted to shake itself to pieces, before I could reply with something resembling indignation:

'What do they mean, no such number? It's my own clinic. Try again, please.'

Despite my effort, my voice sounded unnaturally high, even a little shrill to me, but Buisson hadn't moved. His right hand was still in his pants pocket, closed around his gun—my gun. I didn't have to look at him to know that.

I went back to my table a second time. Fear had boiled so much sweat out of me that my shirt was stuck to my skin. I expected with every step to feel a bullet smash into my back. Right between the shoulder blades. I could feel my sphincter tightening. As though drained by a terrible effort, I slumped into my chair and tossed down the glass of wine in front of me.

'It's a bastard,' Gillard said. 'Doesn't look good.'

I didn't have time to reply, because the proprietress called me again, beaming all over. 'Here it is, sir,' she chortled. 'The operator got the wrong number.'

I walked towards the phone. For the first time, I dared slip into the kitchen without feeling as though I were walking into a gas chamber. I passed within a yard of Buisson but I kept going without looking at him because the killer had pivoted in his chair, following me with his eyes, his hand still out of sight in his pocket. Out of the corner of my eye, I could see the lump the gun made in the cloth.

I turned my back to him when I picked up the phone. 'Hello,' I bellowed. 'The Roses clinic? This is Doctor André. I'll be a little late. I'm on the Deauville road, but I won't get there before one-thirty or so . . . What? No, now listen: continue the strepto for number six—of course as usual! Don't do anything to number twenty-seven until I get there . . . Ask the lab to do the tests I ordered. I'll look at the results when I get there. Thanks.'

I hung up. Throughout the conversation, I was terrified that the person at the other end of the line—the one who kept repeating with growing exasperation that 'this isn't a clinic, it's the cemetery'—would hang up on me (with an audible click).

The proprietress smiled at me. I smiled back. I was calm now, I felt good. It was now or never.

I moved away from the phone, heading towards my table, paying no visible attention to Buisson, who now had both hands on the table. We were a yard apart. Then I jumped, swarming all over him, wrapping my arms around him at waist level so that his arms were pinned. With every ounce of my strength I hung on, squeezed, lifted.

The man was short, but he was strong. I could feel his muscles tensing. He struggled to break my grip, but exhilaration had multiplied my strength; nothing short of a blowtorch could have pried me loose from him. Buisson raged, yelled, wiggled. Half suffocated, he managed to pant out:

'What the hell's got into you? Are you insane?'

'You've had it, Émile,' I told him hoarsely.

He tried one last time to wrench himself free. He almost made it, but I succeeded in holding on. Then his muscles relaxed. Marlyse had rushed into the kitchen, fishing the handcuffs out of her bag. There were two metallic clicks and the killer's wrists were imprisoned in steel bracelets.

Buisson was pale, his mouth was working, uttering unintelligible sounds. With a feeling of relief, I removed the Mauser from his pocket, along with an extra clip of shells and a fake identity card in the name of Ballu.

'Good work,' said Buisson, who had calmed down by then, while I was suddenly convulsed with trembling. 'Have a drink. It'll pick you up.'

'The gentleman's right,' Marlyse chimed in. 'Two cognacs.'

'How about me?' interjected Gillard, who moved to the open window, took out his whistle and blew it to alert Fatso and Hours.

'Three cognacs, then,' Marlyse said calmly, 'and a lime-flower tea for me.'

The proprietor and his wife had watched the entire scene without budging, bug-eyed, open-mouthed, their faces smeared with pâté. 'I'll be damned,' was all he could say—but that repeatedly—when he came out of his trance. 'I'll be damned . . .'

His wife, who had nearly fainted, now drifted like a zombie towards the bar. She came back carrying a tray of glasses and a bottle of cognac. We drank each other's health, offered heartfelt toasts to our success. I hadn't said a word since the bracelets went on Buisson's wrists, which was so unlike me that Marlyse began to worry.

'What are you thinking about, darling?' she asked.

I didn't answer. Capturing Buisson should have satisfied me; I had succeeded where dozens of police officers of all ages and every rank had failed. For a half wit with only a few years' experience, it wasn't bad. Tomorrow, everyone in the Grande Maison would be singing my praises, envying my triumph; my temerity would be criticized, I would be scolded for my heedlessness in involving a young woman not employed by the Maison in my foolish adventure. To some I would be the top cop; others would see me as a cop with a drunk's luck; still others would dismiss the achievement as nothing more than the work of a good informer. What the hell! The 30,000-franc bonus Fatso had promised me meant that at last I was going to be able to buy Marlyse a new stove.

The floor in Buisson's room was littered with cigarette butts. I went through the place methodically as Émile watched. Then I found it: a Colt 11.45; I was sure it was the gun that had been used on Polledri, wounded the jeweller Baudet, blasted the bank employees in Champigny and many others. I was delighted.

Buisson read my thoughts. 'I never used it, you know,' he remarked. 'Have it tested and you'll see.'

My delight faded before his calm assurance.

Three hours later, Émile Buisson entered the driveway at the rue des Saussaies. 'Borniche,' Fatso intoned solemnly, 'from this moment, consider yourself a chief inspector.' It was six-nine p.m., 10 June 1950. It would take him six months to keep that promise, although Fatso himself was promoted to superintendent at once. And top of the list, at that!

ROUND SIX

47

Our interrogation of Buisson went on all through Sunday, although he had still not been formally booked. The call to action stations was sounded at nine o'clock on Monday morning, when Fatso had scheduled a press conference to announce the great news. He called me, nervous. 'Listen, Borniche,' he jittered, 'are you coming or aren't you? I've been calling for an hour.' I went to his office, delaying only long enough to skid on the freshly waxed floor. Fatso was wearing a dark suit and white shirt; his black shoes glittered like glass. Radiant with joy, he never even took time to shake my hand.

'Borniche,' he trumpeted, 'we are going to get our revenge.'

I stared at him, flabbergasted, but he was off again before I could get my mouth open.

'Yes, indeed, my boy, we are going to get even with the PP for those three years it spent spiking our wheels,' he informed me. Then his voice went sly. 'Buisson was not arrested in Claville. Get that, Borniche? He was picked up at the porte de Saint-Cloud, while lunching at the Trois Obus restaurant.'

'What do you mean, chief?' I asked, feeling my face growing longer by the second. Fatso hunched his shoulders nervously and planted himself before me.

'It's really exasperating, the way you refuse to understand,' he said. 'Girier was arrested in Montfermeil, wasn't he? In our territory, where the PP had no business being. All right, then. I arrested Buisson in their own front yard. That way, they're going to find out what it means to get their arses kicked.'

Fatso was tickled pink with the trick he was going to pull on his luckless rivals. 'If I wanted to be really low about it,' he added, letting himself subside into his chair, 'I could do them even dirtier. I could, for example, have arrested Buisson while he was strolling in front of 36 quai des Orfèvres. But I play a gentleman's game.'

Two hours later, the early editions of the afternoon papers told

all France that the elusive Buisson had been lunching peacefully
in a Paris restaurant when Fatso's men jumped him.

It's all a question of luck, whether you're doing police work or
playing billiards. Sometimes one well-placed shot will open up
an incredible break. That's what happened to me in the Buisson
case.

Mathieu Robillard pocketed his million and a half after
Émile's arrest. The PP showed its displeasure at being bested. The
vast dragnet I had thrown out in the underworld enabled me to
make the acquaintance of Vérando, Loubier, Labori and some
thirty other villains, all of whom were locked up for consorting
with undesirables. Only little Orsetti slipped through the net, but
he would only get riper with age.

The wind was still in my sails when I caught up with
René Girier on the place de l'Opéra two months after he had
parted company with his guards by sawing through a police van
floor.

The greatest cop in France, that was me!

Once Buisson was settled in his cell at the Santé, I concentrated
on interrogating him, because he refused to talk to anyone but
me. I hate to admit it, but, over the months, we became attached
to each other. It's stupid, but that's the way it is. We became
almost matey.

Émile and I set up a private, inflexible work schedule. In the
morning, I went to the Santé to fetch him in a Maison car. 'How
are you this morning?' 'Fine, and you?' We shook hands. I handcuffed him and we climbed into the car and drove to the rue des
Saussaies. We didn't say much on the way, except for inane comments on the weather, the French soccer team, the girls we passed
in the street. When we got to my office, I fastened Émile's left
wrist to the radiator and pushed a padded armchair under him.
He sat down and, with his right hand, poured himself a glass of
good Bordeaux wine—I bought him a bottle every morning—took
his horn-rimmed glasses out of his pocket and picked up the
morning *Figaro*, which was lying on my desk waiting for him.
That was at nine o'clock. There was no interrogation until
twelve-thirty. Total silence; live and let live. That was part of our
routine. Calmly, refilling his glass from time to time, Émile read
the paper from front to back, line by line, paying special attention
to the political news.

One day, curious, I asked him why he was so interested in the international situation.

'Monsieur Borniche,' he replied, arching his eyebrows, 'I am trying to decide whether the Russians and the Americans will lay into each other one of these days.'

'Why? Scared?'

'Of course I'm not scared. On the contrary. I'd love to see another scrap—that's my only chance. In 1940, it was only because of our collapse that I was able to skip out of the Troyes prison. But if the peace continues, Monsieur Borniche, I can see it coming: you're going to try every trick in the book to get me to cough up everything I know.'

Towards noon, Buisson would take his nose out of his newspaper and peer at me over his glasses. 'What's for lunch today, Monsieur Borniche?' he'd ask.

'Wait a minute. I'll find out.'

I would phone down to the police station on the ground floor and they would give me the day's menu, which I passed on to Émile. If he approved, he nodded agreement. At one p.m., Émile wiggled in his armchair. He put down his paper, drained his glass, pocketed his glasses and said:

'What about a piss, Monsieur Borniche?'

I agreed. I handcuffed myself to him and we trotted down to the lavatory on the landing. From there, we descended to the basement where he lunched, guarded by two policemen who were not accustomed to having a killer for a table companion. While he was thus occupied, I went and downed a cold lunch at the Santa Maria.

Serious business got under way at two o'clock. Buisson was brought back to my office and again cuffed to the radiator, visibly pleased at having eaten a choicer lunch than the Santé could offer. I began going through the five-foot shelf of dossiers concerning the thirty-six murders and robberies of which he was accused.

'What will we work on today, Monsieur Borniche?'

That was how my interrogation began. Invariably. Everything went with an admirable lack of friction. The tone was friendly. I was up on everything he'd done. With rare exceptions, all his former cronies had talked. I read their confessions to Émile, who listened to them impassively, showing no surprise, no indignation at having been so lavishly betrayed by his friends. They blamed everything on Émile, even things he hadn't done. All France was purged of guilt by this avalanche of accusations. Had a little girl been raped? Émile. A bicycle stolen? Émile again. Had someone's heirloom silver been filched? Why, Émile, naturally. He was linked with every larceny, every killing on the books. I had to get the record straight, and Émile helped me as best he could. At the end of the session, he would sign the statement I typed out without even reading it.

'I'll take your word for it, Monsieur Borniche,' he told me.

He confessed to everything he'd done, admitted everything. Except the murders.

He was already under a life sentence, but he wasn't taking on anything that might lead him to the scaffold. The bank messengers' murders, the Russac and Polledri slayings—he denied flatly having had a hand in any of them. He denied the evidence, denied the witnesses' testimony. When brought face to face with his ex-associates, he would glare at them in rage and contempt.

Only once did I see his cruelty flare up. When it did, his eyes gleamed with such a savage flame, his face was so terrifying that I was glad he was chained to the radiator. That was the day we discussed Mathieu Robillard.

'If I could get my hands on him,' he growled hoarsely, his voice shaking with hatred, 'I'd cut his throat with a hacksaw. And I'd stop sawing from time to time just to listen to him scream.'

Our tête-à-tête went on for three years. When he heard that Girier had escaped from the police van, I saw Buisson's eyes light with a nostalgic gleam. And when he learned that I had captured Girier at the Opéra, he flashed a satisfied little smile. I kept him informed of the arrests I made. All the criminals he had frequented or employed fell to me, one after another.

'You see, Émile,' I said with a hint of pride in my voice, 'I'm up to my thirty-fifth arrest in your case.'

He looked at me, amusement dancing in his eyes. He took a sip of wine, then set his glass down. 'There's still one,' he said in a challenging tone, 'who's got away from you.'

That was a shock. Frowning, a little annoyed, I at first thought of Orsetti. I was curious. 'Which one?' I asked him.

'Courgibet, Monsieur Borniche. You haven't got Courgibet, and it doesn't look as if you will.'

'Courgibet? That's ancient history. It doesn't interest me now.'

'Oh? That's a shame.'

'Why? Do you know where he is?'

'Sure, he's in the United States. But it's a big place, the United States.'

'It's big, but my colleagues of the FBI are well organized. They'll find your Courgibet, take my word for it.'

'That would surprise me, Monsieur Borniche, that would surprise me. The name of Émile Courgibet is unknown there.'

'What are you trying to tell me, Émile?'

'Come now Monsieur Borniche, you're cleverer than that. You know what I mean.'

'He's using another name, is that it?'

'Right on the button. In the United States, Émile Courgibet calls himself Fernand Châtelain and he's a cabinetmaker.'

I sat there studying Buisson for a long moment. He sat quietly in his chair, his left arm dangling from the handcuffs, looking intolerably vain. I thought about the underworld's mythical law of silence, which had been given extremely short shrift in the Buisson case. The number of men who refused to talk, to betray their friends despite threats of heavy sentences, could be counted on the fingers of one hand: Caillaud, Screwball, the Hunchback, Labori. And there had been Buisson. Now Émile was striking himself off my short list. He was acting like a squealer, despite his oft-repeated contempt for the breed.

'Why are you giving me Courgibet?' I asked him.

'Since I'm inside, and since all my friends are too, there's no reason why Courgibet shouldn't be inside with us.'

'Émile,' I told him, 'you are lowering yourself in my esteem.'

48

12 February 1952. A frigid wind blew through the port of Le Havre. With Leclerc, the officer who had joined our section when Hours was transferred to Marseilles, I was waiting for the liner *America* to arrive. We had been notified that Émile Courgibet was aboard, in cabin 324—shipment courtesy of the FBI. As soon as I contacted them after Buisson blabbed, they got on the trail. He was easy to find. He had married a pretty California girl four years before and had opened a shop in New York specializing in copies of Louis XV furniture. He was two months away from naturalization as an American citizen. The American police noted in their report that Courgibet-Châtelain's conduct in the United States had been exemplary. Had Buisson kept his mouth shut, Courgibet could have forgotten his past.

The *America* docked and the gangplank went down. The purser was waiting for us when we went aboard. A steward led us into the belly of the ship, threading down interminable gangways to cabin 324. I opened the door and walked in, with Leclerc behind me. A tall, distinguished-looking man stared at us in surprise.

'All right, Courgibet,' I said, showing him my badge, 'let's go.'

The man flushed, obviously nonplussed. In heavily American-accented French, he murmured something barely comprehensible and handed me his diplomatic passport.

'Very pretty,' I said sarcastically. 'It's a beautiful fake, but it won't wash.' I grabbed him by the arm and was about to drag him out of the cabin when a ship's officer burst in, pale and puffing.

'Let that man go,' he murmured. 'He's the Norwegian ambassador. There's been a mistake. Your man was put into another cabin—number 264.'

It was my turn to redden, but with embarrassment. Leclerc and I mumbled our excuses and fled, at a gallop to Courgibet's cabin. This time we went in without knocking. Émile Courgibet was on his feet, waiting for us. He was pale and sad-looking. His mouth twisted into a melancholy smile when he nodded at the porthole behind him.

'If I was twenty years younger,' he said, 'I'd have tried to skip out that way. But I'm fifty-five now, and my life is finished, for good.'

He was a little guy, Courgibet, with a soft voice. To look at him, well dressed, his hat in his hand, you'd have taken him for a successful store owner, not a fugitive from justice.

In the train taking us back to Paris, Leclerc and I were deeply impressed by this friendly, courteous man. And our feeling turned to genuine pity when we saw tears suddenly trickle down his cheeks.

I had him in my office the next morning to make a statement. He was corpse-white; his first night in prison had shaken him deeply. As I rolled the statement form into my typewriter, I asked him if he wanted a cup of coffee. He waved the offer away. I did not cuff him to the radiator.

'Let's have it,' I said. 'Just as well to get it over with, if you agree.'

'As you like, Inspector.'

'Let's begin at the beginning. You were sentenced on 18 November 1918, in the Seine Criminal Court, to eight years' imprisonment in Cayenne for the murder of the woman you loved. Crime of passion, right?'

'Yes. One evening in 1919, one of a chain gang, I was shipped out to Saint-Laurent-du-Maroni. I landed in Camp Colbert, with men I had no affinity for, nothing in common with.'

Courgibet went on to tell me a pathetic story that another writer, twenty years later, would embroider and assume for his own. A repentant thief, the writer was.

'I had no choice but to adopt some of their ways,' Courgibet recalled, 'to become brutal and violent if I didn't want to get my throat cut in the night or become some other prisoner's "little woman".'

'So you escaped.'

'On the evening of 20 September 1922. A Sunday. With two other prisoners, I pretended to leave camp to do some laundry. We disappeared in the bush and hiked to the Maroni River. On the other side of the water was Dutch Guiana, but we had to get across. We swam it, and I have often wondered how we managed to resist that terrible current. Well, we reached Dutch Guiana. The three of us kept walking, endlessly, eating roots, our clothes in shreds, tortured by fever. That was just the beginning of our misery, but I was willing to put up with it to escape the prison colony.

'We stumbled into a bauxite mine. There were nine other

escapees there already. My companions knew them. They got us jobs there. We were badly paid—we weren't worth any more—but we saved all the money we could. I had only one idea in my head: buy a boat to sail down the coast of British Guiana to Venezuela, which had no extradition treaty with France. The others agreed.

'It was a big-bellied fishing boat, heavy but solid, that a black sold us for next to nothing. We made sails out of a couple of jute bags, loaded aboard food stores and two barrels of water and shoved off. I knew a little about navigation, so the others left it to me.

'It was the eighth or ninth day out that we were surprised by the storm. The sky had grown a blackish grey, the wind rose with increasing force. We had taken in part of the sail, leaving only what we needed to steer with. We fought that storm for two more days. First the sail went, then the mast. We drifted, out of control.

'We sank at dawn. It was all over in a few seconds. An enormous wave picked us up like a giant hand and hurled us into the air. Our cries for help were lost on the wind. God, it was fast. My companions sank one after another, except for me and two others. We swam for hours; the only thing that kept us afloat was a blind determination to stay alive.

'Suddenly, I saw white bellies around us, and black maws. Sharks. It was futile, but I screamed in terror. It was at that moment that I felt a horrible pain in my left arm. A shark had gone for me. I thought I was a goner, and I fainted.

'When I came to, I was stretched out on a beach. There were Indian faces peering down at me. They were fishermen and it was they who had rescued me. They were completely naked except for a tiny loincloth. Hairless. And they were smiling at me. They carried me to their village—ten straw huts. I was on an island and I could see a lighthouse marking the Venezuelan coast.

'I was nursed by a fifteen-year-old Indian girl. Her devotion was touching. She taught me the language of her little tribe. With the chief's consent, I became her husband. I lived with them for six years, learning to make chairs and tables, learning to hunt and fish and dive for pearls. Lila, my wife's name was. She gave me two children. And then, one day, sadly, I left Lila, who cried, left the old chief and the others.'

'Why?'

'I was homesick for Paris, Inspector. I had dreamed the same dreams all the other cons dreamed: breaking out, then going home. I set out for Caracas in a dug-out the chief gave me. "I knew that you would leave one day," he told me when we separated. It took me a month to reach Caracas and I was completely exhausted when I got there.

'I found a job. One of my older brothers was living in Buenos Aires and I wrote to him to send me a little money and some false papers. I knew that all the ships leaving Caracas for Buenos Aires stop in French Guiana. It was too risky for me. I didn't want to be dragged back to Saint-Laurent-du-Maroni. So I decided to travel to Argentina via Peru, the Pacific route. I had to cross the Andes. I didn't reach my brother until 1933—a five-year trip. If I had stayed quietly in the clink I'd have been a free man long since and I'd have lived another life.'

'Why didn't you stay in Argentina?'

'I told you: I was homesick for Paris. My brother gave me the money to take ship for Spain. The Civil War had started there. I was in Barcelona. One evening, I heard two men near me in a bar talking French. It had been years since I'd heard my own language. I struck up an acquaintance. They were the Buisson brothers.'

'And you went to China with them. Later you took part with Émile in the Troyes hold-up.'

'That's right. But there's one thing: I didn't have a gun in Troyes. I didn't threaten anybody. I've always hated killing. When I realized that Émile Buisson was a killer, I broke with him.'

'I know. It was just before the war. You went to the United States.'

'Yes. I wanted to start a new life. Honestly. And I did . . .'

Courgibet fell silent. He retreated into his misery, and a tear ran down his cheek. The elegance of his clothes, his manners, testified to his position and his success. He had escaped his past, had moved up the American social ladder and now here he was again, because of Buisson, dragged back into the sewer only months away from safety under the statute of limitations.

'Listen, Courgibet,' I said, 'I'm going to surprise you.'

He looked up. He licked his lips and bit back a sob, but he quickly got hold of himself again. 'What do you mean, Inspector?'

'I'm going to testify for you at your trial.'

49

There is an end to everything. One Sunday afternoon in September, Marlyse and I were strolling arm in arm along the boulevard Rochechouart. The day was fine.

'Let's walk up to Barbès,' Marlyse suggested. 'We can come back on the other side of the street.'

I knew what that meant. Marlyse loves to window-shop. I don't.

'I've got work to do at home, dear,' I said, making my voice syrupy, 'there are those sink tiles to cement in. Let's go home.'

It was no contest. So we went window-shopping. As we reached the subway entrance, a swarthy, pinched-looking little man came down the steps and began walking in a familiar, jerky stride towards the boulevard Barbès. The build, the hair, the face—I knew them all too well. In two bounds I was alongside Orsetti.

'Well, Jeannot. What a surprise!'

Orsetti stopped dead. Despair shone in his black eyes.

'Monsieur Borniche!'

'The very same. What brings you here, Jeannot?'

Marlyse had flagged down a taxi and was holding the door open.

'See you later, darling,' she said.

While she resumed her walk alone, we rode to my office. A quick frisk, a call to Victor to ask him to bring some clothes and food for his kinsman, a confinement order quickly typed and Jeannot was back in a cell. He hadn't said ten words since his arrest. I knew in advance he wouldn't say anything about anything. I left it up to the magistrate to question him and confront him with his accusers. For me, the circle was closed.

The Champigny robbery case was solved despite Buisson's denials, despite Loubier's lies, despite Labori's loss of memory, despite Grosjean's silence. It was Bolec who broke first. He was able to satisfy his eagerness to commune with his wife from time to time, for which he was touchingly grateful to me. Happy opened up, too, in exchange for a promise to release his mistress. He formally accused Buisson of Polledri's murder, of shooting Baudet, the jeweller, and the bank messengers in Champigny. Buisson insisted on his innocence.

'It's crazy,' he howled, slapping his thighs. 'You know damn well my gun was never fired, Monsieur Borniche.'

That was true. The Colt I had found in his room was virginal. The police lab guaranteed it. The one I took from Vérando when I nabbed him in a café on the rue de Richelieu, on the other hand, had fired the bullets found in the passage Landrieu in Paris, on the avenue Jean-Jaurès in Boulogne, on the avenue Jean-Jaurès in Champigny. But Vérando, an accessory to the Polledri murder and the Boulogne hold-up, had not been involved in the Champigny robbery. Happy and Bolec both told me this, and none of the witnesses identified him, although they all had pointed to Buisson as the man with the Colt. That meant one of two things: either Vérando had lent his gun to Buisson, or there had been an inexplicable swap.

'No,' yelled Buisson, 'I never carried any gun but the Colt you found in my room. Vérando never loaned me his. I was never in Champigny. It was Vérando who shot those two, just like he shot Polledri. And the jeweller.'

Luckily, Happy's mistress gave me the key to the mystery. It was simple:

'When Buisson and Vérando went to my boyfriend's place, they used to take off their guns, which they usually put in the bottom of the chest of drawers.'

Maybe they had merely switched guns unwittingly after the Champigny job. When I suggested this to Buisson, he began to giggle nervously, but the look in his eye told me that there had been nothing accidental about the switch. Vérando hadn't known when he left Happy's that he was carrying the murder weapon.

When the Seine Criminal Court sentenced him to death, Buisson was still fiercely denying his guilt of the slayings with which he'd been charged. Turning to face his former accomplices, he pointed a vengeful finger at them. 'Pigs!' he screamed before he was led out. 'You won't take it with you. You've condemned an innocent man!'

François Marcantoni was caught up with, too. Superintendent Denis suspected the honest tradesman of engaging in activities behind his bar that had nothing to do with lemonade. Despite his protestations of innocence, he was locked up in cell 2.85 in the maximum-security wing. That was the night of 27–28 February

1956. Marcantoni couldn't sleep. He was into his second pack of cigarettes. It was a long, cold night.

Suddenly, he pricked up his ears. He seemed to hear footsteps gliding through the corridor towards the condemned cell in which Buisson had been confined since his trial. He thought he heard whispering, the rustle of clothing.

Marcantoni held his breath. Using the handle of his spoon, which he had filed down on the cement floor of his cell, he succeeded in raising the peephole in his door. He recognized the long, swarthy visage of his fellow Corsican, attorney Charles Carboni, who had defended Buisson; it was Buisson these men had now come to get. The killer was about to keep his date with the Widow.

The bar owner had seen Buisson only once, at the Calanques, with Orsetti, and he had bawled the little Corsican out, one day when they happened to meet on the street, for his imprudence. Oh, yes—there had been a second time: when they shared a prison van taking them to the Palace of Justice. The two had never met, but Marcantoni felt the anguish rising in him at the thought that this man was about to die.

Through the peephole, he saw Buisson, already wearing an other-worldly expression, behaving with surprising calm amidst the group of white-faced men. Marcantoni watched him disappear towards the registrations office, to the place where his neck would be bared, the formalities of discharge fulfilled as though he were going to be released, and he would be offered a tot of rum and a cigarette.

Marcantoni let the lid of the peephole drop back into place. He sat down on his bunk, his chin resting on his fists.

At six-five a.m., Émile Buisson shook hands with his lawyer. As coolly as though he were setting out for another robbery, he turned to the executioner.

'I'm ready, monsieur,' he said. 'You can go ahead. Society will be proud of you.'

The plank seesawed. The blade dropped. The wicker trunk closed on a headless body.

Monsieur Émile had, as the saying goes, paid his debt.

Almost at the same moment, only a few hundred yards away, a man stood sobbing in a room at the Pitié Hospital. Mathieu Robillard's wife, Annick, the woman for whom he had become an informer, for whom he had consented to sell out his friends so that he could pay to keep her alive, was quietly dying.

Medical science was powerless to save her. Annick had been in the Pitié for three weeks, smiling faintly at Mathieu, who never left her side.

At six-ten a.m., Robillard closed his wife's eyes forever.

For one last night, the Buisson case robbed me of sleep. I had spent an exhausting day and I was hoping to get some rest. I was brushing my teeth when the phone began jangling in the flat.

'If it's Fatso I'm not here,' I hissed at Marlyse, who was already in bed. She stretched a naked arm towards the phone and handed me the receiver, covering the mouthpiece with her hand. 'It's Carboni, the lawyer,' she said. 'What does he want you for?'

I knew at once what he wanted. I had exchanged sharp words with Carboni when I testified at Buisson's trial; my testimony had been objective enough, but the defence gave me a going-over. I took the receiver.

'It's for tomorrow morning,' the lawyer told me. 'I've just been told. Is there any message you want me to give him?'

I stood there for a moment, unable to speak. Only Marlyse's regular breathing pierced the silence of the darkened room.

'Just say goodbye to him for me, will you?' I finally murmured. 'I'll call you tomorrow.'

I put the receiver gently back in its cradle and looked at Marlyse, who was peering intently at me.

'Well?'

'Well, he was a swine, Monsieur Émile. But I'll tell you, Marlyse, I really don't think—I mean it!—I really don't think I was cut out for this work.'

Amanda		Alister
	A	3
	2	
		40
	3	
		55
	4	
7		55
	5	
11		55
	6	
16		55
16	7	83
	8	
16		
	9	
	10	
	J	
	Q	
	K	

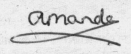

APPENDIX

What Became of Them

Émile BUISSON: Buried in Thiais cemetery, in the section reserved for the condemned.

Jean-Baptiste BUISSON, alias Screwball: Unable to stomach the insulting remarks made about his brother by another criminal named Michel Cardeur, he executed the offender by firing two bullets into him from a Colt on 24 December 1952. Arrested in Juan-les-Pins on 3 April 1953, by Roger Borniche. Sentenced to hard labour for life. Now old and sick, he is in Clairvaux Penitentiary waiting for his troubles to end.

Henri BOLEC: Stunned by the heavy sentence meted out to him and by the idea of being separated from his wife, he lay down and died on 3 August 1957, in Fresnes Prison hospital.

Antoine BORGEOT: Shuttles his nostalgia and his 20 stone between Boulogne-Billancourt, the rue de Lappe and the rue Gît-le-Cœur. Pines for the days when 'men were men'.

Paul BRUTUS, alias the Hunchback: Was granted judicial clemency. Died in total poverty in Paris, 13 October 1962.

Francis CAILLAUD: Condemned to death. Sentence commuted to life imprisonment, then reduced to twenty years hard labour. He was finally granted parole and returned to his native Brittany, where he is working as a blacksmith in a farming community.

Émile COURGIBET: Sentenced on 24 April 1953, to five years' imprisonment and ten years' banishment by the Troyes Criminal Court. On petition of Roger Borniche to Justice Minister François Mitterand, was accorded a suspension of sentence. On 31 May 1954, he returned to the United States, where he rejoined his wife and resumed the life of an honest man.

Roger DEKKER: Sentenced to twenty years hard labour. Escaped from Fontevrault Penitentiary, 15 June 1955, after commandeering a guard's uniform and rifle. Located several days later hiding in a wood. Shot to death by gendarmes.

Suzanne FOURREAU: Undermined by sorrow and disease, she survived her former lover, Roger Dekker, by only a few years. Is remembered at 57 rue Bichat as a plucky kid.

René GIRIER, alis René the Exile: His spectacular prison breaks made him a celebrity. Broke completely with the underworld after his release from prison. Runs a metal-polishing shop in the provinces. His skill and his gluttony for work have amazed police officers and judges. None of his customers knows his real name.

Pierre LABORI: Died in Paris, 18 November 1964, soon after his discharge from prison.

Simon LOUBIER: Has made the rounds of the penitentiaries while serving a life sentence. Is scheduled for release shortly.

François MARCANTONI: Is still keeping the wheels of justice grinding. His indictment is the longest-standing in France.

Jean ORSETTI: Appalled by the murderous madness of his former friends Abel Danos and Émile Buisson, he chose to retire to Corsica. Runs a hotel-restaurant near Bonifacio.

Mathieu ROBILLARD, alis the Nantais: Left the Paris region for Dunkerque after his wife's death in 1956. Signed on as a stevedore. In 1962 he sailed aboard a freighter bound for the South Seas. Has not been heard of since.

Jacques VÉRANDO, alias the Niçois: Released on parole, he retired to the Côte d'Azur. Seems to be leading a normal life.

TRUE CRIME – NOW AVAILABLE IN PANTHER BOOKS

Paul Foot

Who Killed Hanratty?   60p ☐

Ludovic Kennedy

A Presumption of Innocence   £1.25 ☐
10 Rillington Place   95p ☐

Stephen Knight

Jack the Ripper: The Final Solution   £1.25 ☐

Peter Maas

The Valachi Papers   75p ☐

John Pearson

The Profession of Violence   95p ☐

Ed Sanders

The Family   95p ☐

All these books are available at your local bookshop or newsagent, or can be ordered direct from the publisher. Just tick the titles you want and fill in the form below.

Name ....

Address ....

....

Write to Panther Cash Sales, PO Box 11, Falmouth, Cornwall TR10 9EN.
Please enclose remittance to the value of the cover price plus:
UK: 22p for the first book plus 10p per copy for each additional book ordered to a maximum charge of 82p.
BFPO and EIRE: 22p for the first book plus 10p per copy for the next 6 books, thereafter 3p per book.
OVERSEAS: 30p for the first book and 10p for each additional book.
~~nada Publishing reserve the right to show new retail prices on covers,
~~may differ from those previously advertised in the text or elsewhere.